Virtual Menageries

Leonardo

Roger F. Malina, Executive Editor

Sean Cubitt, Editor-in-Chief

Synthetics: Aspects of Art and Technology in Australia, 1956–1975, Stephen Jones, 2011

Hybrid Cultures: Japanese Media Arts in Dialogue with the West, Yvonne Spielmann, 2012

Walking and Mapping: Artists as Cartographers, Karen O'Rourke, 2013

The Fourth Dimension and Non-Euclidean Geometry in Modern Art, revised edition, Linda Dalrymple Henderson, 2013

Illusions in Motion: Media Archaeology of the Moving Panorama and Related Spectacles, Erkki Huhtamo, 2013

Relive: Media Art Histories, edited by Sean Cubitt and Paul Thomas, 2013

Re-collection: Art, New Media, and Social Memory, Richard Rinehart and Jon Ippolito, 2014

Biopolitical Screens: Image, Power, and the Neoliberal Brain, Pasi Väliaho, 2014

The Practice of Light: A Genealogy of Visual Technologies from Prints to Pixels, Sean Cubitt, 2014

The Tone of Our Times: Sound, Sense, Economy, and Ecology, Frances Dyson, 2014

The Experience Machine: Stan VanDerBeek's Movie-Drome and Expanded Cinema, Gloria Sutton, 2014

Hanan al-Cinema: Affections for the Moving Image, Laura U. Marks, 2015

Writing and Unwriting (Media) Art History: Erkki Kurenniemi in 2048, edited by Joasia Krysa and Jussi Parikka, 2015

Control: Digitality as Cultural Logic, Seb Franklin, 2015

New Tendencies: Art at the Threshold of the Information Revolution (1961–1978), Armin Medosch, 2016

Screen Ecologies: Art, Media, and the Environment in the Asia-Pacific Region, Larissa Hjorth, Sarah Pink, Kristen Sharp, and Linda Williams, 2016

Pirate Philosophy: For a Digital Posthumanities, Gary Hall, 2016

Social Media Archeology and Poetics, edited by Judy Malloy, 2016

Practicable: From Participation to Interaction in Contemporary Art, edited by Samuel Bianchini and Erik Verhagen, 2016

Machine Art in the Twentieth Century, Andreas Broeckmann, 2016

Here/There: Telepresence, Touch, and Art at the Interface, Kris Paulsen, 2017

Voicetracks: Attuning to Voice in Media and the Arts, Norie Neumark, 2017

Ecstatic Worlds: Media, Utopias, Ecologies, Janine Marchessault, 2017

Interface as Utopia: The Media Art and Activism of Fred Forest, Michael F. Leruth, 2017

Making Sense: Art, Computing, Cognition, and Embodiment, Simon Penny, 2017

Weather as Medium: Toward a Meteorological Art, Janine Randerson, 2018

The Invisible Colors: The Arts of the Atomic Age from Marie Curie to Fukushima, Gabrielle Decamous, 2018

Virtual Menageries: Animals as Mediators in Network Cultures, Jody Berland, 2018

See <http://mitpress.mit.edu> for a complete list of titles in this series.

Virtual Menageries

Animals as Mediators in Network Cultures

Jody Berland

The MIT Press
Cambridge, Massachusetts
London, England

This book was set in Stone by Toppan Best-set Premedia Limited. Printed and bound in the United States of America.

Library of Congress Cataloging-in-Publication Data

Names: Berland, Jody, author.
Title: Virtual menageries : animals as mediators in network cultures / Jody Berland.
Description: Cambridge, MA : The MIT Press, 2019. | Series: Leonardo book series | Includes bibliographical references and index.
Identifiers: LCCN 2018028560 | ISBN 9780262039604 (hardcover : alk. paper)
Subjects: LCSH: Animals in mass media. | Digital media--Social aspects.
Classification: LCC P96.A53 B47 2019 | DDC 179.3--dc23 LC record available at https://lccn.loc.gov/2018028560

10 9 8 7 6 5 4 3 2 1

For David, Jasper, and Lola

Contents

Series Foreword: Leonardo/International Society for the Arts, Sciences, and Technology (ISAST)

Leonardo, the International Society for the Arts, Sciences, and Technology, and the affiliated French organization Association Leonardo, have some very simple goals:

1. To advocate, document, and make known the work of artists, researchers, and scholars developing the new ways in which the contemporary arts interact with science, technology, and society.
2. To create a forum and meeting places where artists, scientists, and engineers can meet, exchange ideas, and, when appropriate, collaborate.
3. To contribute, through the interaction of the arts and sciences, to the creation of the new culture that will be needed to transition to a sustainable planetary society.

When the journal *Leonardo* was started some fifty years ago, these creative disciplines usually existed in segregated institutional and social networks, a situation dramatized at that time by the "Two Cultures" debates initiated by C. P. Snow. Today we live in a different time of cross-disciplinary ferment, collaboration, and intellectual confrontation enabled by new hybrid organizations, new funding sponsors, and the shared tools of computers and the Internet. Sometimes captured in the "STEM to STEAM" movement, new forms of collaboration seem to integrate the arts, humanities, and design with science and engineering practices. Above all, new generations of artist-researchers and researcher-artists are now at work individually and collaboratively bridging the art, science, and technology disciplines. For some of the hard problems in our society, we have no choice but to find new ways to couple the arts and sciences. Perhaps in our lifetime we will see the emergence of "new Leonardos," hybrid creative individuals or teams that will not only develop a meaningful art for our times but also drive new agendas in science and stimulate technological innovation that addresses today's human needs.

For more information on the activities of the Leonardo organizations and networks, please visit our websites at http://www.leonardo.info/ and http://www.olats.org/. The Leonardo Book Series and journals are also available on our ARTECA art science technology aggregator: http://arteca.mit.edu/.

Roger F. Malina
Executive Editor, Leonardo Publications

Acknowledgments

This book benefited from inspiration and help from many sources, sites, and species.

For their invaluable research and editorial contributions to this work over the last few years, I thank image consultant Zoe Lepiansky and awesome research and editorial assistants Sabine Lebel, Jeremy Mathers, Brian McCormack, Ryan Mitchell, Jonathan Osborne, Sugivan Ratneswarran, NT Rowan, and Kelsey Speakman. For their knowledge, support, and capacity to inspire I am grateful to Rob Bennison, Linda Bronfman, Matthew Brower, Bill Burns, Jonathan Burt, Jodey Castricano, Sean Cubitt, Bob Hanke, Ashley Johnson, Rob Laidlaw, Cheryl Lousely, Claire Parkinson, Greg Seigworth, Nicole Shukin, Jonathan Sterne, Tom Tyler, and Joost van Loon.

For their helpful comments and suggestions on the book manuscript, thank you to Bob Hanke, David Hlynsky, Brian McCormack, Jonathan Osborne, and MIT editors Matthew Abbate and Julia Collins. Earlier versions of portions of this work were published in *Cultural Studies*, vol. 8 (2006, ed. Phaedra Pezzullo); *Global South* (ed. Mike Hill); *Antennae* (ed. Giovanni Aloi); *Imaginations* (ed. Adam Lauder and Jacqueline McLeod Rogers); and *Material Cultures* (ed. Tom Allen and Jennifer Blair). I am grateful to these editors and to the anonymous readers for their feedback and suggestions.

Portions of this work in progress were presented at conferences including "Ecologies of War," at University at Albany, SUNY; "Interfaces and Visualizations: A State-of-the-Art Conference on the Humanities in Post-Human Times," at University of Illinois at Urbana-Champaign; "Crossroads 2014," Association of Cultural Studies, at Paris-Sorbonne University; the Canadian Communication Association, Fredericton, NB; "Screening Nature," at Queen Mary University and Whitechapel Gallery, London; "Affect WTF," at Millersville University, Lancaster, PA; The TechnoScience Salon, York University and University of Toronto; "Minding Animals 4,"

Universidad Nacional Autónoma de México, Mexico City; "International Visual Sociology Association Conference," Faculty of Education, Concordia University; and for Toronto Semiotic Circle; Department of Art History and Visual Art, University of British Columbia; McLuhan Centre for Culture and Technology, University of Toronto; School of Media and Cultural Studies, University of Cardiff, Wales; Centre for Human Animal Studies, Edge Hill University, Ormskirk, Lancashire, England; Department of Media and Communications, Goldsmiths, University of London; School of Art and Culture, Carleton University, Ottawa. I thank the organizers and hosts for bringing people and ideas together and the participants and conversants who helped make these collective learning events.

I acknowledge my debt to the formidable work of contributors and activists on the many social media cat sites and animal welfare projects, campaigns, and fun sites that inspired this project to begin with, including the Infinite Cat Project, LOL Cats, Stuff on Cats, Hello Kitty, Grumpy Cats, Cats Against Capitalism, Internet Cat Research Group a/k/a Institute of Kitteh Studies, Kitten Competition, Toronto and Annex Cat Rescues, Zoocheck, Rainforest Action Network, Elephants without Borders, The Audubon Society, The Wildlife Recording Society (UK), April's webcam, Blankets for Baby Rhinos, and other sites too numerous to mention.

This research was funded by the Social Sciences and Humanities Research Council of Canada. My thanks to SSHRC and to Janet Friskney, our indefatigable research officer, Laura Taman, and the Robarts Centre for Canadian Studies for their kind assistance, and the York University Faculty Association, the Faculty of Graduate Studies, and the Department of Humanities, at York University. I thank Handel Wright and the Faculty of Education, University of British Columbia; Sean Cubitt, Lisa Blackman, and the Department of Media and Communications, Goldsmiths, University of London; and the Centre for Human Animal Relations, Edge Hill University. Finally, thanks to David, Jasper, and Lola for the magical times and places they have brought into my life.

Introduction

> To suppose that animals first entered the human imagination as meat or leather or horn is to project a nineteenth-century attitude backwards across the millennia. Animals first entered the imagination as messengers and promises.
>
> John Berger, "Why Look at Animals?"[1]

The simplest images can call for the most complex interpretive strategies. A picture of a smiling goat, say, with a flower in its mouth. Perhaps you have encountered images of a soaring bird, an ingenious beaver, an adorable cat, a noble lion, a stately giraffe. Who doesn't love these pictures? Our species' capacity to be stirred by our encounters with animals defines us as human as much as their fur or feathers define them. This does not explain everything about our relations with nonhuman animals any more than biology alone explains our relations with each other. It certainly doesn't explain how a goat came to advertise a telephone company.

I began this project with a simple question provoked by the images and links suddenly crowding my inbox. Why are there so many cats on the Internet? My curiosity led to a broad interdisciplinary exploration of animal-mediated encounters and how closely these were tied to the emergence of new media technologies (defined in the broadest sense) and spaces. Why people assign these inaugural roles to animals or animal figures; what critical ideas best explain the work they are doing in these contexts; how groups of animals resembling menageries came to launch the tools and platforms of digital culture; what role the animal-technology figure plays in managing the risks of the Anthropocene;[2] what, if an animal is a mediator, it is mediating, and how; and what the current eruption of digital animals means for the future of human-animal relations: these are what this book is about.

In carrying out this research I spent a lot of time looking at the faces of cheerful animals. It is almost impossible to escape such images in our contemporary mediascape, not only online, and not only in children's books and toys. You would think we were all children. I will admit that right now I am not optimistic about the future of human-animal relations. There are fires and floods out of control all over the world; our politicians are madly terminating regulations protecting endangered species and bodies of water; palm oil producers are eliminating so much forest that orangutans, Sumatran tigers, and some parrots will be extinct in the wild in no time, giraffes and elephants the week after that; people eat so much meat they are killing themselves and denuding the planet; hermit crabs are living in tin cans, whales are devouring plastic, every time I go into social media I risk becoming paralyzed with distress.

Perhaps ironically, the screens and virtual spaces on which I read this news launched each of their landmark changes with digital-savvy images of animals, some of them comprised of messages that demanded attention and some squirreled away in brands and interfaces just below the threshold of an ordinary user's perception. *Virtual Menageries* highlights the use of animals in the spread of global communicative networks, and shows how animals and representations of animals have been put to work in changing social configurations and have helped to alter them. These configurations are part of what makes us human—not because we are different from them but because they are an essential part of everything we are and do. We are equally dependent on the technologies of mediation that we use to communicate with one another. "We have committed the fundamental error," Marcel Mauss writes in "The Technologies of the Body," "of only judging there to be technology when there is an instrument." Mauss means that the human body can be understood as a technology, as an instrument or "a living mediation of intersections between orders, artifact, and nature."[3] The same can be said of nonhuman bodies, or even of the parts, fragments, or representations of animal bodies which appear in the following pages.

To elaborate how animals have served as what Mauss calls "instruments" in the emergence of global communicative networks, and to explain how the trope of the menagerie links these events across historical eras, I draw on Régis Debray's outline of a mediological perspective. In his 1996 book *Media Manifestos*, Debray rejects the idea of analyzing a medium in the singular.[4] In a critique that takes aim equally at McLuhan, semiology, and sociology, Debray calls for "looking not for *that which is behind* a symbolic utterance, but rather *that which takes place between.*"[5] His book advocates an approach that reconnects the technological, semantic, and political spheres so as to generate the right questions about a media event:

In the word *"mediology," "medio"* says not media nor medium but mediations, namely the dynamic combination of intermediary procedures and bodies that interpose themselves between a producing of signs and a producing of events. These intermediates are allied with "hybrids" (Bruno Latour's term), mediations at once technological, cultural, and social.[6]

The mediological manner or cast of mind consists in putting one's finger on the intersections between intellectual, material and social life, and in making these two silent hinges grate audibly. [It focuses on] the first appearance of nodes and networks of sociability, interfaces bearing new rituals and exercises, proving worthy as means of producing opinion.[7]

Debray's emphasis on intermediates and intersections is driven by the need to analyze "first appearances" and "events" which hold the potential to remix the configurations of the society in such a way that constituent elements of its "procedures and bodies" are changed. In the occurrences I have chosen to investigate in this book, animals are conscripted to participate in some of the "first appearances of nodes and networks" that Debray describes. In these intersections between the animal, the milieu, and the emergent technology, the animal's presence matters. The animal does not arrive later to symbolize or legitimate what has occurred, or to compensate for what is not there or lost. If the meanings of these events seem to be exclusively the prerogative of humans, this reflects an ethical judgment (and mainly the right one) but not a historical or mediological analysis. The animal is there when the story begins, its presence is essential to the search for new ways of life, and it is an inextricable part of what the story becomes.

Exposing this mediological hinge between the constituent elements of change—between the animal, the milieu, and the emergent technology, for instance—shows how a perceptible event emerges from one set of meanings and conditions while opening doors to new possibilities. Constructing a mediology of the animal also helps to illuminate essential links between our colonial past and our Anthropocenic present. Focusing on animals in these contexts confirms how often the exploitation of animals involves the exploitation of other humans, and how often the exploitation of other humans involves the exploitation of animals. The question of the animal is important to the humanities. In what ways are nonhuman animal lives meaningful, in what ways are human lives shaped by the same instincts or drives we habitually ascribe to those others, and how, where, or when do such distinctions matter? Furthermore, if rational reflection and the ensuing control over one's self are the basis of human superiority, why is the world in such a mess? Can the global proliferation of digital animal images inspire humans to transform their relations with other animals and the natural world? What unanticipated shifts in our relations with the nonhuman world could help make this happen?

The questions that drive this project appear at the intersection of critical animal studies, media studies, postcolonial studies, and environmental humanities. Much of the work in critical animal studies can be located on a spectrum that spans two nominally opposed approaches. In one, the representation of animals mimics and/or reproduces existing forms of domination by hiding or displaying them through the spectacular aesthetics of capitalism and prevents humans from forming less oppressive relationships with animals. With so many layers of technological processing now involved in animal display, it is possible that "the estrangement engendered by this mediation makes it all the easier for humans to dominate, subject and mistreat other animals."[8] In this prognosis, the overriding forms and logics of animal representation are determined by the technological processing and exploitation of industrial capitalism, and such representations carry no meaning outside the logics of domination.[9] Yet on the other hand, the presentation of images of the animal body[10] can function as an "agonistic force" that reasserts the unique and inescapable presence of animal life.[11] The "creaturely" dimension of the depicted animal speaks to us and calls forth an ethical response. In a parallel debate, feminist and STS critics have observed that science researchers are taught to develop a stance of neutrality or "objectivity" involving distance from their subject whose instrumentalism is explicitly antithetical to the cultivation of empathy for animal subjects.[12] And yet, as Alexander Pschera claims in his recent book *Internet Animal*, the development of digital technology enables science to know more about animals than was ever possible in the past. Because of this, scientists and everyday observers can learn about the unique qualities of individual species or animals with their own tracks, habits, and voices, or even discover new species. In this view, the knowledge and visual beauty created by digital technologies will help to save animals from human-caused suffering or extinction.[13] These two approaches form in opposition to one another, and each asks readers to accept its critique of the other side. If a representation of an animal is performing one of these agendas, it can't be implicated in the other. From the vantage point of cultural studies, however, the negotiation of contradictory values or identities is key to the formation of all cultural texts, and we seek to understand them as such.

As inhabitants of a contradictory, strife-ridden world we are drawn to works that seem to accomplish some creative reconciliation of conflicting situations or desires. The same kind of negotiation can be discerned in the worldly ecologies (which are also texts) through which we might encounter such works. Indeed, critical attention to the medium is essential, for otherwise no matter how innovative your aesthetic language your work becomes the "fodder," as Bertolt Brecht put it, for an already compromised medium (in his case, the stage) which must continue to feed its audiences.[14] The sense of freedom and creativity we associate with digital media contains its own contradictory relationship with a powerful apparatus: the concentrated corporate power that produces these devices and inexorably traces our movements and moods while doing so. These tensions haunt our relationships with our devices, as does the presence-absence of the animal. In this context technological innovations (re)mediate our encounters with animals, just as animals (re)mediate our encounters with technology. As the concept of mediology makes clear, thinking of animals as essential figures in these encounters is radically different from viewing animals as part of the content transmitted via a particular medium. Whether in ecological or symbolic terms, we humans can no more be separated from nonhuman animal bodies and meanings now than when our species was new.

While critical animal studies research has taught us a great deal about representations of animals, I see an absence in these accounts: an explicit engagement with mediation itself as a process with its own complex and sometimes unpredictable dimensions and effects. With important exceptions, this work tends to rely on an idealist understanding of the media as a more or less adequate, more or less authentic representation of the world. The critique highlights the ethical framework, visual language, or dominant ideology the critic wishes to expose. While deeply indebted to such work, *Virtual Menageries* asks what insights a focus on mediation such as that outlined by Mauss, Debray, and others can offer to understanding representations of animals in the age of hypermediation and environmental crisis.

In pursuit of this question I draw on my own background in media theory for its insights into materiality and assemblages. But this literature has its own problems; it needs to take better account of the agency or lack of agency (quasi-agency?) of living, nonhuman bodies and meanings. Without acknowledging the central presence and the central problem of animal life, our understanding of mediation is narrowed and restricted, and our understanding of human experience both universalized and animalized.

Does it make a difference to the difference that mediation makes, if the mediator is an animal? McLuhan defines "the medium" as an extension of our limbs and nervous systems that transforms what it extends and alters the sensory balance of the body as a whole. His focus on the sensory transformation of the body by the technological extensions it produces anticipates the thought of posthumanism. When I think about media as an extension of my own activities, I think about what is at the end of my hands: a pen, a fork, a musical or alphabetical keyboard, my cat's fur, my dog. Without them, my participation in the world is diminished; my hands are incomplete, I am not-me. When forms of mediation change, whether from cow to coin, fur to logo, horse to car, stage to cinema, birdsong to relaxing soundtrack, pet cat to Grumpy Cat, people change. To be human doesn't just mean to think or reason; it means to be incomplete, to rely on shoes and coats, pens and glasses, keyboards and cats, and to adapt as best one can when these mediations are changed. To be a better human is to struggle for better awareness not just of our diversity but also of our own inherent mutability, incompleteness, and need for supplementation. Analyzing the human-machine-animal performativity engendering new media spaces might therefore help to ensure a better "ecology of ideas"[15] concerning the interdependence of interspecies and intrahuman lives. With this goal, "nature itself is not faithfully represented but 'our participation *within* nature,' our material-discursive intra-action, is."[16]

I explore these questions in connection with an insight that appears briefly in writings by John Berger, Jonathan Burt, and W. J. T. Mitchell: that new visual capacities have, perhaps from the time of the first cave drawings, been launched with images of animals. My approach to this irresistible hint for further research is to divide this idea into two ideas and then reconnect them. Animals have served as first contact between previously separate societies or entities, and have provided the first images in testing and launching new forms and rhetorics of technological mediation. Bringing these two proximate but distinct themes together helps to fill in some of the continuities between colonial empire-building and capitalist processes of commodification and risk management. To explain this double exposure requires reference to concepts of animal magnetism or animal spirits which play a substantial but slippery role in these events. I use this interdisciplinary stereoscopic mediological lens to analyze the role of animals in the transformation of social space and human-animal relations.

Virtual Menageries begins with the menageries of early modern Europe and follows their traces into the digital menageries that emerged in the 1960s. In this more recent era, early innovators in computing software created an iconography resembling the classical menagerie to identify their products.

The identification of digital tools with images drawn from menageries calls to mind the wonder and acquisitiveness of early colonial exploration. But this confluence of old and new configurations raises unexamined questions about how and why animals have served for so long—and now appear so extensively—as mediums in the growth of networks and technologies of connectivity. What are they mediating? The answer depends profoundly on the context. The convergence of animal theory and medium theory is at an early stage of development. My shorthand for this inquiry is to address the animal as a medium of communication in the contemporary event of technological mobilization, wherein it is dematerialized and repackaged in the name of love.

The events I examine suggest that in the neoliberal era, however, the constellation of animal spirits, love, and desire can transgress boundaries while strangely promising to damage nothing. Defining love as the force that unites multitudes, Michael Hardt and Antonio Negri write in *Empire* that the "creation of a new humanity is the ultimate act of love; ... without this love, we are nothing."[17] It seems wrong to dispute this idea. As Eleanor Wilkinson notes in a discussion of Hardt's own work on love, however, "Hardt is attempting to think affect beyond subjectivity, and to instead focus on the potentia that emerges when bodies come together. Yet, this fails to address the uneven terrain on which bodies encounter each other to begin with. For, as Ahmed notes, affect cannot be separated from issues of power, privilege, and oppression."[18] To imagine a love that brings no disruption, conquest, or pain—as some of these animal figures invite us to do—means moving backward, away from any useful engagement with animals or life or love that can be orchestrated in time to save the world. In any case, it is with moving backward that we begin.

Constituting the Menagerie

While rulers and aristocrats have owned menageries since the time of ancient Rome, the early modern European menagerie was reshaped by new capabilities for capture made possible by transcontinental travel. Charismatic nonhuman animals have since then frequently appeared as inaugural or "first contact" participants in the emergence of new technologies and spaces of connection. The term "first contact" ordinarily refers to colonial agents who organized encounters with others to advance the profits and desires of their patrons. Animals transported to other parts of the world can also be first contacts and agents of change. The practice of international trade in exotic animals led to the creation of menageries as heterotopias in which, following Foucault, diverse and incompatible spaces are brought together in one place.[19] Through such transformative spatial processes, humans and animals entered one another's worlds and altered one another's planes of existence.

Animals have served as mediators for human interaction as far back as records exist. They have been conscripted as sacrifices, symbols, items of trade, gifts, and tokens in the circulation of kinship, wealth, belief, and power. That these objects of exchange predate the mediation of money is evidenced by the inscription of animals onto the faces of coins when they first appeared. With the exchange of animals in these new colonial encounters, agents sought to initiate new connections and to occupy new spaces. Showing animals' importance to these enterprises clarifies the parallel I wish to draw between the animal body as emissary or mediator in early modern colonialism, and the animal image as emissary or mediator in the launching of electronic and digital media. The revival of the menagerie to launch digital communication—subliminal progeny perhaps of the dog and the chimp launched by rocket ships on the first Soviet space missions—bridges these eras and extends the use of the animal emissary to mediate new electronic and digital media spaces.

The menagerie's ability to evoke and supplement power in these historic processes works in part because of the incontestable power of the animal itself. The exotic animal triggers feelings such as amazement, curiosity, enchantment, repulsion, envy, and fear, while containing them within the untouchable bodies of animals and the uncrossable walls of the estate. One does not normally seek to touch a lion or a rhinoceros. The emperor who owns a lion acquires some of its physical and symbolic power, but this is not a power to be shared. The images of animals that appear with new digital devices and virtual spaces inspire a lighter but in the end no less imperative fealty to the technological milieu with which they are associated and the potentialities to which they point. The virtual menagerie reassures late modern spectators of their own power, not just over animals, whose images and sounds gratify users as though they are the new overlords, but more importantly over increasingly touchable technologies, whose powers (and those of their creators) seem increasingly untouchable, and finally over themselves, as they strive continuously to retrain their skills and emotions.

In asking what such animal mediators mediate, though, we must be careful to acknowledge the complexity of the relations in or from which they appear. Both old and new, hard and soft menageries help us to imagine and anticipate an unfolding future, and are in this sense virtual. The potential achievements arising from these magnetic moments require great exertion if their promises are to be realized. The word "virtual" has three usual meanings: (1) cybernetic, simulated, not real; (2) potential, waiting to unfold from the complex material and symbolic planes of social life and become actual; and (3) almost, a meaning that muddies the semantic distinction between the first two. The animal emissary or mediator exemplified by the menagerie calls for a mode of analysis that connects these meanings. All menageries evoke or simulate wild untamed landscapes full of beasts; they open a window onto the possibility of taming that wildness or meeting it halfway; and they (almost) span distances between places, species, and peoples. Exotic animals have been used as emissaries to announce (to perform or simulate) and advance (to unfold or draw near to) the senders' and receivers' desires to transform their worlds in the early modern period. The possibility of a crack emerging between power and desire, like the possibility of fracture between colonizer and subject, never disappears.

As Richard Grusin argues, there are different ways of looking at the future; one is based on a model of prediction, which implies that the future is more or less settled, and the other based on the idea that the future is immanent in the present, that it consists of "potentialities that impact or affect the present whether or not they ever come about."[20] Viewing this past of the future from the future of the present, the menagerie slides forward and backward as a zoological and discursive entity intersecting the tangled threads of colonial conquest, the extraction of wealth from nature, the fissures in modern culture, animal rights, visual and digital media, the loss of species, and climate change. In these processes, animals are not merely the cargo of various media of transport and communication. They play important roles in microscopic and macroscopic shifts in the meaning and governance of human and nonhuman lives. The two nonhuman entities that supplement the human—animals and machines—come together in foundational ways to form the world we are and know today.

From Heterotopias to Money and Mediation

Like early modern menageries, virtual menageries are heterotopias that actualize links between dispersed spaces. The menagerie's original meanings—spectacle, marvel, the exotic, the conquest of distance—anticipate and survive their migration to global digital networks. There are traces of the visceral power of the animal body when it is taken up in graphic and digital forms. These virtual mediators share an admirable semantic economy through their ability to catch our attention while slipping between the tangible and the intangible, and between animal and machine. They model a vision of nature in which such boundaries are increasingly slippery. Unlike representations of raced or gendered people, these virtual animals can sneak social meanings in without controversy; unlike representations of software, they can impart a sense of the vitality of living things; unlike live animals, they can be encountered without risk or fear. Their antics reveal and contain the vulnerabilities that humans share with nonhuman animals.

These virtual menageries play out their mediological roles in the context of a capitalist economy which since John Maynard Keynes, writing in the 1930s, has been characterized as a foundational oscillation between rational deliberation and "animal spirits," the latter describing an outburst of energetic spending that could be fueled by either confidence or uncertainty regarding the health of the economy.[21] The idea of an economy driven by opposing forces in human nature can be traced to Adam Smith, who wrote that "there are some situations which bear so hard upon human nature, that the greatest degree of self-government, which can belong to so imperfect a creature as man, is not able to stifle, altogether, the voice of human weakness, or reduce the violence of the passions to that pitch of moderation, in which the impartial spectator can entirely enter into them."[22] Smith believed in the possibility of moral judgments that could be made in interaction with other people. Like Smith, Keynes characterized judicious self-government and intense passion as opposing forces, but not surprisingly, writing after World War I, he was less confident than Smith in the human capacity for judicious self-government. For Keynes, even the most powerful motivations to defend "our own dignity and honor" could be overtaken by "sufficiently intense passions."[23] Because people driven by animal spirits enact their passions rashly, Keynes argued, government intervention was needed to balance the fluctuations of the market. This position is widely known as Keynesian economics. The connection of animal spirits and capitalist risk was revived for obvious reasons after the 2007 economic crash. A recent commentary uses the "bullish" market after the election of Donald Trump to illustrate the point: "Animal spirits is a component of economics and one that helps to explain why individuals and firms sometimes make poor investment decisions."[24] Once again one side of economic behavior is characterized as rational, self-controlled, and future-oriented, while the other, the impulsive "animal spirits" side, is unpredictable and affect-driven. In this account, both are needed to drive the capitalist economy, which is thus implicitly sustainable.

Keynes's concept of animal spirits was indebted not only to Smith but even more to Freud, whose work was known to Keynes through the latter's involvement with the Bloomsbury circle in the 1920s.[25] Keynes's "animal spirits" is a variation of what Freud called the "animal magnetism" of repressed instincts which hold power through their sublimation. Keynes appropriated Freud's description of the unconscious to explain the role of irrationality, particularly the neurotic love of money, in economic behavior.[26] Keynes writes in *The End of Laissez-Faire* that the "essential character of capitalism" is the dependence on an "intense appeal to the money-making and money-loving instincts of individuals as the main motive force of the economic machine."[27] The fact that capitalism relies on irrational spirits suggests that these individuals base their beliefs on evidence that they know at some level is questionable or false. In another extrapolation of Freud's capitalism, the animal spirit is associated with the movement of electricity and the possibility of its capture.[28] Either way, the animal spirit is not susceptible to reason.

Migrating across our screens, my virtual menageries appear to be speaking the language of these animal spirits, implicitly associating "instinct" (the animal) with naturalized desires to explore, acquire, and own according to the impulse of the moment. Their graphic unification of animality and digitality also conveys the assurance that the decision to own something digital is a rational investment, since the evolution of technology follows the same inexorable logic as the evolution of species.[29] To accept the invitation of the iconic animal spirit is to believe that the warring sides of human nature (and perhaps then of the economy?) can be reconciled through the rational/magical digitalization of capitalism, regardless of what Freud or Keynes might have thought. Unwrapping these syntaxes of form in the images comprising the contemporary menagerie thus involves acknowledging not only the presence of animal spirits but also their intended use in risk management strategies directed at the beliefs and dispositions of its viewers. In this negotiation, government plays an interesting role, if not exactly that which Keynes intended.

In a commercial context, these animal figures vitalize the market for digital devices on which the new security state depends. They have also helped to create online spaces for activists defending animal welfare or endangered species and for bored workers doting on cats' antics. They have enticed young children into using interactive toys—some of them the very embodiment of animal spirits—and prepared them to interact cooperatively with intelligent machines.[30] They have supported the growth of a three-dimensional informatics grid that makes it possible to fight wars with robot dogs and hummingbirds, track endangered wildlife, and monitor any and all forms of life including some as yet undiscovered, with the hope perhaps that they might make up for those being lost. They have provided the sights and sounds of a therapeutic apparatus designed to help humans cope with physical and mental stress. They have helped ensure that the potentially decommodified spaces and devices within digital networks continue to reward the financial and creative investments made in them.[31] These activities reanimate and alter the hinges that connect our material, social, and intellectual life. This summary may oversimplify what animal representations actually do in the world created by digital technologies, but what they actually do cannot be understood without these ideas.

What had to happen for these animal spirits to acquire this agency in the contemporary mediascape? The process follows a definite pattern borrowed from the menagerie. The giraffes we see in the next chapter are not wandering the savannah in the company of their extended families; the industrious beaver from which pelts and logos were extracted is not swimming across a river; the penguin announcing new ways to distribute data is not standing on the ice; the singing bird is not flying through the trees. We encounter them as solitary subjects whose powerful affects and capabilities are enveloped by the social and technological power to extract their life and vitality for human purposes. This mobilization pushes the animal habitus away and locks animal figures into a complex of animal, human, and material entities that act upon one another in sometimes unpredictable ways. The animal that joins and supplements other mediums enhances the powers of some people and groups and depletes the powers of others. The animalization of the technology involves a de-animalization of the animal. As we will see, it can become in the process what Fredric Jameson has termed a "vanishing mediator."[32]

The final question for this introduction concerns the actuality of the objects I am describing. Is this figure an image or a life? A photograph or a map? Animal or mineral? Analog or digital? Smiling goat or binary code? Instinctive peep or musical expression? Once the animal has been removed from its natural environment, and its image removed even further from that ground, what exactly are we looking at, or listening to? Does it even make sense to speak of it as an object? Yuk Hui writes:

> Digital objects appear to human users as colorful and visible beings. At the level of programming they are text files; further down the operating system they are binary codes; finally, at the level of circuit boards they are nothing but signals generated by the values of voltage and the operation of logic gates. How, then, can we think about the voltage differences as being the substance of a digital object? Searching downward we may end up with the mediation of silicon and metal. And finally we

Figure 0.1
T-shirt. Photo by the author, Toronto.

could go into particles and fields. But this kind of reductionism doesn't tell us much about the world.[33]

The "colorful and visible beings" Yuk Hui describes call on researchers to develop new understandings of the syntax of digital images that can "tell us much about the world" without excluding the codes and silicon. These colorful beings seem to point our attention toward what is outside their own codes and signals. At the same time, the lively images and sounds explored in the following chapters deliberately divert our attention from that same outside universe with its lives and deaths and complicated challenges. In this context, "images" refer to a complex interplay of digital data, screen technologies, zoological tropes, scientific rationalities, neurological interventions, design aesthetics, politics, history, and risk management. In this complex interplay, "material images fix mental ones and vice versa."[34]

The images' double-talk tells us something important about the world in which they arise. As a recent study found, for instance, the average French citizen "will see more virtual lions through photos, cartoons, logos and brands in one month than there are wild lions left in west Africa." Said one of the authors of this report, William Ripple, "The appearance of these beloved animals in stores, in movies, on television, and on a variety of products seems to be deluding the public into believing they are doing OK. If we don't act in a concerted effort to save these species, that may soon be the only way anyone will see them." Ripple adds that "a major threat faced by nearly all of them is direct killing by humans, especially from hunting and snaring," a reality he described as "sadly ironic."[35] These colorful beings are thus ambiguous but potent icons in a climate in which the idea of a vanishing mediator takes on new dimensions.

Summary of the Book

Chapter 1 elaborates the history and practice of the menagerie and explains how this collection of animals came to bridge peoples and territories that were previously unconnected. It examines how this precolonial formation opened a space for new routes and heterotopias that continue to build and define the technologies of global connectivity. It traces the menagerie's inaugural role through animals' key appearances in the first moving pictures, the earliest computing software, the commercial adoption of mobile phones, and the spread of social media.

In chapter 2, a ruler in Bengal sends a giraffe captured in Kenya to join an emperor's menagerie in China. This gift of a previously unseen exotic animal serves as a first contact between imperial leaders and opens the door to new transcontinental trade relations. But what about the giraffes? Jameson's concept of the "vanishing mediator" illuminates the suffering, deaths, and disappearances of these animals as they contribute to a global colonial and capitalist network of exploration and exchange. The chapter compares the emperor's giraffe of 1414 with April the pregnant giraffe, the famous online sensation of 2017, to help elaborate the concept of the event that underlines the mediological approach.

Chapter 3 addresses the beaver's body as the central commodity for the Canadian fur trade. Beaver pelts became the currency of new relations between colonial settlers and Indigenous peoples, while the whole beaver became the emblem of a political identity built on the conquest of

Indigenous people and the dead bodies of the animals. The beaver trade generates first contacts between the settlers and the Indigenous people and new relations between colonial representatives and the "home country" to which the pelts are sent. The beaver's role in the colonization and settlement of this dominion is unwrapped as the source of a rich body of narratives, commodities, symbols, and archives. In the process of extracting value from the beaver, first from its body and then through its symbolic proliferation, the history of colonization, the animal's valuable hydrological activities, and the furriness of the animal are all left behind.

Chapters 4 and 5 document the graphic reinvention of the menagerie and its widespread use to advertise virtual spaces and mobile devices. The exotic species featured in these virtual menageries mimic, in more ways than one, and with multiple projections of affect, the exotic animals captured and displayed in the original menageries of ancient and early modern times. These digital heterotopias are promoted as the chosen habitat for a neoliberalized self. As iconic first contact, digital animal emissaries promise liberation from local or social constraints through the fable of digital empowerment. By promising power to users while absorbing them into the matrix, these carefully purified animal spirit-figures are put to work altering geopolitical relations, human experience, and the alchemy of connection. The promise of human transformation is inseparable from the performativity of these nonhuman animals. Whether the primary role of these animal emissaries is to reenchant the secularized, disenchanted (as Max Weber influentially called it) modern world through accomplishments in the technosphere, or to naturalize reliance on mediated communications, infantilize consumers, mimic robot pets, merge pets and small humans together into cell phone hyperactivities, or promote the "coolness" of their creators,[36] a mediological understanding of this animal imagery is vital to the politics of the present.

Cats have drawn millions of people's waking hours into the enticing spaces of social media. Chapter 6 explores this remarkable phenomenon, wherein the domestication of computing technologies has built upon and played havoc with the unique role of cats in the history of religion, philosophy, and gender. Many significant philosophical interventions have been punctuated with references to cats; as companion animals they continue to attract controversy. The Internet cat phenomenon builds on these histories while creating a new phenomenon shaped by the techno-domestic spheres from which it arises. The online cat once again makes explicit the degree to which the animal is central to extending and engaging with social networks.

In chapter 7, I stage an encounter between the history of field recording, musicology, and media emotion research to analyze "nature" soundtracks and their use in therapeutic spaces. The genre is contextualized intersectionally here in relation to debates about animal language and meaning in musicology and evolutionary biology. Do birds sing? The story draws on the technical history of sound recording, the development of experimental neurological and affect research on humans, the transformation of birdsong meanings and silences with the publication of Rachel Carson's *Silent Spring*, and the dislocation, disembodiment, and disempowerment of the bird in the sonic vocabulary of these soundtracks. I follow the collapse of ontological distinctions between human, animal, and machine narrated here into a brief rumination on monsters that concludes the book.

When social groups and human tools move into new configurations, animals often play a significant mediating role. We deny our humanity when we deny our deep connections with these animals. As Gayatri Spivak writes in *An Aesthetic Education*, "To be born human is to be born angled toward an other and others."[37] These others toward which we are angled are not necessarily human. What is at stake here is not just the importance of animal bodies and images in the formation of colonial relations or technological assemblages, or vice versa. What is at stake is our need for new ways of thinking about animality, humanity, nature, culture, and capitalism. It is in our "nature," even when that nature is twisted and skewed, to be intertwined with nonhuman animals and technological entities that are increasingly intertwined with one another. Grappling with questions about these relations is crucial for dealing with the issues of risk and sustainability that confront us all. Hold on to these thoughts as we angle toward the future.

1 Hard and Soft Menageries

Menageries and Power

Menageries were collections of wild and exotic animals displayed for the pleasure and edification of the nobility. They are known to have existed in Roman, Incan, Asian, and early modern aristocratic estates. Owners and visitors could tour the grounds, marvel at the collections, and pay proper obeisance to the owner. In some versions of the menagerie, owners would stage fights to the death between various combinations of domestic and exotic animals for the entertainment of their exclusive audiences. These menageries provided physical evidence of their masters' potential to acquire dominion over faraway lands and over every life—human and nonhuman—that traveled between them. The menagerie was a fascinating space populated by powerful and charismatic animals. The power of the animals themselves was visible but contained, allowing observers to expand their own horizons imaginatively into rich but unknown geographies without fear of injury or harm. These exotic animals bridged distant worlds and at the same time reinforced the differences between them. An animal extracted from one country and displayed as exotica in another imprinted the possibility of spanning space together with the perpetuation of difference onto viewers and became an emblem of that history. All menageries, live or digital, are virtual and heterotopic entities, and all have been shaped by their colonial history.

The explicit purpose of a menagerie was to collect and display animals whose native habitat was often far away. As a luxuriant demonstration of power that consciously imitated the practices of the Roman Empire, the European menagerie between the fifteenth and eighteenth century was, depending on what disciplinary or theoretical lens you use to examine it, a private collection of exotic animals, an unmistakable manifestation of power and wealth, an unfolding imperial project stimulating the

Figure 1.1

View of the Menagerie at Versailles, seventeenth century, print and watercolor, Nicolas de Poilly. Image courtesy of RMN-Grand Palais (Château de Versailles) / Gérard Blot / Thierry Le Mage.

exploration and conquest of distant lands, a negotiation for economic partnership, a performance of containment of the savage natures subdued by conquest, a reorganization of natural and social space, a discursive structure organizing human-animal relationships, a medium of communication, a spectacle of magnetic animal beauty, and finally, to bring our attention back to today, an evolving heterotopia of animal bodies interfacing various technologies and sites.

The shared etymology of the words "species" and "spectacle" encapsulates the idea of the menagerie and zoo as sites for visual pleasure.[1] Menageries were not dedicated to the idea of displaying "species," for taxonomy did not exist until Linnaeus published his work in the mid-eighteenth century. The wildness of exotic animals from distant locations created rather a sense of wonder for people privileged enough to look at them. By the nineteenth century, however, these now-familiar animals could be seen performing in circuses, along with human "monsters" or "freaks," while public zoological gardens were being established to make diverse animal species available for observation and study by scientists. From the viewpoint of early zoos, it mattered little whether the captured specimen was a nonhuman primate or a human member of a "savage" community. What mattered was the display of wildness as a spectacular experience that fascinated audiences and enriched the status or income of private or public owners. As Yi-Fu Tuan writes, these public collections combined a desire for order with a desire to accumulate the heterogeneous and the exotic.[2]

For some animal historians, zoos were a pivotal step forward in human-animal relations because they made it possible to organize and learn about animals more systematically. Endowed with scientific and educational mandates, modern zoos became popular sites for family outings and group entertainment. From the 1970s, some zoos undertook a conservationist role. The American Zoo Association claims that they generate $130 million each year in support of conservation projects and encourage zoogoers to participate in conservation activities.[3] The Toronto Zoo's public relations focus on conservation features iconic animals such as white lions, pandas, and polar bears. How much zoos actually contribute to the viability of species, or whether they have adopted conservation rhetoric as public justification for their continuing existence, are subjects of continuing debate.[4]

In his influential 1964 essay "Why Look at Animals?," John Berger claims that animals, like art, have always been central to human symbolic creation. But the capturing of animals for zoos is merely "a symbolic representation of the conquest of all distant and exotic lands."[5] Berger describes the experience of going from cage to cage as though viewing works in a gallery. But the object, the animal, which you would think would be imbued with the aura of singularity, is barely alive: "You are looking at something that has been rendered absolutely marginal; and all the concentration you can muster will never be enough to centralize it."[6] Berger has been criticized for expressing nostalgic sentiments when he describes the display of animals in zoos and photographs, which Akira Lippitt compares to cinema as "a gesture of mourning for disappearing wildlife."[7] Berger claims that the paucity of animal encounters in urban cultures combined with the constant mediation of cameras and zoos (which arose more or less at the same time) prohibits genuine encounters between human and nonhuman animals. This prognosis leaves only a retreat to premodern life to restore the possibility of exchanging an authentic look with an animal. In fact, Berger did move to the European countryside for the last half-century of his life. I find it more productive, though, to consider other potential openings from Berger's critique. It's useful to revisit "Why Look at Animals" in connection with his BBC book and lecture series *Ways of Seeing*, an extended commentary on visual culture drawn from Walter Benjamin's essay "The Work of Art in the Age of Mechanical Reproduction."[8] Viewed from that angle, Berger's description of the loss of the aura of original art through electronic reproduction is not purely nostalgic. He elaborates Benjamin's argument that when removed from the ritual architectural environments in which they arose, such as churches and cathedrals, paintings began to mean differently to their viewers. A baroque painting could hang in a modern gallery; a reproduction of it could hang in a middle-class home. It became possible to make copies and move them around, to create new aesthetic combinations, to sell image reproductions to ordinary people who could mix them with their own images and memories in their own interiors, and to juxtapose images through photocollage and film editing to create new meanings for images and new sensations for audiences.[9] The original aura is lost with reproduction, as Benjamin argues, but the potential to enchant and find new meanings is potentially more democratic.

Michel Foucault refers to menageries and zoos as "heterotopias," or themed spaces in which entities formerly separated by distance are brought into new relations of proximity to one another.[10] The spaces that are juxtaposed are incompatible—you would not, for example, see polar bears and elephants living in proximity to one another except at the zoo. Galleries and homes can also be heterotopias, or places where spatially diverse items are mixed and their meanings appropriated for a definite purpose. Raymond Williams describes such an experience in a justly famous passage:

> There was this Englishman who worked in the London office of a multinational corporation based in the United States. He drove home one evening in his Japanese car. His wife, who worked in a firm that imported German kitchen equipment, was already at home. Her small Italian car was often quicker through the traffic. After a meal, which included New Zealand lamb, Californian carrots, Mexican honey, French cheese and Spanish wine, they settled down to watch a programme on their television set, which had been made in Finland. The programme was a retrospective celebration of the war to recapture the Falkland Islands. As they watched it they felt warmly patriotic, and very proud to be British.[11]

This depiction of everyday life in the modern world shows how much the global reach of empire together with the heterogeneity of commodities and images have become ordinary. This apparently ironic duality of diversity and centralization was not perceptible when noblemen kept menageries on their estates, but these menageries anticipated and inspired the reach of global capital and the heterotopic world of commodities. They created novel viewing experiences for people who were not familiar with these exotic species and would only ever see them randomly housed together.

As zoo historian Eric Ames writes regarding menageries and zoos, "Whatever their ontological differences each example represents a contradictory site, where one space is transformed into another, real or imagined."[12] They have for this reason been critiqued as "antigeographic" spaces, particularly in the shadow of Disney.[13] It might be equally useful to see them as metageographic spaces, in which animal bodies are used to reference, authenticate, and enchant by proxy their original environments, while making such environments marginal to the spectacle. Menageries thus legitimated, or in Benjamin's term, aestheticized, acts of violent appropriation. Their bodies became beautiful living symbols of the rich lands from which they originated, while these same habitats and ecosystems were robbed and disrupted in order to enrich the tastes and coffers of the imperial centers. The "charismatic megafauna" collected in the menageries were the sacrificial prize of colonization, and the material foundation of what we now call the Anthropocene.[14]

For Berger and Benjamin, seeing a reproduction or an original work of art hung in a gallery cannot fully restore the aura of its lost status as a holistic part of a unique environment. Similarly, seeing an animal in a zoo can never be the same as encountering it in the wild. The wild space of the exotic animal is simultaneously romanticized and marginalized in the semantic structure of the zoo. As Benjamin understands the effects of such reproduction, the ritual function of art (such as one sees in a church) aestheticizes politics; but when art is mechanically reproduced, when it becomes part of a heterotopic collection of space images as one sees in a snapshot or video, it creates the opportunity to politicize aesthetics. Like paintings or mosaics, animals in zoos have been extracted from the spaces and activities from which they emerged and which made their being possible. Their capture and confinement in these heterotopic spaces multiplies their special value as objects of display. Animals in zoos can never mean what we expect them to mean, Berger argues, because their wildness has been amputated. Depending on what viewers do expect them to mean, this is incontrovertible. Similarly, the virtual menageries populating our present heterotopias aestheticize the syntax of de-animalization. Just as we can catch glimpses of the power, movement, and beauty of animals even in zoos, photographs, cinema, or digital media, so we can see these bodies and traces reconfigured. Images can be juxtaposed or layered or mediated to defend the offerings of existing society or to argue for a new culture, a new society. Then the image of the animal becomes emblematic of the vistas of human domination that have spread across the planet—at least until animals disappear altogether, but then, so would we.

Figure 1.2

The Royal Menagerie, 1777, etching, Jean-Baptiste Nicolet. © Frankfurt Historical Museum.

Just as a menagerie is, but is not only, a collection of animals, so the virtual menagerie is, but is not only, a reiteration of animal collections in virtual space. Among its primary differences from living menageries is the fact that it is not made to be looked at in the way we think of looking. For this reason, there is still more to say about the constitution of the earlier menagerie and its critical implications for the present. The exotic animals they housed can no more be separated from the ship or team of oxen that transported them than a cart can be separated from a horse. The ship was built to explore different lands. It carried a giraffe across the ocean to enchant its recipients and to open the door to new trade relations, taking important first steps to colonizing the lands from which the animals were taken. The animal becomes a medium of colonization through its attachment of other mediums.

Why are there so many images of animals now demanding our attention? What and who are they mediating, and what do they want of us? In the 1950s, advertising billboards were filled with kitchen appliances, which, as Susan Buck-Morss has shown, were instrumental in celebrating and consolidating the utopian imaginary called America, not just across the United States but also across the dreamscape of the Soviet empire.[15] In the 1990s, more angels than would fit on the head of a pin crowded the surfaces of museum and gallery exhibitions, postcards, calendars, dishes, and kitsch commodities. I interpreted them then as disenchanted souvenirs from a distant space once known as heaven, now conquered by the Pentagon's so-called Strategic Defense Initiative (popularly known as "Star Wars") and military optical probes.[16] These angel "messengers" were earthbound prisoners of war, trapped from flight. The military-industrial complex leading the "revolution in military affairs" in the late 1990s wanted more than souvenirs from their space adventures. Just as satellites needed the income generated by weather forecasting, so these three-dimensional military communication and surveillance capacities needed a vast network of and market for digital devices that could carry people with them. While the proportion of military budgets assigned to telecommunications soared, the network of devices, people, and animals grew. In a materialist vocabulary such as this, it might be tangential to argue about whether people "really" looked at those animals or spoke to those callers. Either way, the proliferation of animal interfaces has shaped how people relate to their digital devices, to animals, and to the world in general.

Cultural representations are symbolic responses to deeply conflicting social and aesthetic positions that can be negotiated through the process of creation, textual form, reception of the work, and the meanings that situate it in the world. Perhaps the same can be said of the mediums through which we encounter these works. For instance, the autonomy and mobility we seek in mobile devices coexists with the concentrated corporate power that produces these devices, and our felt sense of freedom is contradicted by the fact that the technology inexorably traces our movements. Such contradictions haunt our relationships with the networks in which we find ourselves. The inchoate pressure of cumulative human technological extension is widely mediated by the image of an animal that both holds and withholds meaning. Such technological innovations seem to (re)mediate our encounters with animals while animal symbols (re)mediate our encounters with technology. It doesn't really matter whether the user that picks up a phone or game believes that technology restores our proximity to other species. It is not the other species that matter in this encounter. And yet the other species are visible, and even if they are only visible as ghosts, they are reminders that we humans can no more be separated from the nonhuman world now than when our species was new.

Just as the images featured in the following chapters have been set in motion to advance an intent, so there is a pedagogical side to my own undertaking: in Benjamin's words, "To train our image-making faculty to look stereoscopically and dimensionally into the depths of the shadows of history."[17] These animal interfaces don't just speak to relations and negotiations in the present; they also carry traces of what has been combatted or suppressed, harnessed or forgotten, freed or destroyed. Looking at these traces stereoscopically calls for a media archaeology[18] of ubiquitous human-animal-technology mediations. The point is to produce a "layered approach to Internet language that looks for 'insights from past new media, while also accounting for the political economy of contemporary Internet language.'"[19]

If animals confined in menageries and zoos have been "rendered absolutely marginal," and if the animal figures knocking on our virtual doors are even more distant from the *Umwelt* of animal life, these phantoms have also awakened people's fascination with and debates about animal life and wellbeing. For Jonathan Burt, "The theory that the animal is becoming increasingly virtual, that its fate is to disappear into technological reproduction to become nothing more than imagery, would make sense were it not for the fact that this imagery is not uniform but unavoidably fragmented, both in terms of the technical variety of its reproduction and in terms of the various conflicts around the image itself."[20] Thus, Burt adds, "the link between vision and animals should not be reduced to the backward glance of nostalgia, but also acknowledged as 'forward-looking.'"[21] Whether looking backward to the old menageries or forward with the present, whether the menagerie is live or digital, more than one possibility is catalyzed through the mediation of the animal.

Virtual Encounters

Encountering the penguin or lion emissaries that comprise the virtual menagerie is far removed from a first encounter with a penguin or lion in the fifteenth or sixteenth century. The earliest virtual menageries nonetheless borrowed species and graphic design elements from the menageries that preceded them. By recuperating early modern animal display to promote the technologies and values of late modernity (speed, convenience, mobility, connection), digital entrepreneurs and designers confirmed Burt's claim that "there is no doubting the significance of the visual animal body to the technologies of modernity."[22] The animals that entice us into connecting with electronic media are designed to animate the magic, admiration, and sense of control over life and distance that was promised by those earlier menageries. Their backward-looking forward-looking design suggestively blurs the passage of time that flowed through the chaotic progress of capitalist modernity and the ways this era distanced humans from most animals through urbanization, deforestation, hunting, industrialized agriculture, habitat loss, and extinction. Like their living predecessors, these digital creatures can be seen as chimeras. I borrow this term from descriptions of the giraffe that arrived in China in 1414 as a "monster," a chimera, a previously unseen creature combined from other species. Digital menageries are like their predecessors' chimeras in reorganizing the spaces and horizons known to their observers, and they too present viewers with dreams of exploration. These virtual menageries do not require physical transport from one continent to another to be assembled, and they do not need physical spaces to be housed in. The animals in our contemporary mediascape inhabit an environment vastly different from that of their predecessors, but their mediation of worlds to bring them closer together parallels in some ways the purpose of the early modern menagerie. Both menageries formed first contacts between previously distinct spaces and offered enticing tokens of things to come.

Like the animals displayed in early modern menageries, the animals displayed online co-constitute new spatial and sociotechnical imaginaries with various trajectories of power, desire, and belief. Like the real and imaginary animals illustrating medieval maps, these figures promise to open, bridge, and subdue the marvelous but potentially dangerous places of the "New World" online. Virtual menageries channel these wondrous capacities into the life of the technocratic present. Despite such images' cheerful populism, the aristocracy for whom live animals were captured to populate

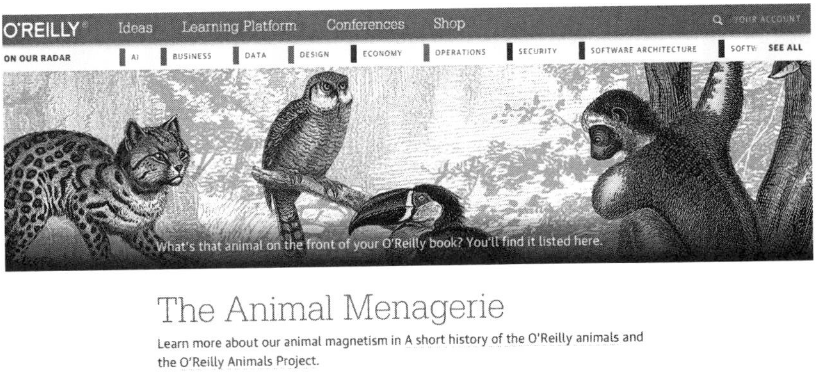

Figure 1.3
The Animal Menagerie, 2018, screenshot. Image courtesy of O'Reilly Media.

early modern menageries is not gone. Many twentieth-century millionaires and celebrities have owned personal menageries, from Randolph Hearst, newspaper mogul, to Richard Branson, former owner of Virgin Air, who lost many of his animals in Hurricane Irma,[23] to Michael Jackson, whose affection for his exotic animals is memorialized in Jeff Koons's unsettling sculpture of the singer and his chimp Bubbles. Readers may recall the exorbitantly expensive menagerie owned by the Rosen Corporation in Philip K. Dick's prescient novel *Do Androids Dream of Electric Sheep?*[24] These owners are reenacting the iconic lifestyle of the outdated landed aristocracy through possession of exotic animals, but their menageries are susceptible to environmental risks that seventeenth-century owners could not have imagined. Aside from these archaic personal menageries, the aristocracy is being resurrected through the unprecedented concentration of wealth by the largest corporations in the world, many of which brand themselves with animal images. Apple "has" wild cats; Disney has Mickey Mouse, the Lion King, and the Animal Kingdom; Coca-Cola has polar bears; companies producing cell phones claim copyright for images of pandas, lions, rhinos, dogs, goats, monkeys, and beavers. The impact of the circulation of such figures is not as benign as these happy images suggest.

But I am pursuing a different kind of connection between colonial menageries and contemporary mediascapes. Let's look more closely at the genealogy of animal imagery in the era of technological reproducibility. Film critics rightly emphasize the synchronicity between moving animals and moving pictures, but the history of these first contacts demonstrates a longstanding tendency to connect animals with exploration.

The first moving picture, made by Muybridge, featured a running horse; in 1894, both Étienne-Jules Marey and Thomas Edison made short films of cats in motion to illustrate the exciting potential of the new medium (see figure 1.4).[25] The cinematic editing techniques of the early 1900s were, according to one critic, derived from trying to make zoo enclosures appear contiguous with wilderness, so that explorers could be filmed heroically discovering or shooting animals in what appeared to be wild spaces. The wild spaces in which the animals cinematically appear supplanted the confined spaces in which the animals were kept and filmed. These wild and confined spaces were merged through editing, but the shooting to death of the animals was real.[26] The creation of seamless movement between wild and confined spaces was not simply a technical creation of film editing, and not simply a way to simplify the portrayal of hunting and exploration. It was also a reenactment of the power to capture and move animals, retracing electronically the history of colonizing new spaces for which

Figure 1.4
Boxing Cats, 1894, screenshot, Thomas Edison.

the animal has functioned as a crucial emblem. Whether cinematic artists found animals the most convenient or magical vehicle for conveying motion and so demonstrating the superiority of film over photography, or intuited that animals were the best means to stir viewers and elicit their desire to watch these new technologies, or some combination of creative and mythic impulses promising new exciting but ultimately safe vistas, this strategy of using animals to draw viewers into new spaces or technologies appears repeatedly in twentieth- and twenty-first-century media.

Animals appearing in the first demonstrations of moving and digital media promised a reenergized relationship between machinic and human life. Early cinematic achievements were populated by boxing cats and electrocuted elephants. American animation was launched in 1913 with the image of Gertie the Dinosaur strolling out of a cave, drawn by Winsor McKay, creator of the popular "Little Nemo" comic strip (1905–1914). Early American animation featured many inescapable animal characters, including Felix the Cat, Mickey Mouse, Pluto the Dog, Bimbo the companion of Betty Boop (racial stereotype or animal?),[27] and later, when wartime came, boxing beagles, armed insects, eagles, bulldogs, and other conscripted species. Animators' dependence on images of animals to construct their stories was amazingly not explored or even acknowledged by documents and studies of American cinema until animation scholar Paul Wells published *Animated Bestiaries* in 2009. (In a sabbatical research trip to the Library of the Academy of Motion Pictures in Los Angeles in 2008, I spent days scouring magazines and the indexes of book monographs and anthologies dedicated to the analysis of animation. I found that in eighty years of animation commentary, the word "animal" did not appear once! Since the entire history of animation relies on anthropomorphic animal characters, the omission is remarkable.)

Beginning in the 1960s, software products were branded with graphic images of penguins, monkeys, birds, snakes, and other species designed to look like the older menageries, a story elaborated in chapter 4. The first commercially successful interactive toys were Tamagotchi and Furby, both animal-like robots developed to be interactive and alive-like. The first amateur video posted on YouTube, "At the Zoo," displayed the maker, one of the founders of YouTube, posed in front of an elephant at the zoo. The second and third YouTube posts were cat videos produced by Steven Chen, software engineer/graphic designer and another of YouTube's founders, titled "Stinky the Cat I" and "Stinky the Cat 2." Apple produced a series of wildcat images to signal its serial innovations, while iPhone 5 was launched with a GIF of a splashing elephant. A 2009 exhibition entitled "Fauxy the fake-fur-with-feelings" presented haptic touchscreen technologies as a way to translate between digital and animal neurologies. This was not only a creative expansion of the digital animal-robot pet affordances, but also, for Pramod Nayar, the launch of "a new era in several areas: haptic technologies, body image issues and textile technology."[28] "If you want an artificially intelligent system to reason like a person, model it after an octopus," says Jim Crowder from the U.S. company Raytheon Intelligence and Services.[29] Similarly, the British company Octopus Ventures invests extensively in research in artificial intelligence. Identified by a logo that encapsulates this same idea of the octopus as a model for distributed intelligence, the British company has financed at least fifty separate AI ventures.[30] These ventures will ultimately be connected by intelligent robots whose development has become the holy grail of universities and corporations seeking major research funding today.

While animals mediate our relations with other humans and spaces, then, they also mediate relations between people and machines. Electronic and digital images, telecommunications hardware and software, and computer and new mobile and haptic technology products have been widely tested, branded, advertised, and disseminated with images of animals, presumably to help encourage their "adoption." The anti-spyware encryption technology famously used to open a locked iPhone 6 in 2006 was first used against an animal rights campaign in 2002, showing that the relationship between animals and communication technologies is always close but often dynamic and unpredictable. There is no such thing as a free flow of images. The conflict Marx outlined between the relations of production and the means of production did not end when the production of images went online. If an animal has the power to animate a narrative and enrich its investors, it also has the power to interrupt it. Anecdotal evidence of this power is popularly circulated through iconic images of dogs or cats sitting on or chewing up our domestic machineries of textual production. Part of us wants the animal to win. The trope is similar to the scene in which the movie protagonist chooses love and throws his cell phone into a pond, but when a puppy chews up your essay or a kitten sits on your keyboard, it's not your decision, what can you do?

The Animal Is the Medium Is the Message

Animals and animal imagery have been indispensable to building material connectivities and collective imaginaries and differences, whether among tribes, monarchies, nation-states, childhood, or the information society that emerged in the 1970s. Every new technology introduces changes in the space and scale of human relations.[31] The giraffes, beavers, cats, and birds that appear in the following chapters arrive in concert with emergent technologies and are united by their role in the inauguration of new social relations. The subsumption and abstraction of animal power, the mediation of new spaces, and the production of risk and reassurance come together as a field of forces from which these animal-technology-human images emerge.

What defines these menageries as an outcome of these developments is not only their status as representation of animals but also their syntax, their relations with viewers, and their capacity to vanish. As I began to unravel the language of these virtual animals, I realized that they could only be understood as the product of a history of human-animal relations that was cumulatively encapsulated and layered into the contradictory graphic language of virtual, profit-driven networks. The duality of the menagerie anticipates what Applegate and Cohen describe in their analysis of graphical interfaces on the Internet. They refer to a "political economy of Internet communication that functions solely on the commodification of reference and, by its opposite, the destruction of signifiers."[32] That is to say, there are two opposing, co-constitutive forces at work in the political economy of Internet communication: the commodification of information (software, for instance) and the devaluation of how information can be represented in language (the abstraction of the animal image, for instance). The animal symbol refers to something that is commodifiable; it conveys less and less information itself, while offering up the insight that it is itself dispensable, and yet special or lively enough to (appear to) resist this same process.

The syntax of these images is a residue of the past shaped by contemporary networks and economies. Looking at how images of giraffes, beavers, or birds become abstractions of animal bodies through digital iconography tells us something about how the circulation of such imagery reinscribes and disrupts the logics of contemporary life. Media encompass both actual and virtual realities in their production of "the real." When a media storm moves across and shakes up the platforms and possibilities from which it arises, and the categories and experiences through which nature and technology were once understood are rewritten, you arguably have a media event. To describe the virtual menagerie as a media event is to explore how it arises from and reconfigures multiple and overlapping systems of order and agency.

This virtual menagerie arose in the 1960s from a confluence of events described in chapter 5. It continues to circulate within an increasingly dense network of technological and ecological transformations which would be impossible to encapsulate in a single book. A contemporary theory of media would ask, How does the material culture built through these social and technological processes determine what kinds of variations or changes can be produced by media events? What can emerge from such an event, and what possibilities are constrained from playing out? In reconfiguring the practices and potentials of mediating technologies, the media event alters what McLuhan calls the "shared situation" of human (and nonhuman) collectivities.

In a 1953 article published in the Toronto journal *Explorations*, McLuhan introduced an early version of the idea that made him famous, that "the medium is the message." Critiquing his contemporaries' tendency to interpret media in terms of the contents transmitted by them, he wrote: "This assumption blinds people to the aspect of communication as participation in a common situation. It leads to ignoring the *form* of communication as the basic art situation which is more important than the basic idea or information 'transmitted.'"[33]

This introductory remark gives us a slightly different portal to the idea that "the medium is the message," or that the animal can be a medium. McLuhan is not always asking us to focus on a single medium as a tool of connection, even one that mutates our nervous systems; he is asking us to investigate how they shape our "participation in a common situation." That is to say, the medium together with the process of mediation unites people in a common language, experience, or place. No medium works alone, but in combination: thus the term "media ecology," whose principles apply to both living and technological entities. Every medium works together with others to inscribe new perceptions and possibilities onto our social and affective experiences, while diminishing others. Echoing what he learned from Innis, McLuhan writes: "Every medium is in some sense a universal, pressing toward realization. But its expressive pressures disturb existing balances and patterns in other media and cultures." Today, when the technical and aesthetic forms of the media multiply so fast that we must constantly adjust, we may be more aware of such disturbances, although for those for whom "new" media have always framed their "common situation," such disturbances are surely experienced differently.[34] In any case, a medium doesn't just transmit something from one party to another, or from one to many; it participates in a relationship, sensually and socially shaping and being shaped by the subjects who participate in it and of course the power relations extant among those subjects.

In trying to encapsulate these ideas, McLuhan, like Benjamin, sought to identify a deeper connection between media as art form and media as political process. To consider an animal in a mediological perspective is to pursue the same connection. McLuhan explained the "expressive pressures" of a medium in terms of how its materiality and informational process equally shape and reshape users' sensory and haptic dimensions. As he elaborates in *Understanding Media*, each medium absorbs and extends our body and focuses our attention in specific ways. One could apply this principle equally to clothes, cameras, cars, or cats, all of which we live among, all of which are interactive participants in a "common situation" of media involvement. Mediated in all directions, the human body no longer coincides with itself. Like the material object conceived by Marx, it only has a life, it is only productive, in the context of its relationships.[35] By applying this concept to the body, McLuhan had taken a first step toward posthumanism.

For McLuhan, "The body, in sum, is a capacity for relationality that literally requires mediation and that, in a sense, cannot be conceptualized without it."[36] If this ideational body is incomplete, it is for McLuhan, just as it is for Marx or Stiegler, the reliance on technology that makes us human. This human dance of mediated becoming does not only intersect with technology, however. Animals are also mediators of social relations: between humans, between social groups, between humans and technologies, between power, space, and resources. In the context of display, these virtual animals, like their predecessors in the menagerie, are doing something—mediating—while metaphorically standing in for the vitality and affect of this activity. This double duty of the multilayered menagerie produces the impression that the symbolic, the material, and the vital can coincide in a world beyond the screen just as they do in our bodies. Of course the vitality of these virtual entities is questionable when they fulfill so many of the characteristics of an inert object and invite their viewers to do the same.[37]

Media theorist Friedrich Kittler was strongly influenced by McLuhan's ideas, but drew a sharp dividing line between them on the issue of what he perceived as McLuhan's anthropocentrism.[38] For McLuhan, media are the "extensions of man." As Geoffrey Winthrop-Young comments, "This prosthetic logic has its point of origin in the human body and nervous system. From Kittler's point of view, McLuhan still subscribes to the anthropocentric delusion that man is the measure of all media, even when the latter reshape the former."[39] But Kittler's critique of anthropocentrism does not extend to a consideration of nonhuman species. Kittler does not propose that if a train or a light bulb can be a medium, so can a horse or a giraffe, and yet horses transported people and mail for centuries before faster, automated "horsepower" machines were invented to replace them. Giraffes and cats can also be mediums of communication, whose relations with humans are thoroughly mediated and multiplied by communication technologies that are in turn thoroughly mediated and changed by the animal's presence. McLuhan invites us to look at ourselves as changed beings from the perspective of the media through which we construct and view the world; critical animal studies scholars invite us to look at ourselves from the imagined perspectives of nonhuman animals as we watch, cuddle, or eat them. Thinking of the animal as a mediator allows us to begin to ask what they see looking back at us, and what they might want to tell us.

For McLuhan, "man" is constituted by "his" extensions but is still the measure of meaning. And yet there is nothing in McLuhan's argument that excludes the nonhuman animal from the definition of a medium. As Lawrence Grossberg suggests, we need to enlarge our scope for conceptualizing media "both as category and object."[40] In *Cultural Studies in the Future Tense,*

Grossberg aligns the analysis of mediation with the cultural studies project of analyzing the complexity of "affective apparatuses and mediations." Mediation belongs to "reality itself," he argues, not to "media" or "culture."[41] We can extend this concept of mediation not only beyond objects of representation but also beyond the human. The animal medium charges and focuses our attention, mediates our relationships, extends our capacities, alters our nervous systems and indeed our lives.

Consider this premise at the simplest level: if you have a dog, your relationship with neighbors and the neighborhood is different than if you do not have a dog. You share a particular "common situation" (McLuhan's term) with other people and animals and with the spaces through which you move. When you meet through dogs, your dog is an essential medium of communication, as evidenced by the probability that you know the name of the dog sooner than the name of the person on the other side of its leash. As you stroll the neighborhood at various times of day and night, you are acting as the servomechanism of the four-legged creature leading you on, just as McLuhan says, in one of his more histrionic phrases, that humans act as the "servomechanisms of the machine world."[42] Human incompleteness works in many directions. Your awareness of your environment is unquestionably changed by the presence of the dog whose awareness of his environment is unquestionably changed by the leash. You are recognizing and participating in the physical and affective reciprocity of bodies through which humans and animals become companion species.[43]

You also share a common situation with people online who post cat pictures that you like to view and share. In the Facebook site "Cats Against Capitalism,"[44] for instance, thousands of members creatively twist (unleash?) cats, comradery, comedy, and anticapitalist politics into new tropes. Someone took a picture, capitalism is the enemy, the cat is the object, the screen is the subject, the people are the verb … wait, is it the other way around? As I will argue in chapter 6, cats mediate human relationships with interfaces and people as much as the screen is mediating viewers' relationship with cats. Both are mediating connections to the world online via a community of amenable multispecies comrades whose surrogates ostentatiously refuse the logic of capital that brings them to the screen. "When I am playing with my cat, how do I know the cat is not toying with me?"[45] There is more than one history haunting this activity. These cats mediate different spirits than those burned with the witches in earlier inquisitions, but together with the people who live with cats or post their pictures, they are also animating an opposition to population management strategies at a microlevel.

Rather than attend to the finely textured and sometimes bewildering phenomenologies of these experiences, I want to explore more closely what it means to identify an animal as a mediator, and to connect this idea with affect. If an animal can be a medium, and not just the content of a photograph, painting, or advertisement, and not just the body of an animal, what is it mediating? What constitutes its agency within the context of human domination, the nonlinear trajectory of global culture, and the emergence of compulsory connectivity connecting the planet? The 1414 giraffe featured in the next chapter, together with the ship that transported it, mediated between two imperial courts and established new possibilities for future relations between them. The Canadian beaver, together with ships and canoes and other materials enumerated in chapter 3, mediated an empire and its colonies, and thus settler-Indigenous relations, and contributed monetarily and symbolically to the proliferation of new political and corporate entities and icons. The beaver was a central (unwilling) player in the pilfering of the territories of the First Nations and the transformation of the corporate territory of the fur trade into the political territory of the nation state. Similarly, the digital menageries explored in chapters 4 and 5 mediate emergent relationships between software designers, personal computing, informational and technological corporations, military and civilian research, new forms of life online and off, and the emergence of nonhuman intelligence. These bits of animals arise from and circulate through different regimes and habitats and meet with different destinies. The larger-than-life lion whose portrait appears behind Steve Jobs to reiterate the Apple brand is not the same lion chosen to fight with horses and bulls in ancient menageries or captured for display in an aristocratic menagerie. This is not only because one is possibly still alive and the other isn't, although this difference has enormous consequence for the lion in question. The lion whose photograph provides a background to Jobs is interchangeable with any other lion. In this respect, it is an object, not an animal, and Jobs does not need to look at it. Jobs was arguably more powerful than any emperor, but he didn't require a living lion to prove it. His expression of power sought to engender a more modern response. Corporate billionaires are like and unlike emperors, just as tech users who love the animals on their screens and phones are like and unlike others who find such compliance demeaning. In 2005, for instance, the mobile phone operator Meteor prompted protests from Irish animal protection groups over the use of an orangutan called Harry in its advertising.[46] They felt that it was inappropriate to reduce such an animal to an object for the purpose of manipulating consumers. Such protests are part of a shift in attitudes toward the exploitation of animals from which emperors would have been exempt. This shift is related in complicated and unfinished ways to the velocity and lack of velocity in the animal imagery that circulates on a daily basis.

Behind all these interesting details is a central argument. Understanding animals as co-constitutive entities in the imbrication of machines and humans is fundamentally different from viewing animals as the content or text transmitted via a particular medium. This argument has implications for thinking about mediation, about affect, about risk management, and about the human-animal relations so desperately in need of repair. From writing implements to transport vehicles, scents, flavors, musical instruments, clothing, and even film and telecommunications, as Nicole Shukin and Jonathan Sterne have demonstrated, many of our mediating materials have depended upon or been "rendered" from animal bodies.[47] We have a country that was "built on dead beavers" (see chapter 3): we have film because of the rendering of horses' body parts, we have audio transmitters because of experimental surgeries on cats' brains, we have exquisite carvings and piano keys because of the slaughter of elephants.[48] Animals, animal parts, and animal images and sounds have been indispensable to building our social bonds, material connectivities, and collective imaginaries. In some instances, it is precisely the fact that the object is rendered from animal parts that constitutes it as an object of desire. Although representations of animals are increasingly de-animalized, we humans should not imagine that we are exempt from these processes. Just as an animal or a picture of an animal can be objectified, so its instrumental use on us can have a similar effect.

Stereoscopic History

Writing in the mid-nineteenth century, Karl Marx makes use of the rhetorical triangulation of humans, technology, and animals to illustrate and justify his identification of humans as a unique species. His discussion of labor is based on a fundamental distinction between humans and other animals: both are builders, but humans are unique in that they can conceptualize an object before they build it, he argues.[49] The human appropriation of nature is legitimated by our species' intelligence and adept development of tools. Marx's juxtaposition of humans, animals, and machines at work is at the same time the basis for his critique of industrial capitalism and its suffocation and exploitation of human capacities. Humans only produce what they produce, objects only mean what they mean, Marx insists, in the wider context of social relations. For Hannah Arendt, however, Marx's emphasis on toolmaking to define human potentiality presupposes a production-oriented life world that reverses the relationship between means and ends. With the emphasis on productivity fueling modern society, she writes in *The Human Condition*, "it was ultimately the life of the species which asserted itself. … What was left was a 'natural force,' the force of the life process itself, to which all means and all human activities were equally submitted … and whose only aim, if it had an aim at all, was survival of the animal species man."[50] In this scenario, the "natural force" of the life process, that is to say our human species being, forces all other aspects of human nature to submit to it. This is quite different from the post-World War II description of "animal spirits," which it appeared to be the responsibility of governments and psychologists to control. For Arendt, in any case, Marx's positive emphasis on the "natural force" accumulated by the human species has justified greater interdependency with technologies of production that were not sustaining of the potentialities of human nature or of nature as a whole. One wonders whether Marx's influence has been so great that it has shaped both the means of production and our ideas about them, but that is beyond the purview of this discussion.

Like Arendt, media historian Carolyn Marvin challenges the nineteenth-century emphasis on production, the idea that subsistence is the sole foundation of the "natural force" of man's species being. For Marvin, the emphasis on subsistence as the destiny of life raises the question as to "whether men were fundamentally different from electrical machines after all," which in turn raises the prospect of "a contest for supremacy between automation and evolution."[51] These critical inquiries into Marx's understanding of the relationship between humans, nature, and technology suggest that under capitalism, "man" has so thoroughly and parasitically summoned the powers of animals and machines and interwoven them into his instrumental productive being that "he" has lost "himself."

Later thinkers allow us to wonder whether man had newly "lost" himself or was always incomplete, always in need of the supplementation of tools and nonhuman animals. The "man" summoned by the industrial capitalist regime with its ability to marshal animals and machines willy-nilly turns out to be less sovereign than our philosophy has claimed. With the increasing sophistication and power of such tools, theorists like Arendt and Marvin conclude that complicity with the power their machines wield over them is rendering humans more akin to animals than to sovereign subjects. If that is the case, the virtual menageries circulating on our screens are extensions, fantasies, or even hauntings of ourselves.

Whether lack of sovereignty is a good or a bad finding depends entirely on how human relationships with animals and technologies are understood, organized, and lived. This is a central question, given how colonial and commodity relations have underwritten the history of these practices and ideas. It is also a central question in terms of how the relationship between animality, work, and desire is configured and experienced through the virtual menagerie.

Speculation about the machine's animalization of human nature did not end in the nineteenth century. Drawing on Deleuze and Guattari's "becoming-animal," Jane Bennett suggests that the flights of freedom we find through animals offer an escape from order and instrumentality. She suggests that "the fugitive thoughts that pass through our brain with extraordinary speed" can be compared to Thoreau's encounter with a flock of birds that interrupt and enchant the horizon.[52] Here freedom is equivalent to contact with the phenomenology of animal life, a kind of homeopathic resolution for the reduction of the human potential. This identification of the animal with freedom can be contrasted with the imagery of surrealist artists such as Max Ernst and his contemporaries, for whom the meaning of the animal fragment is far more elusive. In Bennett's remedy, animal spirits can elicit enchantment or philosophy but not fear, pity, or terror. As allegories or guarantors for human ingenuity and freedom, they cannot be monstrous symptoms or repressive entities or subjected bodies crushed by machinic appropriations of life and time, and they (we) cannot be culpable agents for that appropriative project. Perhaps, though, it is not mechanization in itself, or rationality either, but capitalism, parasitism, and precarity that render humans, animals, or means of production vulnerable to instrumentalization? These forces seek to overcome the potential liberation promised by these processed animal spirits, and more profoundly by their joined trajectory.

Affect, Risk, Mediation

Animals, images of animals, and ideas about animals increasingly provide crucial hinges for our relations with global networks and their strategic processes of reconfiguration. A giraffe or a bird can extend our relationality and change our "common situation," as McLuhan said of media, and the animal does this differently than a computer or a car. But when you combine a giraffe with a ship, a horse with moving images, a cat with a camera and social media, a bird with an industrialized therapeutic sound recording, or monsters with the financialization of everything,[53] you have created a shift, even an event. In such cases, everything—geopolitical boundaries, communication technologies, media platforms, relations with animals, modes of governance—is subject to change. When a shift becomes an event, it arises from but also alters the geopolitical contexts from which it emerges. In the contemporary mediasphere, what the animal has introduced is affect, and what the affect is mobilized with/against is risk.

Commenting on McLuhan's work on the occasion of its half-centenary, Richard Grusin writes: "In the first decades of the 21st century, we find ourselves in the midst of a shift in our dominant cultural logic of mediation away from a predominantly visual, late 20th-century focus on remediation toward a more embodied affectivity of premediation generated by the mobile, socially networked media everyday of the 21st century."[54] The greatest contribution of McLuhan's *Understanding Media*, Grusin suggests, is "to turn our attention away from a primarily visual analysis of media and toward an understanding of how media operate as objects within the world, impacting both the human sensorium and the nonhuman environment alike."[55] Media are heterotopic machines directed toward the cultivation and management of affect. Animal figures enact and symbolize this turn in particularly important ways. This is not to say that there was no affect in human encounters with animals in the distant past. But affect is a subtler concept for talking about how people are touched by mediated encounters with animals than purely historical accounts or McLuhan's speculative cybernetic physiology. If animals are in some ways premediating the technologies we adopt, they are not just stimulating affective responses, or issuing an invitation into the portals of mobile digital computing; they are also providing a means to reconcile contradictory responses to the risky worlds we have constructed.

Affect signals a shift or alteration in how, and with what, we are attached. The concept of affect is drawn originally from research in neuroscience, whose practitioners developed early in the twentieth century an interest in testing responses to external stimuli in human and other bodies. I discuss this research further in chapter 7. The use of its methods to research human and nonhuman bodies in terms of their responses to various stimuli made it possible to think of affect and the somatic realm as tied to the measurable realm of the body, rather than to the mind or to culture, resulting in an understanding of affect as naturalistic, instinctive, or involuntary. In the context of this discussion, affect needs to be understood not only in relation to neuroscientific concepts like sensation or technogenetic perception, but also in relation to chronic affective states like anxiety, mourning, and rage. These are sane responses to the world we share with animals. Writers working at the intersection of science, nature, and the humanities, such as Donna Haraway, Mary Midgley, and Rachel Carson, have rejected the carefully policed distinction between science and other forms of knowledge. In her world-changing book *Silent Spring*,[56] which plays a central role in chapter 7, Carson provided an "eloquent and emotional description of the destructive effects of pesticide use on habitats and birds."[57] In this way, Andrew Whitehouse suggests, she introduced affect into science and nature writing. Since Carson, "The Anthropocene has ambiguity and anxiety at its heart. … The Anthropocene represents the public death of the modern understanding of Nature removed from society."[58]

These developments raise questions about how these menageries make us feel. The idea that animals "stir" human emotions underlies the entire modern enterprise of creating menageries and zoos in which to display them, and helps to explain the common identification of sports teams, nation-states, and leading telecommunications companies with their animal icons. Affect theory recognizes the possibility of a fissure between our cognitive assumptions or commitments and what happens in a moment of felt experience. The insistence on this nonperceptual experience reinforces the critique of naive realism in empirical epistemology, which argues that we know what we know because of direct perception. Not all reality is outside the body, however, and not all making of reality is visible or audible.

In the 1990s, the work and influence of Deleuze and Guattari brought the challenging question of relationships between bodies and social worlds into dialogue with affect theory. Widely cited as a principal source for the use of affect theory in the humanities, Deleuze and Guattari draw on the work of Spinoza and Whitehead to develop a conceptual language for human experience that departs from the idea of the unified subject. Deleuze writes that *affectus* is a "melodic line of continuous variation" or "force of existing" or *potentia agendi*, the lived power or potential to act.[59] He distinguishes this affect from feeling and affection. If Deleuze's description relies on a distinction between mind and body that Spinoza disputes, both philosophers emphasize affect as a relation: "a pre-conscious, proto-social moment in which the multitude of potential, but still virtual, interactions crystallize into the actuality of a specific interaction or response."[60] An affective passage is "an increase or decrease of capacity, *puissance* or lived power, rather than an affection per se." Emotions like fear and hope can be traced back to the "affective dynamics of increasing and decreasing ability to act."[61] In this literature affect is largely precognitive, akin to the experience of the

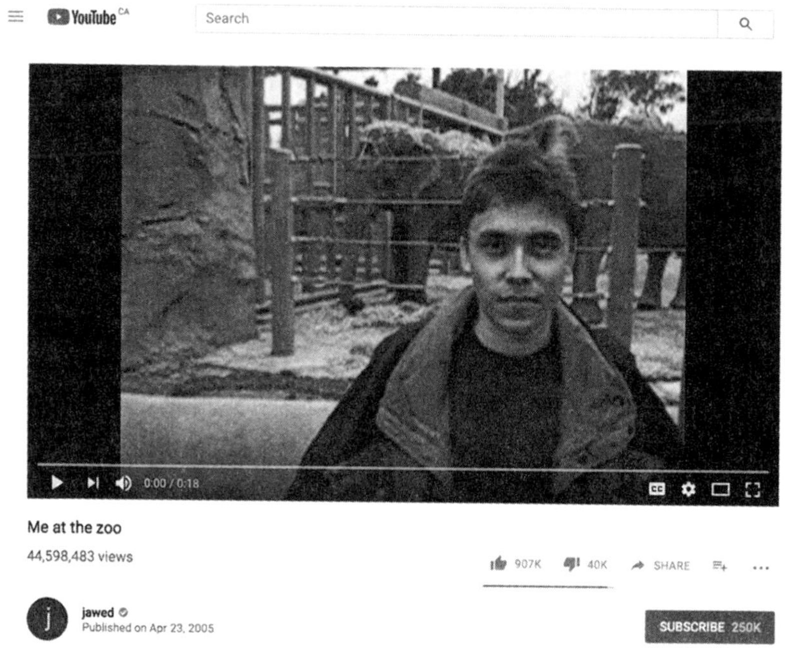

Figure 1.5
Me at the Zoo, 2005, screenshot, Jawed Karim.

startled animal or the intense process of becoming-animal. The naturalist approach to human response has been taken up in cultural theory in terms of the concepts of assemblages of human and nonhuman actors (a trope owing much to Bruno Latour's actor network theory) and the vitalist trope of "lines of flight" which describes humans as becoming other. Also drawing on Deleuze and Guattari's work on assemblages, for instance, Matthew Tiessen argues that the path of human desire is formed by multiple agents, not all of them human. "My suggestion is that reflecting on how desire lines come into being—upon the conditions of their emergence—can provide us with a way to understand the degree to which humans (and human 'desires,' etc.) are interpenetrated, riven, and always already mediated—and even determined—by relationships with human and nonhuman 'objects' that might not conventionally be thought to have agency of their own."[62]

At the same time, the cognitive science on which the discussion of affect and desire has drawn is itself strongly reliant on computing metaphors that were elaborated in research on evolutionary biology, creating rich analogical layers of interpretation in which biology and information increasingly resemble one another. It became possible to temper modern science's absolutist distinctions between humans and animals only when the human-animal connection was remediated by research methods that were modeled on digital data structures. The most visible icons of virtual menageries can be viewed as celebrations of this fusion. This reframing of the "psychosocial interface" to incorporate ideas of evolutionary structure influenced by both computing and models of human cognition is not without its problems. It can lead, as Lisa Blackman argues, "to a rather too hasty dismissal of the concept of subjectivity as such and there is a related tendency to 'flatten out' any would-be distinctions between human and non-human entities."[63] For Western humanism, the animal body had been purely a body, driven instinctively by its evolution-driven genetic programming. The nonhuman animal in this paradigm lacks consciousness or the ability to choose beyond what is required by biological function.[64] Animal "affect" does not become, it just is, which raises interesting issues for the idea of "becoming-animal."

At the same time, electronic and digital depictions of animals can evoke what Anat Pick calls the powerful affect of "creaturely, experiential life," which has been excluded from consideration in research on politics, aesthetics, identity, and the body.[65] Perhaps the experience she describes contributes to the reconciliation of affect and thought, and of technology and human kindness. Our encounter with the animal calls attention literally and figuratively to experiences of embodied life, and potentially opens human experience to more sustainable and compassionate connections with the lives we imagine among nonhuman subjects. But this is still not the end of the story of entanglement, because the study of animal-human-technology mediations also reveals an intensifying management of risk through these same technologies and affects of mediation. Affect is management mediated by tools and relations outside the body; it is a central tool of the present mode of governance sometimes termed biopolitics. Ben Anderson delineates three modes of connection involved in this biopolitical function: "how affective capacities and relations are the 'object-target' of techniques; how affective life may be an 'outside' that exceeds biopolitical mechanisms; and how collective affects become part of the 'conditions' for the birth of forms of biopower."[66]

The research on affect spanning the last century makes it possible, as Patricia Clough argues, to "grasp and to manipulate the imperceptible dynamism of affect."[67] Those birds enlivening your imagination might be, in other words, agents of risk management, as I argue in chapter 7. Connecting Clough's observation to the increased deployment of neuroscience in consumer research and branding, Anderson comments:

Through the promise of imagining what is termed the "reptile brain," neuro-marketing companies sell the holy grail of consumer research: access to the pre-conscious emotional reactions that escape the reflexive subject and yet, supposedly, determine decision making. [Echoes of the "subliminal advertising" warned against in previous decades are surely evident here.] Once these "emotional reactions" have been imaged then "subliminal primes" can be manipulated by changing product design or branding strategy. The consumer is addressed affectively.[68]

Similarly, Mark Hansen points to the sophisticated targeting of human media responses, whereby "today's data and culture industries are increasingly able simply to cut our conscious deliberation out of the loop."[69] With their costly deployment of neurological research along with complex user algorithms, these industries have made good use of media affect research. This "pharmacological dimension" cannot be overemphasized: "In their conquest of deliberative time, today's data-driven culture industries develop research tools and techniques that can also be deployed in the development of delayed cognitive-perceptual systems rooted in the power of data and the capacity for feeding it forward. ... Human-technology couplings that bypass consciousness are already in operation in our world."[70] As a consequence, "humans become implicated within larger causal and technical networks in relation to which they can no longer claim any kind of transcendence."[71] Or as Hiroki Azuma put it, we are becoming animal.[72]

In his *Cultural Studies in the Future Tense,* Lawrence Grossberg specifically aligns the theorization of mediation with the cultural studies project of analyzing the complexity of "affective apparatuses and mediations."[73] This alignment is needed to get at the complexity of the politics of life today. Cultural studies scholar Jeremy Gilbert evokes biopolitics by referring to the "level of interaction at which all relationships (even those between non-human entities such as animals, plants or even, arguably, sub-atomic particles) might be described as political insofar as they can involve relative stabilizations, alterations, augmentations, diminutions or transfers of power."[74] But the industrial cultivation of affect can also lead to what Negri terms "affect from below," the emergence of a world in which new relations, subjectivities, and commonalities may be created and organized.[75] Even when it is manipulated on behalf of the industrial or animal sublime, affect can be productive in multiple directions, and the emergence of alternative potentialities for relating to animals, or to each other through animals, can create a counterneed to exert further biopolitical manipulation as a form of risk management. When you invent the ship, said Virilio, "you also invent the shipwreck; when you invent the plane you also invent the plane crash; and when you invent electricity, you invent electrocution."[76]

When images of animals are used in a calculated manner to capture and absorb affect and attention into the vortex of technological "progress" and capitalist profit, the affective experiences and relations that arise from such entanglement may be different from what was intended.

The animal figures circulated through and in reference to digital networks in the studies that follow invite potential users to join a virtual collectivity through devices that are semiotically and affectively linked with animals. These digital devices extend senses, they are extensions of us, they extend us into some "common situation" that is us and more-than-us. These extensions enhance our powers, but they also deplete them. The digital-animal hybrids emerge within a culture in which the use of technology requires ever more developed techniques, constant innovations in what Edward Tenner calls "the performative use of technology, the skills and know-how that go into the effective operation of devices."[77] Given the economic and political contexts in which such innovation occurs, it is crucial that users *want* to adapt to these new techniques. Users must feel welcome and optimistic in these ever-changing environments and be prepared to lose their earlier forms of knowledge and uses of their bodies. They must respond to technological innovations as simultaneously indispensable to them and capable of freeing them from the implication or effects of being so confined. Otherwise those financiers and engineers will have built their networks, devices, and intelligent prototypes for nothing.

Visible and Invisible Animalities

If animals are essential mediators of our relations with distant others and with our technologies, they are also essential mediators of our relations with ourselves. As Erica Fudge writes, animals "are the limit case, if you like, of all of our structures of understanding. They stand between us and our sense of ourselves, but they also allow us to think about ourselves."[78] Many animal welfare critics pursue this line of thinking by challenging our ravenous slaughter of animals for food. As scientists discover that animals possess more and more of the traits we once defined as singularly human, if, as Montaigne and Derrida write, it is important to consider that the cat is playing with us, as well as the other way around,[79] it is also the case that humans are more animal than we once pretended, and not always in a good way. "We" use our enlightenment to build social and economic structures that sentence millions of animals to slaughter and millions of people to impoverishment, servitude, and alienation. Unlike most animal species, humans murder one another and destroy the planet's resources, and as we consider the precipice associated with the Anthropocene, we continue to do what we have always done because that is what we do. "We have met the enemy and he is us," as Pogo, the inimitable comic-strip possum created by Walt Kelly, exclaimed in 1970 while staring at his polluted swamp.[80]

The representation of animals in contemporary culture echoes the practice of appropriating the power of wild animals by separating them from their natural habitats and reassembling them with others in a new space. Taking the availability of these animals for granted is a cornerstone of colonial power that is massively intensified by the capitalist exploitation of animal bodies. The menagerie relies on the process of making the animal visible without mention of its suffering, poaching, confinement, natural habitats, or ecosystems. The foregrounding of the animal as an object of display obscures the labor involved in this selective process of making visible. Our potential for seeing through these processes, and for feeling empathy for the animals or people suffering because of them, is a social risk that the production of animal representations perpetually seeks to counteract. The bad feelings that we might experience when we look at images of exotic and endangered animals potentially destabilize and disrupt their commercial and entertainment functions; and various risk management strategies, including those that mediate our relations with ourselves, must accommodate these experiences and affects in order to control them. The contemporary menagerie is not only a symptom of modernity, then, or a compensation or substitute for animals or habitats that are lost. As a popular site for the inauguration and mediation of divergent commitments and spaces, the menagerie today has also become a design strategy for the management of a culture increasingly defined by risk. This is another way of saying that, as Fudge writes in another context, "We want animals to speak—this is an overriding desire that many of us share—and yet a speaking animal could be a very disturbing thing."[81] The risks that need to be managed through representation include but are not limited to the anguish that a speaking animal might convey. They also include evidence of the "accidents" of postindustrial capitalism, including hyperfinancialization and crashes, precarity and insecurity, technological obsolescence, toxic e-waste, resource exploitation, leaks and spills, industrial animal agriculture, climate change, rage, loneliness, and the unpredictable eruptions of social media themselves. The ongoing adaptation of risk and changing management strategies is part of the expansion and militarization of global capitalism, but it also engenders popular and potential opposition. This is why so many companies relying on animal imagery donate to zoos and animal welfare associations. They want to be associated with good feelings.

While the animals collected for early menageries were shipped across oceans to help bridge the periphery to the center, the animals of the virtual menagerie travel in multiple directions and help to transform the communicative spaces within which they appear. In both instances, as shown with beavers, birds, and giraffes in later pages, each step of an animal being made visible has relied on something else being made invisible. The animal's interdependence with its habitat; its experience of being captured; the killing of the mothers in order to capture young giraffes or other exotic animals for display; the animal's soul-destroying confinement in menageries and zoos; the viewer's memory of its astonishing powers when first encountered; the work and mistreatment of the local and Indigenous trappers; the smell, the feel, the feathers and fur of the animal; what or who it eats and what animal or person kills and eats it, all these evaporate. Finally, the images of animals fronting these interfaces lose all traces of their natural habits and predatory relations. The predatory fascination with exotic animals and body parts has been tempered homeopathically by a drive to de-animalize them in the context of display. Humans celebrated their power over nonhuman animals well before the invention of electronic and digital technologies, but this celebration and management of the visible through hard and soft menageries has unique features. As rendering images of animals becomes more technically complex, so does the management of what is seen. By merging heterotopic spaces, digital media dramatically advance the project undertaken by producers of all menageries, to wrest control of the "relations between material and immaterial, biological and semiotic, that define the parasitic production of life."[82] For Michel Serres, cybernetics is parasitic because "it is founded on the theft of information, quite a simple thing." This "simple" process of capture is realized, Pasquinelli observes, by "the transformation and exploitation of the bios by the technological and semiotic domain … a dispositive that extracts surplus through the technological infrastructure that connects the semiotic with the biological sphere."[83]

Wielding power through use or "extraction" of the animal as a commodity, symbol, or medium does not just valorize the animal by making it more visible; it makes invisible the very process of making-visible. Clinging to the fantasy of feeing good associated with the love of animals, participant-observers prefer not to see or hear the animals' savage hunts for dinner, their shrinking and endangered habitats, their capture in the burden of history through relationships between trappers and traders, software corporations and workers, platforms and users, desktops and work disciplines, until artists and activists push back with strategies that reanimate these histories and relations—in other words, us—in a different way.

2 Attending the Giraffe

She was a Phantom of delight
When first she gleamed upon my sight;
A lovely Apparition, sent
To be a moment's ornament.
William Wordsworth, 1807[1]

Captive wildlife brings to man, its king, the tribute of its subjection.
Paul Boulineau, 1934[2]

Imagine being one of the first persons outside of Africa ever to see a giraffe. No one you know has ever seen such a thing, it is entirely strange. This beautiful but unusual creature with the long neck and painterly skin seems to belong more to the kingdom of monsters illustrating medieval maps than to the collection of exotic animals roaming the estate menageries of the time. If you belonged to the inner circle of a powerful emperor's estate, you might have seen elephants, rhinos, monkeys, lions, and other exotic species arrive from distant places you would never see. Captured from their natural habitats and isolated from other members of their species, these new animals' appearance in the menageries and zoos of Europe and beyond was part of the display of wealth and power by which the aristocracy kept itself apart. These animals also served to create new relationships between emperors and kings, between nascent empires and their distant territories. What the animals "meant" to collectors and viewers in these early menageries was not so much examples of "species"—a concept that did not yet exist—as curiosities, exotic treasures, a wordless demonstration of the value of something to which no price could be set and of the sender's imagination and power to bridge such distant worlds.

In 1414, a ruler in Bengal shipped a giraffe to the emperor of China. The gift was a tribute, a gesture of good will cementing the special powers and potential economic relations of two rulers. Sparse records of this event include an ancient painting and some brief academic commentaries tracing the story of "the emperor's giraffe." In its first special appearance, the emperor's giraffe was decisively misunderstood as a species. The only communication that preceded it was a rumor, a word that translated as "monster," and since the recipients had never seen a giraffe, this is what they saw. Nonetheless the Chinese court welcomed this "camelopard"—the term, implying a mixed species, was widely used until the late nineteenth century—with great fanfare. It was exotic, it was a gift, and it was a tribute to their greatness. The painting made of it is considered historically important today. The fate of the giraffe featured in this painting is unknown. There is no record of affectionate relations between humans and giraffes in this or other early menageries, which is not to say that such relations did not exist—only that those who had personal encounters with the animals were not those trained or authorized to record such events for posterity. The giraffe continued to be a precious commodity gifted to aristocrats of various courts, including Lorenzo de' Medici, in 1486, who loved his new giraffe so greatly that he built a special high-roofed barn for her, whereupon the precious giraffe entered and almost immediately broke her neck on a cross beam.

We know very little about how exotic animals arrived to populate these early modern menageries. How the African giraffe arrived in Bengal, who accompanied her to China, who saw her, how long she lived, what she thought about her experience, all this is unknown. Why was there only one? What kind of ship would carry a giraffe from the coast of Kenya, where it originated, first to Bengal and then to China, in the fifteenth century? If the ship changed the life of the giraffe, didn't the giraffe also change the shape and purpose of the ship? Imagine them together, the ship and the giraffe, crossing an ocean, crossing cultures, and launching a new world order.

The tribute of a giraffe was a ritual exchange performed in anticipation of an altered future. Aristocrats procured their capture and shipping in order to demonstrate both the inviting mystery of a distant natural world, embodied by the animal, and their growing human mastery over nature, embodied by the ship. The dispatch of this giraffe in 1414 altered relations between two imperial powers and helped to precipitate the emergence of transcontinental trade, an enterprise that became, through complex historical processes, world capitalism. To better understand the modern world and its organization of people, places, and animals, it is important to establish that the giraffe was a medium of communication between these distant people and places. To elaborate this idea and consider some of its

Figure 2.1
The Arrival of the Giraffe Zarafa, nineteenth century, etching, provenance unknown.

implications, this chapter compares the story of the 1414 tribute giraffe with the story of April, the famous pregnant giraffe of 2017. Both giraffes were conscripted to enact a social ritual that brought together and changed the people involved in the event. To play this role, both giraffes had to be conveyed from their natural distance from human society into quasi-intimacy with global observers, from being members of a matriarchal family structure into individuals with faces that could at least hypothetically look back at their human viewer. As with every animal appearance described in this book, each step of being made visible relied on something else being made invisible. This double act of foregrounding and disappearing has discursively shaped both our relations with animals and the visual aesthetics of modern culture.

Let's start with the visible. Giraffes are so oddly crooked, so lovely with their earthy savanna colors and placid herbivore demeanor, so unreachable and tall. The 1414 giraffe launched new topographical imaginations and powers associated with its arrival, which in turn led to "new ways of organizing nature," as Jason Moore writes in "The Rise of Cheap Nature." Encompassing humans, animals, and geopolitical space, these new powers laid the groundwork for the emergence of capitalism as a "world-ecology" in which resources could be extracted from poorer regions for the benefit of the imperial centers.[3] In the contemporary world ecology in which this subsumption

Figure 2.2

Tribute Giraffe with Attendant, ink and color on silk, mounted as a hanging scroll, sixteenth century, formerly attributed to Shen Du. Courtesy of the Philadelphia Museum of Art, Gift of John T. Dorrance, 1977-42-1.

occurs, giraffes are associated with menageries and zoos, children's toys, textile designs, and African safaris. Only recently has the prospect of extinction touched the way we see them. April the pregnant giraffe of 2017 did not have to cross an ocean to become famous. The global desire to witness April's prolonged pregnancy day after day can only be understood in relation to the largely unspoken and unseen effects of loss among endangered animals, and the simultaneous embrace of the article of faith that zoos are the solution to conserving them. Giraffe populations have dropped so dramatically that the International Union for Conservation of Nature and Natural Resources (IUCN) calls it a "silent extinction."[4] It's unfortunate that this extinction is described as silent, given that so many powerful Americans came together to preserve the species in the mid-twentieth century.[5] (This is such a familiar path to rage.) The prominent place of giraffes in tourist eco-safaris confirms their charisma and importance to viewers for whom contact with wildlife is largely symbolic. For a few brief weeks in 2017, in any case, a live giraffe was virtually embraced around the world.

Six hundred years passed between these two events, a passage of time marked by the emergence of a capitalist world order, the spread of modernity, the rise of electronic and digital media, the declaration of the Anthropocene, and growing public anxiety about precarity and environmental risk. This sense of precarity, a consequence of human-caused environmental change, is widely conceptualized as the result of human domination of and estrangement from nature. The Anthropocene has been attributed to factors such as the global expansion of farming, the onset of colonialism, the industrial revolution, the questionable applications of modern science, and the urbanization and deforestation of large parts of the world.[6] At whatever historical point you choose to situate the beginning of the Anthropocene, the story of the tribute giraffe reminds us of the shortcomings of the term. The term "Anthropo-" implies that all members of the human species are equally responsible for a historical process that has been most destructive for those populations that least generated its causes and effects.

Through colonization, some groups and regions were privileged to be estranged from nature while others were defined and exploited precisely by their proximity to its resources. These "others" had to develop ways to capture, kill, and transport animals for purposes that were previously unknown to them. In some cases, they had to be taught new techniques for slaughter to fulfill other peoples' purposes. The wealth and colonial subjectivity that fueled the social and material "advancement" of the imperial nations were extracted from these others, and from their habitats and lands. The giraffe sent to China in 1414 represented and extended the influence of Bengal's nobility, but not that of the Africans who captured the giraffe and arranged for its export to Bengal, or the agents who arranged for its export to China, or the animal keepers who accompanied the giraffe to its final destination. This giraffe reminds us that it is important when we talk about human agency to ask, Whose Anthropocene? Which humans? As Dipesh Chakrabarty reminds us, "The story of capital, the contingent history of our falling into the Anthropocene, cannot be denied by recourse to the idea of species, for the Anthropocene would not have been possible, even as a theory, without the history of industrialization."[7] Put the probing postcolonial query of the "Anthropo-" together with McLuhan's investigation of the mediated human, and you have begun to bridge the lives and surrounding cultures of two celebrity giraffes separated by six centuries.

The 1414 giraffe, sent from one Asian ruler to another, represented both difference and the new possibility to cross that difference. Nonhuman animals have mediated and literally and figuratively fed social relations throughout history. They have played a significant role in mediating relations between rulers, between families, between landowners and peasants, colonial invaders and Indigenous peoples, governments and subjects, technologies and users, environmentalists and climate change deniers. In conditions of movement across territories they sometimes function as what cultural anthropologists and *Star Trek* fans call first contacts between groups or territories. First contact mediators and the narratives that surround them help make sense of the unknown, and they have important but diverse semiotic consequences. As Alan Liu observes, "first contact" encounters also arise in relation to new media when familiar images help users to befriend and navigate the daunting technology and to imagine where such interaction might lead.[8] However familiar these new contact figures might seem, they are not the same things we knew before, and no one can predict or fully control how their appearance in new situations or new media will reshape the cultures or subjectivities of the people who encounter them.[9] Liu himself is not thinking of animals when he describes the familiarity of first contact narratives drawing users into new media. As I will show, however, many designers and entrepreneurs in the dawn of the so-called information age, and even today, put this idea into practice. Tigers, penguins, monkeys, birds, lizards, lions, and domestic cats, all (except the last, of course) prized specimens in past and present menageries of the rich and powerful, have served as mediators for people looking to navigate their way through the interfaces of new media. Such mediators mean something different from the early menageries, and they span different kinds of distance, but they would not be conceivable without them.

GIRAFFE DE SENNAAR.
Agée de 2 ans et demi, haute de 14 pieds, envoyée par le Pacha d'Egypte au Roi de France : elle lui a été présentée à Saint-Cloud le 9 Juillet 1827.
A Chartres, chez GARNIER-ALLABRE, Libraire et Fabricant d'images, Place des Halles, n.° 17. (Imprimerie de FÉLIX DURAND).
ADIEUX
DE LA GIRAFFE
A SON PAYS NATAL.
AIR : Pégaze est un cheval qui porte.
Adieu, beaux déserts de l'Afrique ;
Adieu, plaines de Sennaar ;
De l'admiration publique
Je vais me livrer au regard :
Le moment est très-favorable
Pour occuper peuples et Rois :
Puis, à leur paraître admirable
La grandeur donne tant de droits !
Cette grandeur qu'ici je cite,
Ne saurait prolonger les jours ;
Les hôtes des lieux que je quitte
Ne la respectent pas toujours :
Plus d'un a prouvé qu'il s'en moque ;
On peut juger par ce seul fait
Que la Giraffe, que l'on croque,
Doit être bien rare en effet.
C'est pour changer ma destinée
Que de l'Egypte le Pacha
Au Roi de France m'a donnée ;
En cela rien ne me fâcha.
Dans cette Europe qui raisonne,
N'ai-je pas vu de tous les rangs
Accourir pour voir ma personne ?
Honneur qu'on ne fait qu'aux plus grands.
Mais pourtant, ô douleur amère !
Pour me procurer cet honneur,
On a tué ma pauvre mère ;
Cela trouble un peu mon bonheur.
En vain d'un vif éclat je brille,
Peut-être on doit plaindre mon sort ;
Je suis seule de ma famille,
Mon pauvre petit frère est mort.
Lorsque de la Seine surprise
J'allais m'offrir au Souverain,
Vers les rives de la Tamise
Mon jeune frère allait bon train :
Mais j'ai pu contempler l'image
Du puissant Monarque français ;
Mon frère, mort dans le voyage,
N'a pas vu le Roi des Anglais.
Peut-être à tort je me désole
Quand la mort brise un doux lien ;
De tous les maux on se console
Dès qu'il en résulte un seul bien :
Chaque jour je suis visitée
Par le bon peuple de Paris ;
Par-dessus tout je suis fêtée :
Cet avantage a bien son prix.
Les amans de la renommée
Peuvent envier mon destin ;
Partout ma gloire est proclamée,
Et mon avenir est certain.
Après ma mort cette épitaphe
Sera mise sur mon tombeau :
« Ci-gît l'immortelle Giraffe
« Qui jouit du sort le plus beau. »

Figure 2.3

A Giraffe from Sennaar, Africa, Presented by the Pasha of Egypt to King Charles X of France at Saint-Cloud, July 9, 1827, stencil-colored wood engraving, A. Thiébault. Courtesy of the Philadelphia Museum of Art, Gift of Alice Newton Osborg, 1958-133-14.

Identifying the animal as a medium is a contribution to the relatively new project of media archaeology, which seeks to rewrite the archives of human culture in search of their underlying material histories. Despite this project's notable attempts to counter anthropocentrism, it has rarely accommodated the nonhuman animal as part of such histories. Reframing this initiative to include the nonhuman animal highlights the animal's role as what Derrida calls a supplement to the social relationship in which it appears. The supplement both enhances and takes the place of the human subject to which it is added, thus rebalancing, or unbalancing, the architecture of personal and political relations in which it appears. A text adds a layer of meaning to a field of knowledge, and potentially diminishes the established authority of its most venerated experts; a new child expands and disrupts a relationship or a family; a new technology enhances and displaces the bodies, work practices, and self-conceptions of people who engage with it. The way human limbs and senses require supplementation in order to flourish is the comparative strength and weakness of the species.

Animals, like technologies, supplement the powers and capacities of the human body while confirming and declaring its frailty and incompleteness. Under the biopolitical conditions under which all forms of life are subsumed or recolonized by money, the connection between technological and nonhuman supplementation of human powers becomes ever more salient. At the beginning of the modern period, the emperors and kings sending tributes and gifts to other countries were seeking to expand their influence and power. A revised view of this act might employ the concept of supplementation to suggest that they were not only declaring their own potency and the singularity of their power but also inferring that their territory might be or become inadequate on its own. Kings and aristocrats of the time were known to keep menageries. By sending a beautiful animal as tribute to a potential ally, a ruler could convey the exotic richness of his country. By seeking the supplementation of this power, however, he made it vulnerable to acquisitive interest, through or despite the friendliness of his expansionary drive. As territories or countries such as Kenya or Canada were colonized through the modern period, they were (inequitably) enriched by the export of material resources, and yet diminished by dependency on external powers for the wealth and "advances" brought by this trade. This colonial relationship of uneven development has been commonly expressed in the representation of the colony through images of wild nature, of "otherness," so that a country's destiny seems to be "defined by—and perhaps limited to—its beauty, wildness and natural wealth."[10]

Advocating for a dramaturgical approach to human behavior, Goffman shows in *The Presentation of Self in Everyday Life* that the "presentation of self" entails the strategic employment of select personal features and behaviors or "faces" that are distinct from those lived and more or less hidden "back stage."[11] Modern countries continue to symbolize themselves with images of their most symbolically potent animals just as ancient rulers placed pictures of such animals on their coats of arms. We do not see the labor, exploitation, or violence that enables these others to appear on command in the guise of wilderness and wonder even in modern representations. These ideas can be accommodated within an expanded field of media archaeology enriched by the recognition that the history of natural resources is also a history of colonialism. But the animal body is different from dust, copper, chemicals, or gold; it does not disappear quietly into the image-making apparatus and has never done so. Its purpose here is to be visible. As a mediator of social exchange, then, a giraffe performing the role of animal medium might be simultaneously a body of bones and blood, a political tribute, a theatrical supplement, a ritual event, a resource for financial exploitation, and a resource for hope in the face of an ominous future. Recognizing animals in human cultures as both symbolic negotiation and material infrastructure is essential to understanding how and why animals appear so often in the midst of social relations and cultural events.

Welcoming the Exotic

Ownership of menageries was a common feature of aristocratic life in Roman and medieval times. Records of these collections mention elephants and lions, but not giraffes.[12] Despite the promising reception of the 1414 tribute giraffe, Chinese trade with the world ended by the middle of the fifteenth century.[13] But the new career of giraffes as emissaries of international trade had just begun. Egyptian rulers sent several giraffes to Europe, first to Lorenzo de' Medici in Florence in 1486, and then, several centuries later, to King George IV of England and King Charles X of France, in 1827. During this same period, the capture and difficult, often fatal transport of wild animals reached enormous proportions. Giraffes were among the most valuable of these animals, more expensive than hippos, chimps, elephants, or polar bears, though less than giant pandas.[14] Note the dates of the giraffe gifts, advises Eric Ringmar. If these giraffes were not the first to arrive in Europe, they held particular historical importance.

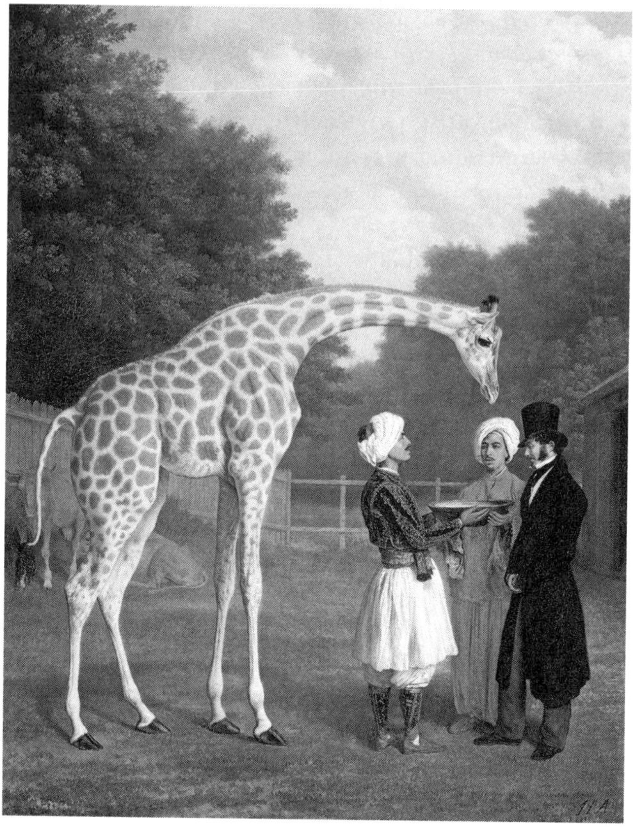

Figure 2.4

The Nubian Giraffe, oil on canvas, Jacques-Laurent Agasse, 1827. Courtesy of Royal Collection Trust/© Her Majesty Queen Elizabeth II 2018.

The first giraffe in Europe appeared in 1486, right before the Europeans—Florentine explorers prominently among them—went off to discover what was to become "America." And the second giraffe appeared only three years before France's first imperialist venture began—the bloody war in, and subsequent occupation of, Algeria. By studying how the Europeans reacted to these two animals, we should be able to better understand how they regarded the extra-European world right at the cusp of the two waves of expansion.[15]

Sent from one ruler to another, the giraffe could have been interchangeable with, and was often accompanied by, gold or silk brocade. But the giraffe is a live animal possessing special persuasive powers. Like other curiosities it stimulated a combination of visceral acquisitiveness and an interest in natural science that was characteristic of the time.[16] It was an even more curious curiosity because giraffes do not fight or eat other animals, making them a novel addition to the pugilistic arena of courtly entertainment. Their peaceful disposition disrupted what people expected of exotic animals.[17] But this did not reduce the giraffe's charismatic power. As Ringmar writes:

> When suddenly seeing something that surpassed the expected in beauty, diversity, or abundance, the mind was overwhelmed. People were first astonished, then delighted, and finally excited. Clearly there was something highly addictive in this mixture of emotions. It piqued people's curiosity, and once they had seen a little, they wanted to see more. Obviously, in terms of height and sheer impact, there was no more marvelous, or more curious, animal than a giraffe.[18]

Giraffes convey the quality of the marvelous even after they have ceased to be "curiosities" as such, that is to say, after acquiring them has ceased to be novel or exclusive to the private amassment of wealth and knowledge.

As my thinking about giraffes and about animals as emissaries and mediators in the midst of these changes unfolded, I began to wonder whether we should be thinking of these animals as "vanishing mediators." Fredric Jameson introduced this concept in a 1977 publication in order to summarize Max Weber's foundational analysis of bureaucracy, and in particular the role of religious authority in the development of modern industrialization.[19] In this analysis, the priest in religious Europe represented and was seen to mediate the spiritual and administrative authority endowed by God. This spiritual authority authorized the birth of modern bureaucratic organization which originated in the Church but, with the aid of capital, spread beyond it. As organizations were further rationalized to manage the more spatially and technically complex processes of industrialization and urbanization, modern bureaucracy abandoned its fealty to religion and made the priest's religious power obsolete in the administration of everyday life. The priest is the vanishing mediator of bureaucratic industrialism.

In this way of telling the story, the giraffe is presented as a tribute or gift from a ruler hoping to be included in new mercenary ventures into the unknown. This exchange precipitates new ways of seeing, transporting, owning, and connecting with other cultures for which finally the giraffe will no longer be needed. The prospect of extinction seems to make the utility of the vanishing mediator concept uncontroversial. But the process of vanishing began much earlier. While giraffes were welcomed in Europe, they did not always flourish there; the death of a beloved giraffe after eighteen years in the Jardin du Roi was, according to painter Eugène Delacroix, "as obscure as her entry into the world had been brilliant."[20] Her fortune was at least better than that of Lorenzo de' Medici's giraffe. Even before these public events, there were disappearances; in order to capture the tribute giraffe, hunters had likely killed its mother.[21] To continue the export of giraffes, Africans had to adapt or modify their practices in order to capture and transport the young giraffe in aid of a purpose previously unknown to them. The capacity to exchange the tribute giraffe thus involved seizing power not only over the animal but also over the people who shared its habitat. This ritual performance of colonial power over the bodies of animals is vividly documented in the 1988 film *From the Pole to the Equator*, compiled by two Italian collectors from the film archives of global explorer Luca Comerio (1874–1940).[22] Comerio had traveled the world recording exotic locations and peoples with his Lumière camera. "Generally speaking," writes Scott MacDonald, "the film hovers on the line between stop-action and the illusion of motion; it is as though we are continually watching the images come alive, slow down, come alive—as if we are witnessing the events we see through a medium which is itself just coming to life."[23] The film's depictions of the performative killing of animals before local hunters is unusually gruesome.

The animals depicted in this unique cinematic record of conquest were rarely exported as live animals, but rather hunted, killed, and rendered into parts as trophies and other products. Such practices (documented in the next chapter with the case of the beaver) entrenched the colonized African or Indigenous person as a dual figure: both the inhabitant of a rich land capable of supplying wealth in the form of animal bodies, and a sacrificial figure represented metonymically by the animal it has forfeited. The animal extended and symbolically displaced the Indigenous person, so that Indigenous and tribal peoples became vanishing mediators in the dissemination of wild animals to diverse parts of the globe. The giraffe came to represent Africa, just as the beaver came to represent Canada, without visible evidence of the colonial and Indigenous trappers who traded them. The colonial origin of an exotic animal is, in short, both a crucial part of its perceived meaning and a referential background rendered invisible by the same technologies and discourses through which it appears. Colonies are often called "frontiers" for intrepid explorers, but this process keeps colonized places and peoples backstage, as Goffman describes it, and whatever happens there, as Edward Said writes in *Culture and Imperialism*, usually (if not in the film just described) remains unseen.

Ringmar's reference to the heightened desire to *see* something marvelous forms an important link between fifteenth-century giraffes and the animals circulating today in media culture. Giraffes have become more accessible by means of their presence in zoos, natural history museums, films, and pictures. Their unique shape is almost normalized, insofar as it is ever possible to normalize a giraffe outside of its natural habitat. In contemporary consumer culture, animals play an important function for children, providing anthropomorphized figures for early object attachment while linking them to a commodity market that is more and more child-centered. The giraffe is reduced to its most recognizable features, so that hypothetically any one of them can be replaced with another. This is not true of the species as a whole. In a study conducted in France, 800,000 Sophie the giraffe baby toys were sold in 2010, more than eight times the numbers of giraffes living in Africa. "Unknowingly, companies using giraffes, cheetahs or polar bears for marketing purposes may be actively contributing to the false perception that these animals are not at risk of extinction, and therefore not in need of conservation," the study co-author Franck Courchamp said.[24]

By combining mass mediation, childhood attachment and release, and ecological vulnerability, the giraffe's meanings have again changed. This transformation alters what we understand to be its mode of mediation: how it mediates, and what it is mediating.

The story of the tribute giraffe is a starting point for rethinking the animal-medium relation, both as a historical project and as an important task for media and animal studies. Scholars have written a great deal about the essential yet sometimes surprising role that communication has played in human history. But to understand the historical changes that occurred in the fifteenth century, and to consider their complicated relationship to the present, we need to establish that the giraffe can be as much a mediator in a particular intersection of material and social dynamics as the ship that carried the giraffe to a country that had never seen one. The coming and going of ships and giraffes together helped to alter their environments by simultaneously demonstrating human mastery through new technology and embodying the exotic and untouched. Only by reading the event as the imbrication of the animal and the technological, that is to say, of two different but interdependent relational processes, can we understand its effects on how humans think and feel about animals, or how the venture of world trade was launched that later became, through various complex historical processes, global capitalism.

Taking up the idea of the animal as mediator or medium means acknowledging, as Jon Durham Peters argues in his book *The Marvelous Clouds*,[25] that thinking about animals in the context of mediation isn't just important for our consideration of human animal relations; it also expands our understandings of mediation itself. If "media are not only carriers of symbolic freight but also crafters of existence,"[26] this insight applies to animals regardless of whether they occupy terrestrial, aqueous, pictorial, digital, or philosophical environments. This doesn't mean that animals are always mediators, willing or otherwise. As Peters notes, "Because media are in the middle, their definition is a matter of position, such that the status of something as a medium can fade once its position shifts."[27]

That is to say, giraffes were once undisturbed members of matriarchal families, as well as food for human and animal predators. Some were removed from their families to send as tribute to an emperor. Others were displayed behind the bars of a zoo. Yet another giraffe becomes a figure on a T-shirt where before there were mainly eagles and tigers or elephants. Before colonization a giraffe might have been a medium of some kind within her own habitus, but today there can be no undisturbed giraffes. The question is not whether we will interact with them, but whether we will see them and how we do interact with them. Recognizing that one entity changes through interaction with others is the foundation of ecology, a term that refers not only to the interactions of species and habitats but also to the interactions of communication media with one another and with their users. Giraffes are mediators when, as Peter writes, they appear in the middle of things, when they intertwine the ecology of species and the ecology of media, when endangered species meet webcams that meet motherhood, when movement from one territory to another shifts the geopolitics of nature and the grammar of looking. As always, what is hidden in these arrangements colors what is visible.

A Giraffe in Mediation in the Anthropocene-Capitalocene

For several months in the spring of 2017, a global audience waited for April the giraffe to give birth in a small zoo in upstate New York. The owner mounted a camera and transmitted a live feed of April as she paced back and forth in her pen, separated by a fence from Oliver, the father, to ensure the safety of the calf. This is not the first time a zoo has sought to capitalize from a prospective birth, but this event broke all viewing records, creating a news sensation and a financial coup for the zoo. According to counts of online views, April's prospective calf became briefly more famous than any human baby in history, including his contemporaries Prince George, heir to the British throne, and Beyoncé's unborn twins. April was not mediating two emperors, but millions of viewers joined together by her image on the Internet. Their participation in this prospective event confirmed their passionate commitment to nature and rebirth along with a degree of collective narcissism expressed in watching the numbers climb.

Viewers' comments heightened the intensity of waiting and reinforced the sense of a significant event. They confessed that they were hooked, they were addicted, they could not believe what they were doing, the incredulity echoing in some strange way the marvel that must have been felt when people saw their first giraffe. But this time, the description of enchantment is darkened by the frequent reference to addiction. This addiction is voluntary and involuntary at the same time; it is experienced as contagious, like a virus. The apparent need of participants to confess as well as to watch this amazing animal indicates the viral qualities of this event. For such viewers, the enchantment of encountering the giraffe empowered and disempowered them at the same time.

This enchanting April contagion was both personal and public in its effects. Thousands shared online their conviction that they could not sleep until April had given birth to her baby giraffe. All the public feelings about the future of the giraffe as a species, the complicity of humans in the endangerment of wild animals, the confusion about what could be done to reverse an unthinkably huge extinction event, the unfortunate and unnatural everyday existence of giraffes penned in small spaces, and the unspoken boredom or loneliness of the watchers—all these were condensed and poured into the need to watch and talk about April. Through this process, the giraffe ceased to be an object posted to enhance visitors to the zoo and became a living female animal visible to anyone. The "event" gave participants an opportunity to express their own sense of being captured along with their hopes for a birth as affirmation of the vitality of nature. This love for April was expressed not only in online professions of insomnia, excitement, and addiction, but also in the vigorous sales of mother giraffe memes and April-themed shirts and maternity clothes.

This community of April fans is not the elite milieu shared by the royal owners of tribute and Medici giraffes—quite the opposite. In this affective entanglement, anyone with a computer could look at April; anyone could express their feelings online. The vulnerability of endangered species has become the principal public rationale for animal captivity, but this context was rarely mentioned in the course of this media event. April's craftily produced celebrity returned sovereignty to individual viewers who invested love and hope in this giraffe, this baby, not all giraffes. April's maternal body thus became a mediator between two powerful discourses, two potential world orders: neoliberalism, with its necrophiliac emphasis on the sovereignty of individual human subjects, and political ecology, with its

Figure 2.5
April the giraffe giving birth, 2017, screenshot. Image courtesy of Animal Adventure Park.

Figure 2.6
Google search result for April T-shirts, 2017, screenshot.

emphasis on habitats, cross-species entanglements, meaningful life, and collective survival. Shared motherhood aside, these logics are irreconcilable outside the space of the zoo. The affectionate alliance between April and her fans failed (at least in the short term), to the extent that it confirmed and naturalized the zoo's authority in the management of life within the posited order of things. Their feelings about risk, an essential component of this event, were discharged through the carefully orchestrated love for an individual animal who once again, once her calf was born, would disappear from their screens.

Watching April didn't just absorb the attention of enchanted animal lovers and create a market for T-shirts and memorabilia; it also served to endorse unseen intermediaries (such as the zoo owner, who hovers on the edge of the screen, and of course YouTube) as benign institutions entrusted with animal salvation. These audiences were prepared for this encounter by their previously established relationship with her species and other charismatic animals through toys, picture books, television and computer screens, smartphones, and websites. Users are enticed to interact with these resources by images of animals that convey appropriate proportions of lovability, cuteness, mobility, autonomy, and adaptability. In this animal-instrument entanglement, the magic of one is enhanced by the magic of the other. The zoo owner calculated all this in his decision to mount a web cam. But seeing this animal move towards birth had other effects.

As viewers watched April pace, the live feed joined the giraffe's body to our feelings of protectiveness and affection and our need for diversion and pleasure. Joined together by the optics of the zoo almost without walls, a million people waited for her to do what giraffes must do (and we apparently cannot), and what ensures the viability of the zoos that contain them, and that is to save the species. As an expectant mother, April is the captured agent of a biopolitical economy that mediates and seems to resolve the conflict we experience every day as we negotiate between money, geopolitics, and the conflicted impulses within our hearts. These layers of meaning challenge our attempts to understand the April experience.

What is notable for me in this comparison of April with the 1414 giraffe is not whether we love giraffes or elephants, or how well April evokes the past, or even the technological mediation of the encounter. Rather, it is the intensity of her affect given the triple commodification—by the zoo, the advertiser, and the measurement of online hits—and its careful management of responses. These frames shaped what could appear (April and the zoo), what could not appear (Where did April came from, and how? What kind of life does she have? Where are her ancestors and where do they fit in the process of silent extinction? How much money is this guy making?), and how the animal is permitted to mean. Describing the April event as risk management is not the same as talking about how cameras document the risks animals themselves face in interactions with humans, or the way such risks are represented explicitly in human images or texts, or even the security of April herself as a widely celebrated, privately owned commodity. April's global profile calls for a more socially and politically grounded theory of risk management in the Anthropocene, together with a revitalized theory of mediation.

The millions of people who watched April were, like the spectators of the unnamed giraffe in 1414, enchanted and delighted by her presence, and by the way the feelings she evoked seemed to exceed her status as a possession and object of display. By (almost) transcending her captivity, this giraffe helped to assuage a number of related risks during her brief global fame. Such risks might include skepticism toward zoos and declining profits for zoos; bad feelings about the capitalization of the Internet; politically volatile uses of online spaces; boredom and indifference with life online; users' nonparticipation in social media, with a negative effect on user data monetization; spreading animal rights activism; and a volatile concern about climate change and the devastated landscapes of the Anthropocenic environment that catalyzes a need to act, somehow. A million individual users sharing the April experience can ameliorate some of these risks. But risk management in the age of silent extinctions and inexorable climate change can only produce new risks, political and economic as well as ecological. April's viewers might find themselves increasingly concerned about animals and their habitats, a concern that would require the cultivation of new techniques, and we are subject to another cascading series of techniques to follow the waves and mediations.[28] In other words, her commercial value is at odds with her referential meaning, her actual conditions of existence, and without this tension neither the value nor the meaning could exist in this network in this way.

This twenty-first-century giraffe is performing a different kind of political mediation than the precious menagerie giraffes of the early modern period. She provides an appropriate subject for an analysis of modern governmentality as a discursive process within which the complicated constitution and practice of human subjectivity are managed. Through these processes, humans formed in (what I am calling without getting distracted by nomenclature) a neoliberal regime learn to think of and to regulate themselves as autonomous subjects expected to take full possession of their own lives. Because of the degree to which the idea of possessive individualism or self-governance has been internalized, people seek out its directives,

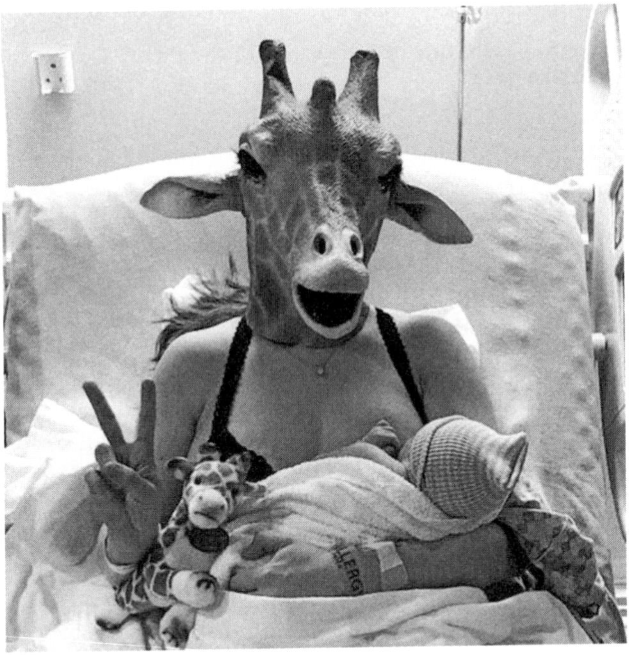

Figure 2.7
Mom posing as April the giraffe with newborn son, Erin Dietrich, 2017. Image courtesy of the artist.

even more so as the actual legitimating logic of individual agency collapses before them. This situation is the foundation for self-healing strategies like connecting with Internet cats, pregnant giraffes, and birds singing on nature soundtracks. The sense of being enmeshed in a state of precarity can increase normalizing strategies of self-care, but it can also engender recognition of the precarity of others—engendering compassion toward April and her other viewers—and a sense of "being with" in Jean-Luc Nancy's sense. "Precariousness designates something that is existentially shared. … What is problematized here is not what makes everyone the same, but rather what is *shared* by all."[29]

April reminds us how much these new techniques of human governance and their imbrication with our self-care concern our feelings for animals. Just as the 1414 giraffe and the ship were entangled in a performative event, so the animal imagery in social media plays an important role in our dominant cultural logics of mediation. It forms affective links between digital media, animals, and us that promise to help us manage and push beyond our everyday lives and feelings. Just as the 1414 giraffe was sent to advocate for friendly relations between two rulers, so contemporary celebrity animals advocate for friendly relations between us and the technologies and institutions that frame their presence. The giraffes and other beloved species of the virtual menagerie are part of a new "digital nature" that, as Charlie Gere observes, is helping to naturalize institutional arrangements with complicated political repercussions.[30] If April's glorious sweetness and fame reenchanted a disenchanted world, such enchantment has become the primary purpose of this lovely endangered species. According to the Giraffe Conservation Foundation, writing in 2017, "The giraffe's primary economic benefit is its evolutionary uniqueness"; its recognizable image has been used to sell "anything from children's apparel or wine, or the promotion of social media fads and the FIFA World Cup."[31] People wishing to see live giraffes are contributing billions to the African economy, but the World Economic Forum recognizes declining African wildlife populations as a threat to the continent's tourism industry.[32] Driven by sectors such as safari tourism and nature/adventure tourism, international tourism receipts in Africa totaled US$36 billion in 2014. The continent of Africa received 56 million international tourists according to numbers from the United Nations World Tourism Organization.[33] Africa needs its giraffes, but they are disappearing; and more than anything, more than zoos, more than T-shirts, more than millions of fans, they need their habitats preserved.

Like other animal figures populating the virtual menagerie, April has been dramaturgically shaped to perform in an aesthetic regime that simulates and contains the human-(quasi)animal interactions we long for while generating profits from them. This multimedia regime interacts with our perceptual capacities and affective states in ways that come to feel natural, like the artificial plants mimicking nature when you walk into a bank. Our "common situation," as McLuhan termed it, draws viewers into a scopic regime that foregrounds an animal's charismatic beauty and gathers us together under its spell. They spell out this spell as evidence of the power of the network, which is ostensibly the power of us, while encouraging us to look away from what the giraffe really references, the endangered fate of the species and their natural milieus.

As Cheryl Lousley writes:

> Distilling ecological relationships into icons of charismatic life displaces how biodiversity is one of the most contested areas of environmental politics where the decidedly social questions of sovereignty, property rights, justice, livelihoods, and the capacity to shape a future are all at stake. ... The slippage from vitality to commodity enchantment is especially hard to avoid, I argue, because capitalist economies thrive on the appearance of flourishing objects of desire, available for intimate appropriation.[34]

As we set our eyes upon these beautiful creatures, we participate in a now habitual process of staged and regularly updated interactions with animals that once referenced faraway and exotic places. It is crucial to this "capitalist subsumption of life" as Negri describes it[35] that viewers want to look, that viewers cannot look away as the giraffe paces and waits, her head moving gently, her tail flipping as she walks in the way that only the tail of a giraffe can flip. Like April, viewers are trapped by the wait, by the sight of the unusual animal, and by the intimate techniques and temporalities of viewing. When the pleasure of watching is all the evidence you need of love for this animal, it is possible to forgo political or ethical concerns about the implications of one's own desires. In this festival of looking, it is not only the animal who is potentially sacrificed. As bodies and images are detached from the nature that makes them animal, the force of the imagery inveigles us to abandon the thoughtfulness that makes us human. But images of animals can also awaken an enriched sense of the beauty and singularity of the natural world. They can stir deeply ethical responses to our shared creatureliness and precarious futures.[36] The experience of being joined to millions of viewers by a common passionate feeling for an animal is arguably as unique and potentially transformative an experience as seeing a live giraffe for the first time.

Conclusion: Nature Shots

McLuhan used watchdog and fish metaphors to describe the state of distraction humans experience when they focus on the content of a medium rather than the transformative power of the medium itself. Peters rejects this metaphorical use of the animal, for it teaches us nothing about them. "One thing about which fish know exactly nothing is water, since they have no anti-environment which would enable them to perceive the element they live in," claimed McLuhan. "In fact," Peters interjects, "fish probably know a lot about water's temperature, clarity, currents, weather, purity, and so on, but the point was that they did not recognize it as water."[37] One has to leave it to know what it is, just as a person has to leave a country or language in order to know it. Taking up the insight that "the medium is the message" without abandoning the squids or giraffes means acknowledging how much animals expand our understanding of mediation itself. How and what animals mediate is contingent on more than their biological niche, more than the technologies within which they appear, more than the feelings and ethics of individual people looking at them, although each of these plays a role in the moments and outcomes of mediation. McLuhan asks us to reverse our perspective on images so that we view ourselves from the perspective of the media, that is, with "attentiveness to the agency of the medium in the analysis of social change."[38] It's like asking, with W. J. T. Mitchell, "What do pictures want?," as though they are alive, while looking through the picture to see ourselves being made by their making.[39] This "attentiveness to the medium" invites us to look at ourselves from the point of view of the animal, acknowledging how little we know about what they know or feel but hoping to nurture more empathic relations nonetheless. Delving into mediation challenges us to multiply our gaze on ourselves. This is a profoundly political task of cultural and ontological reorientation.

What might animals need to flourish in the environments of the future? They need us to see and feel the animals we encounter and to resist perceiving them as objects. We are as embedded in the world of natural and digital habitats as animals are, and we need to find more complex ways to render these realities and more sustainable modes of entanglement with them. Nurturing awareness of how animal and technological media shape our embodied cognition of the world provides a chance to practice living with their eyes on us, and to realize how images that produce the greatest wonder are entangled with the politics of nature and desire in contemporary risk culture. Intertwining them differently offers a chance to focus not just on charismatic giraffes needing to be saved, but also on the visual languages, discursive mediations, and reconfigured human-animal ecologies that can make the future of diverse species viable.

3 The Work of the Beaver

In Margaret Atwood's early novel *Surfacing*, the male protagonist, David, makes a comment that has become one of the most widely circulated citations in Canadian literature. "Canada was built on dead beavers," he says; indeed, "the beaver is to this country what the black man is to the United States."[1] My online search found a ten-page list of sites on which this emblematic citation has appeared, including great-quotes.com, think-quotes.com, famousquotes.com, brainyquote, and animalquotes. It also appears in book collections of "great Canadian quotes" and "great literary quotes," and in one or two academic essays. Most of these citations name the author but not the book that is the source of the quote, suggesting that collections of popular quotes are not invitations to read the books from which they were abstracted.[2] The way this quote recurs without the aid of context or commentary is symptomatic of a larger process at the heart of this chapter, by means of which representations of beavers have been cumulatively severed and abstracted from the bodies and habitats of the animals by the economic tides of colonial history.

This study takes David's (Atwood's) claim as a starting point for a series of questions about what it means to say that a country built by settler colonialism is built on the bodies of animals. The widely disseminated inscription of Atwood as author onto beaver as sacrificial subject conveys a blend of melancholy and irony so characteristic as to make the imprint of Atwood onto beaver, beaver onto Canada, Canada onto Atwood seem inevitable. Through the frequent citation of this remark in digital and literary archives, the association between Canada and dead beavers acquires a life of its own, forming an uneasy undertow to the popular iconography of the Canadian subject as cheerfully busy beaver. The direction of the undertow is undecidable. There is clearly a literal truth to the claim; the Dominion of Canada was founded on the territory and economy of the fur trade, which means not only that beavers were killed, accumulated, and sold as body parts, but also that beavers were instrumental (that is to say, conscripted) as "first contacts" between colonialists and Indigenous people. Arguably, though, the passage also conveys a metaphorical intent. Atwood's character's comment describes not only long-gone piles of bodies but also, as in so many of her fictions, the way historical relations and delusions make an imprint on human relationships. When we are invited to identify collectively with the beaver as the totem of our country, what relationship are we reenacting? Are we readers akin to the animals' dead bodies, to their killers, or to smart amphibious subjects? Simultaneously awakening and imploding popular imperialist nostalgia, one step removed from the story while undermining that very distance, and introducing a bad conscience into the mix, Atwood's words continue to strike a chord.

This chapter addresses the conditions of the beaver's appearance in the country's history. It revisits the animal's role as mediator of cultural and economic systems, its changing historical status as material and semiotic object, and its relevance to contemporary animal and postcolonial theory. The image of the beaver has been appropriated through multiple forces and practices and has appeared again and again as an icon and mediator

LA LOUTRE DU CANADA. LES CASTORS DU CANADA

Figure 3.1
Otter of Canada, Beavers of Canada, 1798–1856, color engraving on wove paper, Jacques Christophe Werner. Image courtesy of Library and Archives Canada and the Peter Winkworth Collection of Canadiana.

of colonial and postcolonial history. It has nourished a compulsive search for meaning to confirm the validity of a national culture that didactically (but forgetfully) identifies itself through that same imagery. Like the Liberal Canadian government that passed its role as national animal in legislation, the beaver symbol is capable of producing diverse and deeply contradictory meanings. It references the originary colonial settlement and its reliance on Indigenous knowledge of land and animals; the movement of currency, trappers, canoes, pelts, corporations, ships, and other long-distance haulers of goods; the symbolic ecology of Canada's famous wilderness; the industrious builder of farms and cities on top of that wilderness; fashion and sex, patriots and political skeptics, friendly telecommunications and costly leather goods. The beaver image thus doubles back on itself and betrays, mocks, and challenges the dominant meanings of this complicated valorization and validation process. It is as though the beaver's amphibious body, its smooth head rising to the surface as it swims across a body of water, has a doppelganger in the semiotic body of images that fluidly displays and hides this animal.

The tension between animality and the symbolic and ontological abstraction from animality has been profoundly formative for contemporary culture. Nowhere is this process more visible than in the case of the beaver. The tension between animality and abstraction exemplified by this history is rooted in an extractive economy that enabled colonialism to dominate and define human-animal relations in the establishment of the modern world. Unraveling the material, semiotic, and political threads in this history is part of a search for a redress of colonial violence that must include a reassessment of the roles of animals in ecological history and identity construction.[3]

Given the importance of beavers in the settlement of the country and the ubiquity of beavers in our visual landscapes today, one might assume that the animal's political significance has been understood precisely in terms of such reassessment. This has rarely occurred. The way this popular and variable image has served to condense and obscure the history of colonization, and of the animal's role in this history, corresponds closely to Roland Barthes's description of myth as "de-historicized speech."[4] Not all speeches are made of words, as Barthes pointed out, and behind the potent meanings of mythic images such as this one are semi-intentional connotations that evacuate historical context and complexity from the grammar of representation. The discursive presence-absence of the past actualized by the beaver image is not accidental. The beaver teaches us to be Canadian by simultaneously remembering and forgetting the country's history along with that of the animal.

Figure 3.2
3 pence beaver stamps, issued 1851. © Canada Post Corporation, 1851. Reproduced with permission.

The relations of power mediated by the beaver are not restricted to economic pursuits. The case of the beaver demonstrates the cogency of the argument that modern Western culture sought to suppress or demolish what it defined as animality in a "schema of purification" that justifies supremacy on the basis of uniquely moral and rational behavior.[5] Describing some humans as "animals" places them outside the domain of human civilization and deprives them of its rights and protections. Nonwhite peoples have long been diminished by colonial classification efforts that define them as less than human because of their perceived closer ontological and physical relations with nature.[6] Representatives of such cultures were sometimes displayed in menageries and zoos in the home countries together with nonhuman animals from the same regions.[7] This enactment of social classification requires those who describe other humans as animals to know as little as possible about purpose and agency in nonhuman animals' interactions with their own environments.[8] The beaver's own mediation of colonial history relies on its being diminished to the status of a useless rodent. As noted by some fur trade commentators and nineteenth-century cultural anthropologists, though, beavers fundamentally challenge the anthropocentric assumptions of Western thought, employing engineering abilities that Europeans had learned to attribute exclusively to human purposeful behavior.[9]

It has become important for all these reasons to look backward from today's iconic beaver, seeking to illuminate a shadowed history of visibility and invisibility that affected the animal, the trappers, the traders, and the colonial overseers who turned them into commodities in the new world. This is a complicated history. In her study of whiteness and Indigeneity, Margot Francis addresses the semantically unstable role played by national symbols such as the beaver:

> On the one hand, we have banal national emblems: the hard-working beaver, the enterprising railway, the majestic mountains—all of which present the values, technologies, and landscapes of white enterprise and manly accomplishment. On the other hand, we have a national literature and popular discourse that suggest we couldn't possibly be associated with the more rapacious aspects of imperialist adventure because the Canadian character is best expressed by anti-heroes absorbed in a struggle for survival. Might these seemingly oppositional images express the state of play between the renewed respectability of an innocent white Anglo-Canadian identity versus our fear of annihilation? And is the outcome of this tension a sense of Canadianness so riven by contradiction as to be a blank and formless void?[10]

As Francis observes, this semantic oscillation and rhetorical emptiness are a function of Canada's status and experience as a second-world empire that has both colonized and been colonized throughout its history.[11] The "blank and formless void" Francis describes is nothing less than the suppressed consciousness of our own rapacious acquisition of a country "built on dead beavers." Anxiety about this void drives the compulsion to multiply enough images to fill multiple archives and containers to ground an identity that threatens to disperse.[12] In this sense, the proliferation of beaver images both expresses and manages our sense of ontological and collective risk.

Mythic symbols like beavers and canoes are examples of what Barthes calls de-historicized speech. They play an important role in rituals of subject formation that involve social purification and what we now call risk management. The beaver image mobilizes our tacit identification with an unglamorous beast that makes loyalty to other citizens gathered under its sign seem both natural and intelligible. The desire to identify collectively via an animal totem is not unique; it dominates but also precedes the iconography of modern nations. If we choose living entities like beavers or polar bears (or later, more fluidly, cats) as symbols of our collective identities, according to the totemic thinking that postcolonial cultures congratulate themselves for having left behind, then the nation congregated under its sign is equally vital, natural, and distinct. Animal images populate a comparable iconography in many countries.[13] Indeed, modern nation-states have created a fascinating zoological inventory of animal symbols—kangaroo, bear, lion, tiger, elephant, parrot, bison, flamingo—many of which, like the beaver, have been at risk of extinction through extensive hunting and habitat loss. Admittedly the beaver is not a lion, a bear, an eagle, or an elephant. Yet we share with modern national subjects gathered under the signs of these more powerful animal figures the need for a symbol of de-animalized animality to convince us that there is something certain, grounded, *natural* in our shared citizenship. But what nature? While these images mutate through various political, cultural, and commercial networks, their physical habitats, kinship structures, and species viability are being destroyed.

The hard-working beaver is a symbol, but it is also more than a symbol. To reconnect these iconic images with living entities requires the de-reification of the animal commodity and the constitution of a new taxonomy that situates these images of animals in a more politically and ecologically reflexive context. In her recent *Beaver Manifesto*, Glynnis Hood insists that "beavers truly are the shapers of the physical and ecological landscapes of North America. ... They and these landscapes have evolved together for millennia and much of our natural environment has really only known a world that has beavers in it. ... Without them, one can imagine the ecological desert left behind."[14] Hood's pointed inability to imagine a landscape without beavers in it, and her reliance on evolution to emphasize this interdependency, echoes the argument that it is impossible to understand human culture without accepting the use and development of technology at the heart of it. (However different in purpose, the two arguments are equally valid.) Hood addresses her manifesto to readers whose ambidextrous commitment to modern wilderness aesthetics and modern individual property rights (not so cordially joined, in some contexts) leads them to decry beavers' destruction of their trees and rivers. This individualized assertion of control over the "natural" landscape obscures the larger significance of beavers: they shape and clean the flow of rivers to lakes, trees to dams, water to us. More recently, the warming of the climate has sent the beaver north, where their dam-building activity threatens to release methane gas and hasten the process of climate change. Decrying their animal presence pushes aside the ways we humans act far more destructively in this milieu.

Skins and Signs

From federal law to social media, from postage stamp to parody, the beaver is an iconographic figure standing unmistakably for the nation.[15] Its status as totem of Canadian identity has been advanced through all the material items appearing in the list that follows. Recently, a hideous inflated beaver

Figure 3.3
Sorting Furs at the Raw Fur Department, Hudson Bay Company, Vancouver, ca. 1930s, photograph, Alfred Krausee. Image courtesy of the Hudson Bay Company Archives, Archives of Manitoba.

appeared as a corporate symbol advertising Bell Media, a corporate telecommunications giant that provides access to television, Internet, and telephone accounts to millions of Canadians, at the same time as Parks Canada officially adopted a beaver as its mascot and corporate emblem. Both organizations, one a large corporate monopoly and the other a government-managed public service, released parodic oversized figures of beavers into urban centers. Released at more or less the same time, the beaver simulacra separately promoted Canada's technological friendliness and famous wilderness as though to acknowledge and cement the triumphant reconciliation of these two interdependent, Greimasian binaries: wild and urban space; public and private management of space. Unaddressed in this geometry is the unfinished reconciliation of the two social groups that brought the beaver's status into being, the Indigenous peoples and the settlers. So physically grotesque is this parodic beaver that it doesn't need to mean anything once the spark of recognition has passed.

The schematized figures of the federal government beaver and the telecommunications giant's beaver are a ghostly reiteration of the doppelganger maps associated with the fur trade in earlier times, for they showed clearly how closely linked the fur trade and political unification were in the unfolding of the new Dominion. The corpuscular plasticine beaver has a history, then, that compels it to oscillate between semiotic power and meaninglessness.

When the Government of Canada passed a Federal Act in 1975 naming the beaver the country's official national animal, the animal was already a popular national symbol, successfully rooting Canada in early colonial trade relations between the new world and the old. Its image efficiently constellated ideas about nature, colonization, domestic life, global trade, and the masculine accumulation of wealth, women, and sex, which thereby came to represent the foundation of the new dominion. Unlike the lions and bears chosen to represent the imperial countries of Europe, the beaver lacks ferocity; it will not bite off the heads of its past and present colonial masters. The government's official conscription of beaver as national symbol enhanced and reconciled its dual status as national icon and friendly mascot of corporate globalization. Like other animals populating the virtual menagerie, Canada's beaver imagery succeeds because it remains indeterminate in its meanings and effects. If, as Steve Baker argues, animal symbolism has lost its connection with animals, and thus its semiotic reliability,[16] the beaver symbol does not seem to mind. Appearing everywhere, it continues to be busy and productive.

Atwood's claim that the country is built on dead beavers isn't just popular because it confirms the slipperiness of the animal's semiotic ground, however, or even because it displays the semantic resilience that we like to attribute to Canadian writers and readers.[17] It shows her readers that we are at least half-conscious of the nation's historical dependence on a sacrificial economy of animal and human lives. This is a complicated half-recognition. The citizenry's cheerful identification with the iconographic animal rubs up against its amnesia and indifference regarding the historic violence through which country and animal were merged. Through the indeterminate speech of this figure, we are simultaneously inheritors of the fur trade and the walking ghosts of its dead remains.

A live beaver is an amphibious rodent; a dead beaver is a pelt. Whether live or dead, beavers with fur are different from beavers without fur (whether the beaver has been literally skinned or symbolically disembodied). The live animal is capitalized in the form of the fur it is killed to relinquish. In the dead or graphically disembodied beaver, the commodity transformation has already occurred. Then we have a fur without a body, a body without a skin, or an animal-like image graphically released from its mortality. The fur without a body, the necessary cause and effect of the animal's death, becomes a hat or coat. The body without a fur is either the corpse of the beaver with its fur removed—extracting the oil of the anal glands was a byproduct of this same process—or the pared-down, hairless, digitally de-animalized image proliferating in the contemporary mediascape.[18] Both are outcomes of the transformation of animal body into commodity. Not surprisingly, the rendition of one to the other is never shown in public, no matter how often the beaver appears in a drawing or on a map, screen, stamp, coin, toy, or logo. The process of extraction haunts the symbolic landscape by its absence.

The renowned quality of the animal's fur is related directly to the animal's amphibious capabilities, so the preference for showing the beaver in water should not be surprising. Uniquely among fur trade historians, Harold Adams Innis explains the beaver fur's value in relation to its activities in water. As an amphibious mammal, its pelt is fine and thick, with two layers of hair; "examined through a microscope," Innis comments, "the fur has numerous small barbs. It was these barbs which made it unusually suitable for the manufacture of felt and of felt hats."[19] Protected by this special fur, the beaver moves easily between land and water, collecting wood to build strong dams which create new bodies of clean water, and then, below the surfaces of this water, it builds lodges of solid and complex construction. Having constructed such well-crafted homes, the beaver has no inclination to travel; he moves in and raises his family. "In the language of the economists," Innis observes, as though this is not his language, "the heavy fixed capital of the beaver became a serious handicap with the improved technique of Indian hunting methods, incidental to the borrowing of iron from the Europeans."[20] That is to say, the amphibious beaver is a profitable resource for Europeans, and European technologies make it easier to kill beavers, which (my Word program's grammar checker won't let me say "who") are too fixed, too home- and family-oriented, not mobile enough to evade their European hunters.

Citing an undated journal by David Thompson, Innis explains:

> When the arrival of the White People had changed all their weapons from stone to iron and steel and added the fatal Gun, every animal fell before the Indian ... the Beaver became a desirable animal for food and clothing, and the fur a valuable article of trade, and as the Beaver is a stationary animal, it could be attacked at any convenient time in all seasons, and thus their numbers soon became reduced.[21]

As Innis well understood, the beaver's aquatic habitat, the value of its fur, the seasonal nature of hunting, the solidity of the beaver's home and family, the Indigenous familiarity with the animal's habits and habitat, the success of traditional practices of trapping and hunting, the expansion north and west of the colonists, the building of settlements and stores allowing trappers to store valuable furs and glandular secretions and trade them for goods brought from Europe by the same boats that were bringing traders and weapons, and the Indigenous adaptation to new goods such as guns and blankets—all these environmental and economic factors form part of the human-land-animal assemblage through which the beaver enters this present history. Innis's account brings together biopolitical economy and assemblage theory half a century before the latter's arrival. In the cumulative mythification of its image, we see the beaver severed not only from its embodiment but also from its essential hydrological activities. While visual images historically show beavers swimming through water, commercial graphics now largely depict beavers on land, or without any material context at all. The beaver has followed the path of the giraffe, in that its mediating role has shifted from a reliance on its body to a reliance on its image.

We read this history along with its absences as foundational to Canada's origin story, its management of people, its sense of place. But the beaver trade did not actually start in Canada. Because of the quality of their fur, beavers have been hunted since the ninth century. By 1240, in areas of what is now Ukraine, the supply of fur-bearing animals was already exhausted. As Clive Ponting records in *The New Green History of the World*, the decline of fur imports into London was evident by the early fifteenth century—around the same time the "emperor's giraffe" was en route to China. "By the sixteenth century," Ponting writes, "the beaver trade from Southern Europe had collapsed and only low-quality skins such as rabbit were available."[22] European merchants employing both Russian and native trappers then expanded into Siberia. By the end of the eighteenth century, the trade in what had been a plentiful population of friendly animals had "denuded" this vast area of these animals. Writing of the European settlement of North America, Ponting argues that "the search for [beaver] furs was one of the driving forces behind trade and expansion across the continent."[23]

The exporting of the species in these waves of hunting and settlement involved not only the depletion of the animal population but also an alteration of its habitus. This is because a dropping beaver population reduces their ecological activity and changes the landscape. The animal was extinct for some years in parts of the United States.[24] Just as well, according to frustrated humans in search of rural harmony whose territorial pleasures and

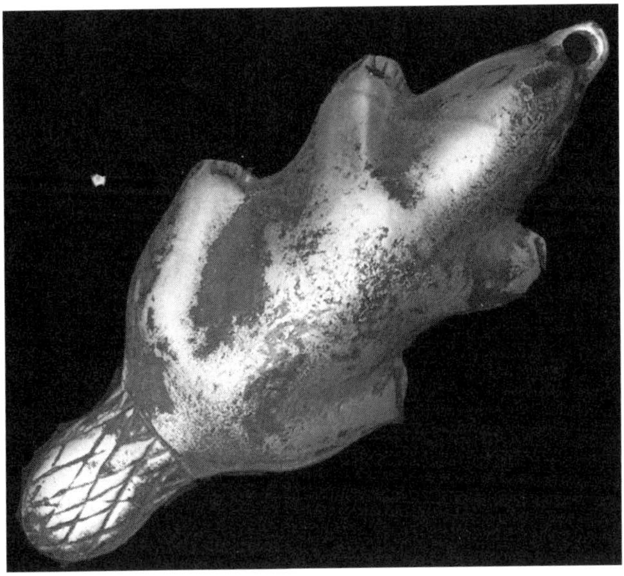

Figure 3.4
Trade beaver silver. Image courtesy of the National Bank of Canada.

investments are marred by beavers. This ambivalence throws further light on the kinship between the beaver and the bear, tiger, elephant, and many other species whose semiosis on behalf of modern nation-states obscures the human struggle for territory and resources that so destructively diminishes the possibilities for animal futures. By symbolizing our collective identity with their images, rationalizing the spaces in which they can live, and clothing ourselves in the skins and scents of these species, we humans announce our conquest of space along with nature and time. While the animal, the pelt, the fashionable hat, the stamp, the coin, the perfume, the dam, and the popular image of the beaver are materially different, they are part of one history and continue to act as mediums in a changing discursive regime.

Material Assemblage: The Fur Trade

Maps
Canoes
Ships, horses, sleds
Home offices: Toronto, Montreal, London, Paris

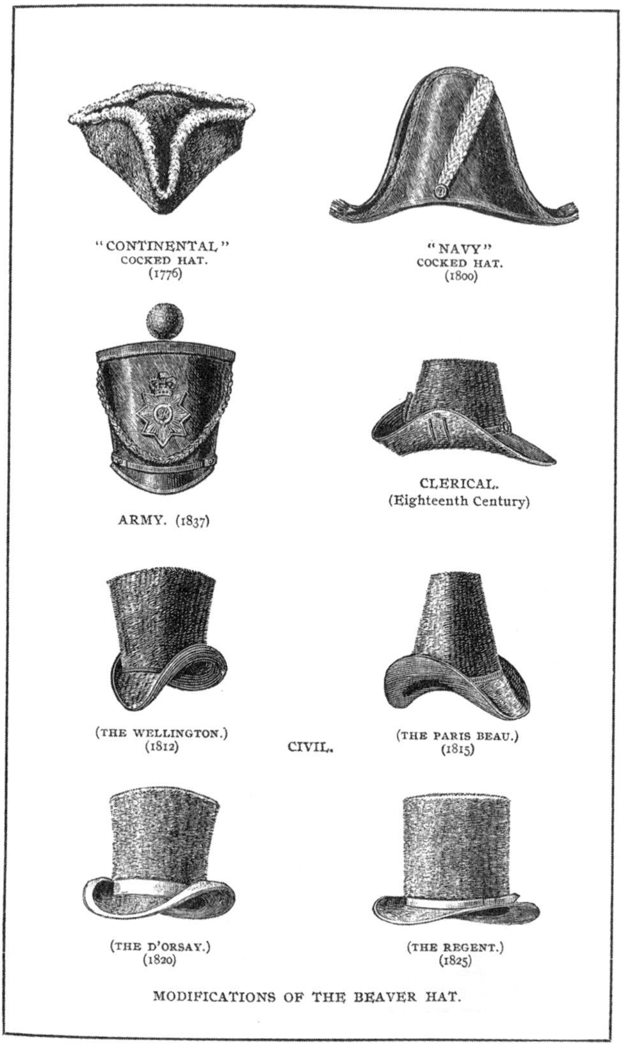

Figure 3.5

Modifications of the Beaver Hat, 1892, illustration. From *Castorologia* by H. T. Martin. Image courtesy of the Hudson Bay Company Archive, Archives of Manitoba.

Clerks, accountants
Guns
Blankets
Stamped coins, gold, silver, beads, trade medallions, money (Canada's nickel features a beaver)
Rivers, lakes, trees, bridges, canoes
Beavers
Dams
Traps
Pelts
Castoreum (rendered beaver anal gland): perfumes, scents (eighteenth and nineteenth centuries), natural and artificial flavors, ice cream, jams, today the major commodity produced from beavers, purchasable in three FDA-approved grades
Birds, fish, algae, insects, rocks
Trees, pulp, paper, pens, ink
Fur coats, collars, muffs, hats
Account books, itemized records
Drawings, letters, mail
Postage stamps (Canada's first featured a beaver)
Company stores, company representatives
Department stores, clerks, administrators and their families
Coats of arms: trading stores, corporations, universities
Lumber, steel, railways, train stations
Journals, novels, books
Totems, carvings, artworks
Taxidermy, museums, diasporas, glass
Artworks (Indigenous and European): totem, soapstone, drawing, print, painting, installation, sculpture, posters
Cameras, photographs, nature photography, documentaries
Parks, conservation areas, rivers, roads, Parks Canada logo
Government policy, insignia, political communications
Pornographic, feminist, and lesbian writing ("beaver" as women's genitalia, lesbian websites)
Corporate logos (Roots, Canadian Trucking, Bell, and others)
Natural history magazines, picture books, textbooks, encyclopedias
Leather and wood embossments and engravings
Vintage fashions
Etched granite
Truck stencils, spray paint, packing crates

Print, television, billboard, plasticine, cloth, photoshop advertisements
Coloring books
Cottages, docks, trees, campgrounds, cameras
Archives, binders, documents, shelves
Cotton, cotton-polyester T-shirts
Internet, home pages, digital image production
Newspapers, editorial pages, political cartoons
Scholarly and popular books
Manifestos
Absences, spirits, hauntings

History of the Fur Trade

The Hudson Bay Company (HBC) was formed by a royal charter from Prince Rupert in 1670, almost exactly three hundred years before the Federal Act that declared the beaver the country's national animal. The period between 1670 and 1975 was characterized by close partnership between HBC and the "mother country" whose progeny was the Dominion of Canada, to such an extent that their territories are cartographically almost indistinguishable. As Innis points out in *The Fur Trade in Canada*,

> The Northwest Co. and its successor the HBC established a centralized organization which covered the northern half of North America from the Atlantic to the Pacific. ... It is no mere accident that the present Dominion coincides roughly with the fur-trading areas of northern North America. The bases of supplies for the trade in Quebec, in western Ontario, and in British Columbia represent the agricultural areas of the present Dominion. The Northwest Company was the forerunner of the present confederation.[25]

It was the beaver that brought the Northwest Company to the northern part of the continent, and fur traders for the Northwest Company and the HBC who followed the rivers in their canoes and created the outlines and travel routes for the new dominion. "The pursuit of beaver allowed access to even the most remote areas of what was to become Canada," Hood explains. "At profits of 1000 to 2000 per cent during the most successful years of the trade, it was a lucrative means to claim a country. It is amazing that the beaver survived at all."[26] In geopolitical terms, the beaver joined with the canoe was a crucial mediator between the old geography and the new, between Indigenous peoples and white adventurers and entrepreneurs, between the old hunting and trapping cultures and the new organization of international trade.

This mediation is visible not only in terms of the territory charted by these maps, but also in terms of how the language of these maps changed. Early maps of European exploration were commonly illustrated with animal figures, ranging from sea monsters to bears and beavers, illustrating the exotic nature of the new lands and the brave exploits of the explorers. With the establishment of the fur trade, mapping territory became more instrumental, and fanciful animal symbols were evacuated from the cartographic text. The theme of the heroic exploration of exotic lands was thus displaced by a more detached rhetoric of spatial administration mapping which land belonged to whom. The newer maps identified by name and place the location of fur-bearing animals and the specific tribes that trapped them there. The function of these maps was to negotiate and govern trapping rights and rules of exchange, and to represent colonial agreements with Indigenous peoples with a form that rhetorically asserted the colonists' scientific as well as economic superiority over the people on whom they depended to fulfill their goals. Their intent to organize land in terms of property rights, their attitude toward trade relations with local tribes, and the rational culling of the beaver population are realized in the design and circulation of the new maps.

The explorer's maps and journals form an important layer in the production of a colonial topos.[27] Belton's elaboration of this concept allows us to see place as a spatial and textual archive of colonial (and other) inscriptions. Maps, journals, and company records are not only the stuff of archives; they are also the means of topographical inscriptions. The management of land, resources, and bodies accomplished through this topographic inscription was the precondition for both corporate success and national sovereignty. By realizing such sovereignty, as Foucault argues, governance enters into the era of biopolitics which involves the management of life as well as death.[28] The emergence of this era becomes visible in the correspondence and records of the Northwest Company and HBC, where they address the size and ecological health and sustainability of the beaver population. Their assessments obviously differ from the way this topic might be taken up in twenty-first-century critical animal studies, whose participants aim to trouble human-centered uses and assumptions. The fur traders would release beavers into an area and measure their local progress through the sizes of beaver houses. They would wait until the population was sufficiently developed, then they (or their trappers) would measure the beaver population, trap them, buy and sell the pelts, measure the houses. They were careful not to exhaust the population of their prey; they sought to ensure that the animal would live, even if this was a purely instrumental and quantitative assurance. Just as their maps marked boundaries between landowners rather

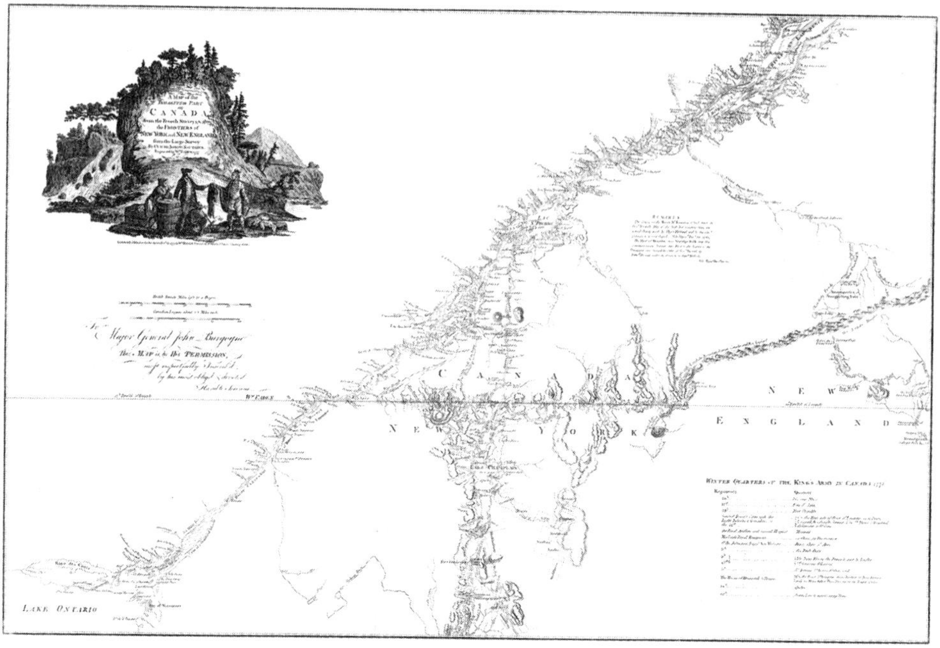

Figure 3.6

A map of the inhabited part of Canada from the French surveys, with the frontiers of New York and New England from the large survey by Claude Joseph Sauthier, 1777, William Faden. Image courtesy of the National Archives of Canada.

than habitats or bioregions, so their correspondence refers to "pelts," never "beavers" or "muskrats." As the beaver is counted, measured, and extracted from its milieu so that its pelt can be extracted from its body, its living body symptomatically disappears from the language of representation, just as the weather disappears, as I show in "Weathering the North," in representations of the country's history.[29] Both the body and its modes of disappearance leave traces whose own materialities must be taken into account.

The Indigenous Animal

"The fur trade," Innis writes "was a phase of a cultural disturbance incidental to the meeting of two civilizations with different cultural traits."[30] Note his use of "incidental"; it does not mean unimportant, but rather, eventful, in the same register that police now speak of "incident reports." This incident arises from the meeting point of two histories, leading to a "disturbance" to the entities that through their collaboration and collision reconstitute one another and themselves. The rhetorical shift in how the land and its occupants are represented reminds us that the fur trade was part of a larger process of global modernization in which the production of maps, reports, accounts, and reports of Indigenous behavior to send back to imperial sponsors was crucial to legitimating the explorers' travels, expenses, and reliable administrative authority.[31] We could speculate that the erasure of the living animal from the explorers' documentation expressed some ambivalence about the large-scale killing of animals. This would be anachronistic, however, for the concept of the animal as subject to suffering had not yet entered the vocabulary of European thought.[32] Indeed, to hunt, capture, and display animals was evidence of human superiority, and any attempt to ensure their well-being, during the transport of a giraffe or the trapping of the beaver, would have been to ensure that objective. The impetus of early modern thought was to enact a clear division between nature and culture, to purge the human from the nonhuman and the nonhuman from the human, as Latour has argued, in order to establish who was eligible to live within the community of the state. This process was easily reconciled with the establishment of successful managerial relations with animal and human resources in the context of the fur trade. The challenge is to understand how (and how much) this disposition changed in the intervening years.

The separation of human from beaver attributes is not hard to discern in this history. More complicated is understanding how colonial administrators categorized human communities that in their eyes occupied a liminal space between human and nonhuman animals, and that they consequently endowed with characteristics of both. As the colonial agents of the Northwest Company and the HBC mapped, collected, counted, measured, and recorded, they asserted epistemological as well as economic and military superiority over an Indigenous culture that in their perception survived with, as well as through interaction with, the ingenuity of an animal. The animals hunted by Indigenous peoples appear on the corporate coats of arms for the HBC and the Northwest Company next to images of Indigenous hunters as though they are essentially interchangeable as signs of the place. Through colonial representational strategies, Indigenous persons were configured as somewhere between human and animal, just as they appeared in early zoos; they are symbolically defined and diminished by a perceived bond between trapper and animal that is enshrined by those who most profited from it. This practice was extended into the twentieth century in natural history museums, whose dioramas placed costumed replicas of Indigenous people in close proximity to taxidermy displays of animals of the region.

Like other national iconic animals, such as the bald eagle, the snow leopard, or the bear, the beaver was hunted to near extinction with the assistance of local Indigenous populations. But the beaver is unique in some respects, for it lacks the heroic carnivorous qualities of these other animals, qualities that implicitly transfer from the animal to the nation in support of its military or industrial prowess. This anomaly was made explicit in 2011, when a Conservative member of Canada's Senate, Nicole Eaton, proposed that Canada replace the beaver, a "dentally challenged rodent," with the properly aggressive and carnivorous polar bear as its official animal.[33] The beaver icon is the relic of plunder, as Atwood's David makes clear, and it was not beavers doing the plundering. In Eaton's view, the beaver symbol was a pusillanimous residue. Her view of it was uninflected by the powerful semantic tensions between beaver as sacrificial animal, architect and builder, family-oriented mammal who must chew trees or die, as troubled index of colonial power, as national totem, stuffed animal, icon, Boy Scout, finally as toothy, glossy, ironically expressive, and peculiarly loved and disdained symbol set adrift in the static decontextualized multiples of imagery today. In the event, Senator Eaton got nowhere with her plan.

Perhaps her campaign speaks to the absence of representations of the beaver as an entity deserving of respect. During my visit to the HBC Archives in Winnipeg I found many early photographs of Indigenous people posing for the camera with beavers, but very few of whites with (uncrated) live beavers. The photographs of Grey Owl (né Archibald Belaney) with his pet beavers are a famous and deliberate exception to the rule. When other white settlers faced the camera, they modeled their understanding of Indigenous-beaver interdependency not by posing with the animals but rather through mimetic rituals in which they draped themselves in furs and masqueraded as Indians. Clad in the furs that had become their property, in their ethnic drag they enacted the connection between Indigenous and animal entities over which they sartorially declare their supremacy. This performance presupposes both the proximity of colonizer and colonized and the absolute distinction between them, predicated on the Indigenous people's assumed closeness to the world of animals.[34]

In the symbolic triangulation of Indigenous communities, wild animals, and colonial conquest, the beaver could not appear as a live animal capable of suffering. The exclusion of the living animal as a subject worthy of attention is part of the ontological environment of purification already mentioned. The semiconsciousness of a sacrificial economy of animal lives evoked by Atwood in *Surfacing* is managed by a colonial writing of history

Figure 3.7

Miss Gladys Walker Dressed in Native Costumes, 1920, photograph. From Captain George Henry Mead's album. Image courtesy of the Hudson Bay Company Archive, Archives of Manitoba.

endlessly reiterated in pictures, museums, and schoolbooks, through which the beaver and the Indian are so closely associated that the meaning of each entity relies on its connection to the other and neither is given adequate understanding. Rather than affirming the achievements of Indigenous peoples, the beaver figures as part of a discursive milieu in which animality "naturalizes" our conquest of them. Reexamination of the beaver archive in Canada and more generally in Western cultural history makes it possible to trace the creation of this interdependency. It provides testimony to the manner in which the beaver became both site and alibi for the same

Figure 3.8
Rupert's House. Indian Boys with Two Week Old Beaver Kitts, ca. 1942, photograph. Image courtesy of the Hudson Bay Company Archive, Archives of Manitoba.

abjection of Indigeneity that has more broadly been projected onto alterity through the trope of animality.[35]

At the HBC Archives, I requested a book published in 1703 that is cited in Innis's *History of the Fur Trade* as *Different Ways of Hunting the Beaver*. It proved to be a hand-illustrated report, bound in an ancient leather cover, dedicated entirely to an account of the beliefs and practices of local native people. The author, Baron Lahonton, Lord Lieutenant of the French Colonia at Placentia, Newfoundland, is writing in English for a London publisher. His close and respectful study of Indigenous practices and beliefs explicitly contrasts the justice and freedom of native people with the European Christians' injustice against them.[36] By the time he had been unceremoniously relieved of his Canadian duties, he had turned against the goal of vanquishing the Algonquins.[37] Baron Lahonton's critique of European civilization and its colonial objectives was unusual for the time. His decision to document Indigenous knowledge for an English-speaking audience should be read in light of Lewis Saum's more recent observation, in *The Fur Trader and the Indian*, that European explorers and traders oriented their correspondence and reports around the debate as to whether Indians were noble savages or not. Who did they more closely resemble, these traders speculated, the beaver or the white man? Samuel Hearne of the HBC complained that the beaver "had been greatly over-endowed with organizational ability, sagacity and ingenuity,"[38] a mistake for which he blamed the so-called savages. Despite the degree to which traders relied on Indigenous guides and trappers, these commercial representatives perceived them as naive; their too respectful estimation of the animal was proof that they lacked the superior judgement of the Europeans. With little interest in the sagacity of either beavers or trappers, Hearne, for one, readily believed himself to be superior to members of either group.

The colonizers' association of Indigeneity with animality naturally enhanced their own claim to power.[39] In this cultural production of the non-Western as not fully human, beavers and Indigenous peoples were linked not only through the beaver pelts they trapped and traded as commodities, but also through traders' observations of Indigenous peoples as though they were a different species from themselves, as though they were closer to the animals they hunted than to the humans with whom they traded. Were these Indians really projecting too much sagacity onto the animal, I wonder, or were white men projecting this perceived pathology, this primitiveness or animality, onto their Indigenous contacts, assuming that their long-established skill in animal observation was a symptom of their lack of reason?

Traders were generally closer in attitude to Hearne than to Lahonton. Their journals disclosed that "the least unhappy [Indians] are those who approximate the naivete of the beasts"[40] or that when a "red man" took up the white man's ways, his happiness vanished: "like a wild animal in a cage, his luster is gone." "Like a wild animal also," Saum concludes in his summary of the traders' opinions, "the Indian did not readily lend himself to transformation."[41] In other words, colonial observers saw beavers and Indigenous communities as linked and parallel subjects of a natural(ized) history in which white traders were the necessary agents of progress. They believed that the native, ingenious but not intelligent, was incapable of mastering his natural environment, that is to say of modernizing himself, of progress. Indigenous knowledge is thus contained by the concept of the machinic animal, adaptive but not reflexive, defined, as postcolonial critics have argued, outside of history.[42]

This is the rhetorical structure Grey Owl set out to sabotage two centuries later when he withdrew from trapping, married an Indigenous woman, and began to write about the interdependent lives of humans and animals in the north. Writing just before Innis first published *The Fur Trade in Canada*, Grey Owl was eager to demonstrate the beaver's ingenuity and the complex spiritual and ecological relationship between trapper and prey. His focus was as much on improving the relationship between species as between races. As he showed in his fiction as well as in his well-documented life, the narrative of the Indigene as living outside of history had less to do with actual encounters through which native and colonial inhabitants were connected by trade, friendship, marriage, and mutual aid than with fixed ideas about Western civilization. In the colonial imaginary, Indigenous people and animals were linked by function, physical proximity, and racist anthropocentrism. White commentators prejudicially underestimated the sagacity of the beaver and did more or less the same in relation to its trappers, and more broadly with regard to the Indigenous communities engaged in the fur trade. In their accounts Indigenous people trapped animals, prepared the pelts, and brought them to fur trade sites, but never contributed food, building materials, advice, or other objects or knowledges.[43] In their lives as well as the documents they produced, Indigenous people were discursively marginalized and contained not only by their links to animals and plants but more pointedly by their perceived reluctance to transform their environments. Like the beaver, the Indian is always already in a failed transitive mode in this narrative, always already both busy and dead. Unlike the beaver, First Nations peoples continue to articulate and enact a critical anticolonial response to this discourse.

The Beaver Archive

As Laura Peers has noted, "fur trade history has always been closely connected to public history sites."[44] Writing of reconstructed fur trade posts built in the 1960s and 1970s, Peers observes that such sites have been contentious because they failed to take Indigenous perspectives and memories into account. "It seems simplistic and misleading," she argues, "to represent the complexity of the fur trade by an insistently repetitive set of artifacts consisting of a blanket, a beaver hide on a stretcher, some beads, and a musket." Peers suggests that the repetitious display of these few visible tokens "connote[s] the still-popular assumption that Native people became dependent on European trade goods; and they thus affirm the underlying assumption that European cultures have always been superior to those of 'Others'"[45]

Such displays of past times reinforce the symbiotic association between Indigenous person and animal entity already embedded in colonial culture. But the "insistently repetitive" quality of such displays has a more general force; it enacts the impulse or "desire" that Derrida describes in *Archive Fever*.[46] Insisting that the archive arises from an active process of inscription, rather than a simple process of collection, Derrida suggests that one can find in the genealogy of the term both "commencement" and "commandment." The curator's display of evidence authorizes the telling of a particular story based on the enactment ("commencement") of specific memories and the abandonment of others. Underlying this drive to collect and display, Derrida suggests, is the felt lack of a fully authoritative space of identity. The individual or communal subject seeks to reconstitute its identity, to separate itself from that which it is not, through memory, through keeping together the contents of its archive. Derrida's understanding of the archive parallels and draws from Freud's understanding of the subject, whose individual constitution through memory relies on the evacuation of what is to be forgotten. "Nothing is less reliable, nothing is less clear than the word 'archive,'" Derrida writes:

> The *trouble d'archive* stems from a *mal d'archive*. ... It is to turn with a passion. It is never to rest, interminably, from searching for the archive right where it slips away. It is to run for the archive, even if there is too much of it, right where in it something anarchives itself. It is to have a compulsive, repetitive, and nostalgic desire for the archive, an irrepressible desire to return to the most archaic place of absolute commencement.[47]

Commencement: the fur trade. As if nothing had been there before, as critics bitterly remarked when Canada recently celebrated its sesquicentennial. Irrepressible desire: pelt, museum, logo, symbol, legislation. Slipping away: the endless receding of history, context, embodiment, animality. Accumulating objects such as pelts or logos as variations of a theme enhances the authority of collective governance but can inhibit new ways of understanding the past. As the space of collective memory spills out into newer technological spaces, the inscription of memory becomes a greater challenge and an even stronger compulsion. The compulsion for the archive seeks to demolish the gap between public record and private psyche. The beaver performatively attaches human subjects to their common national destiny within a permitted range of rhetorical and affective strategies. But the compulsion for thematic closure that informs this archive is undermined in contemporary culture by the detachment from meaning that occurs in the vortex of information. This process also begins

Figure 3.9
Roots logo. © 2018 Roots Corporation. Image courtesy of the brand.

with the beaver, whose representation marks both commencement (the story of Canada's origin) and return (as the beaver pops up in one form or another). If the proliferation of signs might compulsively reassure and entertain anxious citizens, it also succumbs to and secures the cool and differently comforting meaninglessness of the corporate logo.

The beaver at the center of this archive is a commandment to remember and to forget. At the same time, the beaver is a lively animal and won't stand still. It swims from natural history—beaver as architect, builder, and chewer of wood—to cultural anthropology—the beaver is so ingenious! it plans and builds houses much as humans do![48]—to material resource in economic history, token of colonial rights in the new world, index of value on coins and maps, symbol of achievement on Boy Scouts' brands and badges, logo of the nation-state, natural ally of woman, doubling back on itself in a process of increasing stylization and abstraction to provide commercial logos, populist symbols, sarcastic rejoinders, further anarchiving itself in icons of sexuality and lesbian art, indexing diverse realms of the social through commodity fetishism, animal justice activism, advertisements and logos, Canadian studies, contemporary art, political metaphors and cartoons, the latter stripped of any explicit evidence of the animal or its anthropological history, which is at once evoked and dismissed.

The compulsion to multiply and trade beaver images in these changing contexts has produced a lexicon of familiarities, as though the currency can still function as the same kind of exchange even if it is just an abstract database of likenesses, as though meaning, like money, can be proliferated and fully controlled by any mode of governance. But this would be a misinterpretation of what we see. In "Archive Fever and Twentieth Century Critical Theory," Rachel Price writes that "the archive requires imagination. Its prosthetic capacity is insufficient, for it is always a collection of interruptions: more like a container of history, it consists of a few digressive fragments of information which only suggest what was omitted."[49] Having reviewed the important presences and absences in the beaver archive, it is time for us to consider the interruptions this same archive contains. Note Price's use of the word "container," with its multiple meanings: it holds history, contains it from spilling, allows it to speak, contains it from speaking. What does it mean to find a "collection of interruptions" played out in these archival containers? How might we make such interruptions productive in the reconstitution of psyches, territories, and relations?

Let us briefly review recent contributions to the archive as a starting place to address these questions. Jim Cameron's richly illustrated book *The*

Figure 3.10
Parks Canada Celebrated Its 100th Birthday by Bringing a Couple of Beavers into Toronto, 2011, photograph, James Hamilton. Image courtesy of the artist.

Canadian Beaver Book: Fact, Fiction and Fantasy[50] offers an enthusiastic collector's documentation of the beaver as popular visual symbol. This richly illustrated historical resource contains hundreds of images of the beaver drawn from popular, political, and corporate iconography over a hundred years. It contains no reference to natural history or animal life. Chantal Nadeau's adventurous book *Fur Nation*[51] teaches us a great deal about intimate relations between fur, masculine power, feminine sexuality, performativity, and photography, but has nothing to say about trapping or beavers. In *The Sexual Politics of Fur*, Julia Emberley writes with pointed eloquence about the fur trade's devastating effects on North America's Indigenous peoples and about the "abject animalization" of fur-clad women,[52] but the word "beaver" rarely appears, and then only when annexed to the word "fur." Margot Francis's eloquent study of the heritage of white-Indigenous relations attends closely to the beaver as a symbol but does not speak of it as an animal; there is no sense of a shared biosphere from which the symbol emerges and upon which it continues to act. Hood's *The Beaver Manifesto* by contrast builds on the author's work with Parks Canada and her "long and interesting acquaintanceship" with the Canadian beaver.[53] Her contribution fills in some of the beaver's absent nature, enacting a shift from sexual and racial to environmental politics.

Hood's "manifesto" registers two important shifts or interruptions in the production of the beaver archive. As this quick summary suggests, the inescapable masculinity of earlier writing on the fur trade, which emphasizes conquest, profit, and adventure, gave way to the publication of studies by women that attend more closely to culture and power. Given that fur coats enact a longstanding relationship between money and sex, and that the name of the beaver has a longstanding double entendre relating to women's privates, it is perhaps not surprising that animal meanings and metaphors shifted in another direction in twentieth-century women's writing and in lesbian and feminist culture, where "beaver" stands metonymically for women's genitals. In both bodies of literature, the body of the animal disappears into the background. From works like *The Cultural Politics of Fur*, *Fur Nation*, and *Creative Subversion*[54] to lesbian websites like The Beaver, the beaver performs a work of double substitution wherein the animal is subsumed and remediated by mainly white women as part of the act of repossessing their own sexual bodies. More recently, as colonial and anthropocentric discursive structures are subjected to critical scrutiny, writing on the beaver is beginning to retrieve and incorporate the history and the question of the animal itself. It constitutes its subject as beaver, not just pelt or fur, and further questions the historical processes that translated animals into property, money, and power.

This brief review opens a window to a more purposeful approach to the "collection of interruptions" found in the beaver archive. The political contest between Canada's founding narratives and the counternarratives of the First Nations has foregrounded the colonization of Indigenous lands and cultures and exposed the sacrifice of animal and human bodies. By reminding us of this history, beaver imagery plays an important role in the production of postcolonial and anticolonial pleasures. Growing animal awareness reminds us that however much the beaver indexes and entertains the nation-state, this same state does not offer the nonhuman animal the right to assert its own right to rights, as Wolfe puts it.[55] While provincial laws vary, one generally needs a permit or process of consultation to destroy a beaver dam because of potential damage to property or wildlife downstream, but one needs no license to trap or kill a beaver.[56] Given the tension between the animal's symbolic and legal status, the beaver poses a challenge to law as well as to history and culture. Acknowledging this tension challenges the complacency of our feelings when we glimpse its familiar silhouette. Feminism and environmental activism have challenged the conventional valorization of the special relationship between the bodies of fur-bearing animals and fur-wearing women. Left unspoken for the most part has been the beaver's role as medium between two cultures in an often violent process of colonial settlement. As fur returns to the fashion mainstream, how do we interrupt the anthropocentric elision between fur, sex, and power without undermining the traditional cultures and values of Indigenous hunters? Feminism and animal rights activism make their way into the beaver archive through oppositional texts and image productions. But the hybrid animal-human figuration of this archive also poses questions about shared habitats. We have barely begun to redress colonial violence, much less consider ourselves in relation to species diversity or ecological risk, or what such thinking does for our understanding of animal subjects. Timothy Morton poses this last challenge when he asks, "Does the beaver phenotype stop at the end of its whiskers or at the end of a beaver's dam?"[57]

My review of recent contributions to the beaver archive suggests that we have a lot to learn before we can better materialize the "important role that animals play in spatial ecology and identity construction," as Wolch and Emel recommend.[58] In this sense our relationship with beavers reiterates the territorial battles that commercial enterprises are now waging with species as diverse as bees, elephants, tigers, slender-snouted crocodiles,

Atlantic cod, and various species of dolphins and whales. To urban postcolonial subjects they are equally remote, if not equally charismatic. How we think about these issues matters in every sense of the term. "Now more than ever," Guattari insists in *The Three Ecologies*, "nature cannot be separated from culture; in order to comprehend the interactions between ecosystems, the mechanosphere and the social and individual Universes of transference, we must learn to think 'transversally.'"[59] In other words, as these interruptions to the beaver archive remind us, we need new mapping strategies that resituate beavers across the violent histories that forced their bodies and images into mediation of diverse populations, ecologies, and economies. We need beaver figurations that acknowledge colonial history, the land rights of Indigenous populations, the nature and spirit of beavers, the rivers polluted beyond recognition, the future of rivers and lakes.

Finally, then, the interruption we most urgently need to make productive concerns our territorial competition with nonhuman animals and our actions and effects as animals ourselves. While water experts like Alice Outwater call beavers "nature's hydrologists"[60] and emphasize their ecological importance to continental waterways, landowning Westerners do not know how to share rivers or trees with them in a sustainable manner. And yet the risks associated with water have never been more urgent than today, when, not surprisingly, those most at risk are Indigenous people living on reservations. Better strategic collaboration with beavers could probably help ensure the sustainability of water, lakes, and rivers. But the beavers' inscriptions of rivers don't yet show up on *our* maps. If there's going to be any interference in our aqueous territories, we proclaim as we define beavers as pests, it will be *our* interference.

This story of human interaction with the beaver can be told through a history of images, through an examination of a still-growing visual and material archive, but as these thoughts suggest, such a telling is not sufficient. It doesn't account for what is exchanged or produced as these images continue to travel, or for how we actually encounter and use the beaver animal. Restoring animality and agency to the beaver challenges us to confront this fragmentary archive from a material and ecological perspective. Comprised of so many different kinds of objects, so many different kinds of mediation, the beaver archive travels energetically between nostalgia and objecthood and entices us to forget that what is at stake is life itself. Just as the beaver's life was strategically sustained by trappers in order for it to be circulated as fur, oil, and tribute laid before the visiting Crown, so newer forms of reproduction are sustained and managed in the new biopolitical order in which economy is more directly interdependent with the production of affect. The changing actualization of the beaver commodity symbolizes new management.[61] But the animal itself is never just commodity. We know that elephants and bees are traumatized by their oppression, but we know nothing of beavers' states in response to urban sprawl. We see it as a brand or a rodent, or as an inconsiderate chewer of trees, not as an architect.

Conclusion

These "interruptions" to the beaver archive show that the beaver's phantom use value derives from its claim to a shared human-animal history and from its sagacious respect for the water it calls home. Both of these use values have something important to teach us. But both values are negatively indexed in the cumulative loss of fur in current symbolic renderings. Through stylistic abstraction, the paradigm of work—the beaver as architect, the trapper as provider—has given way to a paradigm of control in the ongoing commodification of life itself.[62] As Baudrillard observes in *For a Critique of the Political Economy of the Sign*,

> Stylization always signifies the elision of muscular energy and of work. All the processes of elision of primary functions to the profit of the secondary functions of relation and calculation, or of the elision of the drives to the profit of culture (*culturalité*) have for a practical and historical mediation at the level of objects the fundamental elision of the gestures of effort (*gestuel d'effort*), the passage from a *universal gestural paradigm of work* to a *universal gestural paradigm of control*. It is there that a millenarian status of objects, their anthropomorphic status, definitely comes to an end; in the abstraction of the sources of energy.[63]

Here the sources of energy being abstracted include the dam building of the beaver and the physical and social work of the trappers, the traders, the settlers, and so on. Such control is enacted visually through abstraction, repetition, digitization, and affect management. This abstraction/affect management shows up again and again in the animal-technology mediations described in the chapters to come. Just as animal imagery has played a key role in the development of new representational technologies,[64] so the work of the animal and of its image are central to the biopolitics of late capitalism. The beavers put to work in the contemporary knowledge economy are stylized graphic images that resemble the animal just enough to be recognizable in a glimpse. Through such imagery the design environment of corporate capitalism easily dominates the archive.

Alan Liu's critique of the knowledge economy and the production of "cool" usefully supplements this critique of the symbolic abstraction, regulation, and "dematerialization" of animals as historical projects.[65] Liu defines "cool" as "information designed to resist information [or] the incest of information." It has "everything to do with the mythopoetic landscapes of work," he writes, "leading from filmic deserts to screensaver-like digital highways and seas: the mainstream is identified with the pure milieu, ambience or texture of challenge, with style emptied of agents and agency to become a world sufficient unto itself."[66] This is what makes these latest beaver simulations so extreme and yet so weirdly anticlimactic. Their denial of violence and the infantilization of affect suppress both animality and meaning. For Liu, the culture of cool arises from the creative knowledge worker's need to balance her self-concept as an autonomously creative person against the material constraints of her training and employment in the knowledge economy. Forced to distance herself from her highly regulated milieu, she participates in a design vocabulary that articulates and exacerbates her ambivalent relationship with her object. Cool is ironic, inarticulate, narrow-minded, self-centered, and sometimes cruel. It is strongly invested in the meaninglessness of things. Unlike the destructive actions of the Reformation or the Nazis, Liu writes, we do not destroy our archives but rather render them meaningless, non-sense. We could not find a better description of the annoying de-furred, de-animalized beavers promoting Bell phones and Parks Canada in their respective advertising campaigns. These beavers are cool in a bad way. Their pallid irony licenses indifference and cruelty. As Liu concludes, it is our task as educators to show that cool is a historical condition, to help advance understanding of this condition and to consider how its circumstances might be overcome. The growth of empathy toward living creatures is a necessary step in this direction.

Like the giraffe, but differently, the beaver became a mediator in the expansion of global trade. Canoes, hats, trains, corporate logos, and telephones have material histories that contribute to relations of power over space and time that are central to the rise (and fall) of empires. If ancient power was effected primarily through sustainability through time, modern power stretches across ever vaster vistas of space. Through the routes and economics of the fur trade, Canada was brought under French and English colonial management. Beaver bodies were the impetus for and symbol of colonial conquest. Beaver representations, symbols, and logos have subsequently become seemingly indispensable mediators between two distinct but mutually interdependent modes of government, the nation-state and the global corporation, the logic of patriotic difference and the logic of sublimated indifference.

Today, animals need to be accounted for not only as mediators but also as subjects and objects central to how social relations are imagined and formed and how people are connected and differentiated within those relations. Posthumanist thought seeks to realize more diverse accounts of human subjects and objects, but encounters the challenge of applying political theory to nonhuman animals. This problem is not just conceptual and analytical, Nicole Shukin argues, but deeply material, involving not just the semiotic currency or mythic status of animal signs but also "the carnal traffic in animal substances."[67] So much is at stake in this virtual archive of the beaver: colonial history, animal bodies, water, money, the fur trade, maps and correspondences, inequitable encounters between settler and Indigenous cultures, ideas about nature and land, the so-called dematerialization of the global economy, the source of "natural" and "artificial" flavors, fetishism, posthumanism, fashion, sexuality, water, deindustrialization, the aesthetics of cute, the dominance of cool, the biopolitics of colonialism, and the corporatization of national identity are all present there. The virtualization of the beaver "contains" all this, along with traces of diverse interests acting to make other meanings productive in the contending histories of the present. Unraveling these threads is important to revisiting what is remembered and what is forgotten in the inscription of Canada.

In *A Fair Country*, John Ralston Saul claims that Canadian society has become dysfunctional and that we need to rethink its history. For Saul, imagining ourselves differently means letting go of European hierarchies and rationalities and recognizing the degree to which Canada's values and modes of connection are shaped by the influence and proximity of Indigenous cultures with which we have interacted from the start. "We have to learn how to express that reality, the reality of our history. I am not talking about a passive projection of our past, but rather about all of us learning how to imagine ourselves differently."[68] There is something touching and problematic in the commonality that Saul invokes in "all of us." What might this imagining bring to our depiction of beavers, humans, and natural resources?

To alter our shared political trajectory, we need to relearn this history and what its different players know and don't know about water, ecology, land, culture, and species. We need to appreciate the artistry of beavers, as well as our own, and think differently about maps, the ones that got us here and the ones we might remake. The work of the beaver is to live and rebuild the landscape. That is our job as well.

4 Assembling the Virtual Menagerie

The virtual menagerie assembled in this chapter emerged from a number of distinct historical currents that coalesced in the figures of animals created, patented, and circulated during the blurry liminal moment between the 1960s and the dawn of the information age. Some of these images borrowed from the species and designs of early menagerie illustrations; all of them involved animals and all of them were attached to computers and their programs. This chapter explores these iconic figures and the new software universe within which they appeared as an opening sequence in a notable visual-technical event. The animal images mediating these vistas of a virtual future exemplify my premise that the animal figure plays a singular role in mediating (imperial, colonial, capitalist, virtual) spaces, and in launching (visual, electronic, digital) connective technologies. This complicated and remarkable story forms the bridge between the classical and the virtual menagerie, and between modern and whatever we are going to call our contemporary era's ideas about human, animal, and technological capacities.

The primates and wildcats, penguins and gophers chosen to serve as icons for digital communications between 1965 and 2005 hold an obvious and to some degree deliberate relation to the historic menageries described in earlier chapters. These graphic images visibly link the heterotopias of the early modern European menageries with the technotopian ideals motivating the digital engineers and designers of the 1960s and beyond. To examine the vocabularies and affective resonances of these animal emissaries and their span across centuries as well as continents, I draw on Debray's exhortation to "look not for *that which is behind* a symbolic utterance, but rather *that which takes place between*."[1]

As shown in earlier chapters, the attachment of iconic animals to new communication practices and technologies predates the digital age. The emperor's giraffe, the trader's beaver, the lions and deer that figure in so

Figure 4.1
Grid of Twitter, Firefox, GNU, and Linux logos, 2017, screenshot.

many coats of arms, the dog searching for the source of His Master's Voice, MGM's roaring lion, and the penguin logo familiar from Penguin paperback editions of classic fiction are well-known examples of the association between animal graphic and corporate identity. New ways of life and new modes of representation arising together within complex ecosystems of cultural, economic, and environmental conditions are often heralded with bodies, parts, or images of animals. The connection between the technical and the animal was mobilized in unprecedented ways in postwar American culture, when software engineers undertook to design the component parts of the digital sphere. Almost without exception, their innovations were branded with images of animals. The animal and the digital emerged together through an interactive process in which human capacities were asserted, extended, undermined, and reasserted in multiple directions. The reciprocal emergence of digital animals and animalized digitality played an important role in shaping and managing the concepts, practices, and textures of the "information society."

It is a challenge to find a software or computer company on the market between the mid-1960s and the mid-2000s that was not identified with a figure or name of an animal. These figures capture the space midway between the utopian ideals of the 1960s, which I describe as a nascent cybernetic vision of liberation as explored in projects like the *Whole Earth Catalog*, and the corporate trajectories of information management and military cybernetics. The menageries featured by Honeywell, O'Reilly Media, and Canada's Telus, to name several notable examples, were created by designing clear visual icons of species from diverse habitats and displaying them as a series, mimicking the menageries described in earlier chapters. Like their antecedents, these virtual menageries provided heterotopic spaces populated by animal species that were otherwise spatially incompatible. This reiteration of the older practice allowed animals and humans to migrate together, so to speak, to the new heterotopic and virtual spaces being built by digital computing.

As emissaries for user-friendly platforms being produced in an increasingly competitive milieu, these animal icons offered an enticing and efficient way to identify their products. Honeywell Information Systems was the first company to employ this strategic practice, commissioning eerie cybernetic sculptures of exotic animals made from the parts of the computers being advertised to promote the company, its products, and the collaborative but competitive ideals of the computer revolution. While many companies subsequently settled on a single species to represent their corporate identity, others also used menageries in their promotion strategies, and the early and most influential campaigns referred to them as such. The digitally stylized and minimized design of these animal icons marks them as representations of a product or brand identity. In this way, I will argue, they encapsulate the ideology through which personal liberation is reconciled with collectivist ambitions through innovations in computing.[2]

The design of these digital menageries has ranged from the eighteenth-century etching-style graphics chosen to represent the "O'Reilly Menagerie" to photorealistic images and digital animations to ostensibly spontaneous videographic selfies to minimalist graphic silhouettes. Such icons invite contradictory feelings of childlike wonder and visceral attraction, mischievous energy and ironic cool and bland corporate assent. Their muted affect and dalliance with corporate mindset may not be what the original software designers had in mind. To understand this gap between intention and result and to trace its presence through these images is to unravel the trajectories and unfinished impulses of personal computing.

Early software engineering set out to complete the cultural revolution of the 1960s by engineering a reconciliation of the creative individualism and technological pragmatism so deeply embedded in American culture. Its proponents sought to introduce computing software and its affordances to a wider and freer social arena; to encourage individuals to pursue their own innovative geek impulses; and to connect everyone in what Rheingold famously called a virtual community.[3] The mandate of the animal logo was to intensify the impulse to connect while channeling the impulsive spirit into the necessary and naturally evolutionary acquisition of digital software and mobile devices. The introduction of new computer-based commodities associated with animal icons thus propelled users through a force field of conflicting values and intertextual machineries of meaning that vastly exceeded the functional space of any particular product.

Illustrated History

The population and diversity of virtual animals housed in our digital media landscape are incalculably larger than the range of animals most people at any stage of history will see live, in the flesh, unless they visit the zoo. As the populations of lions, elephants, giraffes, primates, and bees heartbreakingly shrink and others disappear altogether, their images proliferate. On any given day, graphic monkeys and chimps, goats, dogs, cats, giraffes, mice, bees, rabbits, parrots, frogs, otters, polar bears, pandas, rhinos, and other species appear in digital form and in various degrees of purposeful visibility. From subjects of films, animation, and toys to software and corporate icons, these new renderings of animals and new technologies of image production have emerged together in a flurry of intertextual proliferation. To put this in context, there were substantially fewer animals shown in the magazine ads, brands, logos, or illustrations circulated in Anglo-American print or audiovisual culture before the 1960s. When an animal was part of a picture, its relationship to the story or product was comparatively direct: a cow advertising milk, a monkey or giraffe signaling the countries to which American Airlines could take you, a mustang evoking the speed of the eponymous car.[4] The subsequent transformation of the visual field was remarkable.

In 1964, Honeywell, a company known for both military and domestic technology manufacture, launched what has been described as "one of the most remarkable and successful industrial-advertising campaigns in America."[5] The campaign, called "Morrie's Menagerie," employing striking images of animals built from computer components, ran from 1964 to 1972. In each print ad, a photographed animal sculpture visibly constructed from computer parts is accompanied by a text that cleverly associates the characteristic spirit of the animal figure with descriptions of the competitive advantages associated with the computers comprised of these same parts. The product's agility is demonstrated by the apparently effortless fitting together of computer parts to achieve the contours of the animal body just as the computer would effortlessly advance a particular company's competitive technical agendas. These shiny hybrid images conveying the Honeywell message that their products would make you leader of the pack appeared in magazine ads, trade shows, billboards, promotional items, brochures, and prints "suitable for framing."[6] This advent of the digital animal—the fur and feathers are fashioned from computer parts—preceded the release of commodities that could draw explorers into a new virtual universe.

O'Reilly Media, founded in 1978, made a fortune publishing software guides which were designed and advertised as their "animal books." They

How does The Other Computer Company compare with Mr. Big?
Them:
Us:
The Other Computer Company:
Honeywell

Figure 4.2
How Does the Other Computer Company Compare with Mr. Big? Honeywell computers advertisement, 1964–1972, Honeywell.

are collectively searchable online as the "O'Reilly Menagerie." These animal drawings, stylistically modeled on eighteenth-century engravings representing the animals of a conventional menagerie, appear prominently on the covers of their guidebooks. In both print and online promotions, the drawings are arranged in a two-dimensional grid of boxes inviting comparison to a zoological collection. These crafty and exotic animals are more artistically stylized than a painting or photograph, less graphically minimalized than those that now populate the Internet. The taxonomy of these early software menageries, combined with the stylistic reference to an earlier form of image making, suggests a preoccupation with the esoteric. Wildcats, pythons, bears, turtles, bats, otters, eagles, squirrels, kangaroos, fish, gophers, and baboons appear along with other more obscure species taken mainly from distant, formerly colonized parts of the world, alongside mythic norns that look like illustrations from the game "Creatures." These beasts were conscripted as techno-evangelist icons for the geeks forming the early architecture of the Internet.

I call these animals "techno-evangelists" because that is the term used by O'Reilly in its introduction to the company's guidebooks or "menageries." According to the author of this introduction, O'Reilly Media "has a long history of advocacy, meme-making, and evangelism" using animal icons "to amplify" the "faint signals" from the "alpha geeks."[7] The animals were designed not just to proselytize for their products, but also to convert potential users to the ideas and intentions, that is to say the geeks' "faint signals," that spawned them. These animals have been made available for viewing through graphic reprocessing just as the creative instincts of the geeks are made available through corporate digital reprocessing. This assimilation creates a slippage from concept to geek, from geek to brand, from brand to animal spirit, and from animal spirit to the purchase of a device and the potential rediscovery of the universe through digital connection. The animal has been conscripted to advocate for a technologically enhanced future in which information will be free, and implicitly the users of this software will be free too, free as a bird but fierce as a lion. This phantasmagoric freedom is the precondition to control of known and unknown worlds alike. The *Born Free* movies made from 1966 to 1972 about Elsa, the African lion, surely enhanced the intelligibility of this narrative. The lyrics to the 1966 Academy Award-winning theme song ("Born free, as free as the wind blows, as free as the grass grows, born free to follow your heart") expressed and amplified the iconically American idea that "animals, like people, cherish their freedom."[8] The techno-evangelist animals featured in the O'Reilly Menagerie are thus conceived as a great orchestra of instruments in which "Life, and especially human life, now appears as a process of self-realization ... the inner, coordinative aspect of which becomes expressed in the crescendo of an ever more fully orchestrated consciousness."[9]

These evangelical animal figures announce a virtual future based on a vision of work as self-realization liberated from the constraints of offices, bosses, routines, desks, and deadlines (if not gender norms) so that users, like the "animal spirits" introduced earlier, can operate freely in a wild zone of geek creativity. The earliest recorded expression of the idea that "information wants to be free" in relation to computing is credited to Stewart Brand, founder of the *Whole Earth Catalog* (1968–1972), speaking at the first Hackers' Conference in 1984. He added (although this proviso is usually forgotten): "But it also wants to be expensive."[10] The theological overtones in this discourse are reconciled rhetorically with the neo-Darwinist subtext of evolutionary informational systems, so that the theological and evolutionary motifs run together as codependent machineries of the technological sublime. This technocratic reconciliation of evangelism and evolutionism is vivified by a significant shift in the biopolitics of American culture. In a landscape dominated by the electrifying "jolts" associated with commercial television in the United States,[11] the advertising lexicon moves from describing the object to evoking a feeling to be associated with that object. Brand's animalized idea of information expresses a desire for freedom against its own logic as a commodity, embodied by the animal spirit that channels the electrified flow of information that can liberate the animal in us.

Figure 4.3
The O'Reilly guidebook menagerie, 2017, digital images. Image courtesy of O'Reilly Media.

By the 1990s, the movement to develop more advanced platforms for mobile communication coalesced around the contradictory objectives of personal freedom, software creativity, corporate growth, technological progress, the acquisition of commodities, and the management of information. Animal brands were evidently the preferred means to reconcile these goals, to manage not only the software but also the user and user data that proliferated from their pursuit. Just as looking at a confined animal in a menagerie or zoo puts the viewer in a position of relative power, so sending a simulated animal figure in search of data assures the searcher that they are essentially in control of the space behind the screen. In 1991, to manage the rapid growth of electronic data, designers at the University of

Figure 4.4
You're Free, 1964–1978, color print ad, Honeywell (detail). Image courtesy of Honeywell.

Minnesota developed the Gopher protocol. You know what gophers do: they dig. Designed to search and retrieve documents from the Internet, Gopher functioned as an interface between the individual user and a potentially overwhelming and exponentially increasing archive of electronic resources. The authors of a 1994 textbook explain that Gopher searches exploded so swiftly that users soon needed new software to organize them, leading to the development of Veronica: "a database of gopher menu items from thousands of gopher servers around the world."[12] The authors offer the following search terms to illustrate Veronica's intelligence: "dog (which retrieves 'dog,' 'dogs,' 'doggedly,' etc.)"; and "(cats or felines) not dogs."[13] Dogs sniff the surfaces; gophers dig below them. In this didactic illustration, the dog represents the mundane surface view of an ordinary researcher, while the eponymous gopher indexes the hidden but crucial work of the programmer. Animal icons were becoming an almost compulsory rhetorical convention signifying both digital and spatial meanings. Soon enough Microsoft introduced its own doggedly digging puppy, Rover, to accompany online searches with its XP program for Windows. The barest animated silhouette of a young dog, Rover would dig excitedly for buried treasure on the side of the screen as the search engine would search for the requested data.

Gopher's success in creating databases from online resources and archives, together with earlier digital animal icons, encouraged other companies to adopt animal icons for their corporate software products. The founder of the Linux brand, also developed in the early 1990s, claimed that its famous mascot, Tux the penguin, "symbolizes the carefree attitude of the total movement."[14] Like the O'Reilly menagerie and the GNU gnu, Tux bore the burden of advocacy, part of a campaign to merge a corporate brand with the idea of animal spirits, or individual freedom. The logo is barely a penguin at all (see figure 4.1). If it were a realistic depiction of a penguin, even photoshopped or pre-photographic, it would not represent freedom in the same way. This penguin is free because it is autonomous; it is alone, it has no habitus, and it has no body. Like any animal, including humans, penguins require specific habitats, they have particular bodies and diets, they are social, they possess capabilities that make them different from other animals. Linux's cool, stripped-down penguin Tux exemplifies and extends the free thinking of the digital entrepreneur precisely through his graphic minimalization. Just as the iconic beaver image gradually lost its fur (as shown in chapter 3) and appears solo in the popular iconography, so the penguin loses its wings and feathers, the gnu its legs, the gopher its teeth, and all of them their species companions.[15] Combined with the virtual spatiality produced by the desktop interface, this quasi-spatial species taxonomy initiated a sense of the database as the foundation of limitless knowledge and knowledge management, and shaped the way the animal could and could not make sense.

This dematerialization of the pixelated animal image visibly parallels the streamlining over time of animation characters such as Mickey Mouse.[16] This reductive process in turn parallels the diminishing volume of the woman's body in twentieth-century fashion photography. Stuart Ewen writes that this process of reduction "speaks for a life that claims to live beyond the consequences of nature. It reflects the pure logic of abstract value—the economy of thin air—transported and implanted within the inner realm of a human subject. ... Regardless of the shape one's body takes, whatever flesh remains is *too much*; image must be freed from the liabilities of substance."[17] Of course the parallel between women's and animal bodies in this history of electronic reproduction is no accident. The white men who have dominated this history of technical innovation and design have mainly believed that escaping or transcending analog, conventional, corporate, domestic, and social routines—and finally, bodies altogether—is the path to liberation.[18]

The disappearance of the corporeal from animated and commercial images of animals has an obvious communicative function: it makes the icon identifiable at a glance. It also offers an allegory for the freedom conferred to the individual whose animal spirits can master and survive the introduction of new technological resources. This is a conditional freedom in that it can only be achieved through adaptation to digitization. The physical costs of this transmogrification are extirpated from the techno-evangelist iconography. As both mediating and myth-making devices, these virtual animals advocate for and reconcile the potentially contradictory values of liberation, mobility, surplus value, work output, computing speed and efficiency, carefree attitudes, animal spirits, creativity, rationality, pleasure, and the "natural" laws of technological evolution.[19] While the digital animal condenses these values into a single image, spelling them out allows their dissonances to surface. For instance, visual enjoyment is not always conducive to greater efficiency, for a desk worker can be easily distracted. The so-called "natural" laws of techno-evolution compromise the carefree attitude of creative workers, for they could so easily be made redundant. The prolific manufacture, dissemination, and rapid obsolescence of personal computing devices is not beneficial to the natural habitats of these animals, which are becoming endangered or extinct just as the device you now see before you or hold in your hand will soon be outdated. None of these processors—human, animal, or technical—has transcended these conditions enough to be truly free.

But virtual animals don't care. After all, how much does a gopher or a penguin think about the future in this post-Heideggerian *Umwelt*? The design of these images conveys the idea that animals do not plan or revise their plans, or think about or share their lives or the lives of others. Perhaps there was a semi-nihilistic delight amongst those who supplanted (raced and gendered) images of humans with the adventurous silhouettes of mammals, amphibians, and birds. However opaque their gaze, however minimal their design, however immediate their affective grab for the viewer's attention, these icons have no obligations. Their power is to make the idea of constant remediation seem natural, inviting, and essential. Alerting us constantly to platform innovations, they beckon us to mimic them as any good colonialist will do and to follow the instincts of our own most adventurous animal spirits.[20] At the same time, they symbolize and collaborate in the ever-increasing acquiescence to technical innovation of a particular kind, illustrating the argument Japanese cultural theorist Hiroki Azuma makes, citing Kojève, that postwar American culture has "animalized" its human subjects.[21] Captivated by the rhetoric, the tools, and the immersive spaces

Honeywell
OEM peripherals
help you devour
the competition.
Honeywell peripherals. Reliable, respected, proven peripherals that help you sell systems.
Honeywell disk pack drives, magnetic tape units, card equipment, and printers in a variety of speeds and capacities.
Honeywell logic design engineers can help with the peripheral interface. Our 1500-man field service force offers in-depth support. Our manufacturing base assures fast delivery.
Get in touch with Honeywell/OEM Sales/ 300 Concord Road/Billerica/Massachusetts 01821. Phone: (617) 729-7759
The Other Computer Company:
Honeywell

Figure 4.5
Honeywell OEM Peripherals Help You Devour the Competition, Honeywell computers advertisement, 1964–1978, color print ad, Honeywell. Images courtesy of Honeywell.

promoted by these techno-evangelists, users can be simultaneously alert and distracted, instrumental and susceptible to impulses. This "becoming-animal" occurs within a multiplying field of images wherein the viewer is interpellated as a distracted consumer whose desire to acquire and to connect arising from the encounter with the animal cools to a pragmatic acquiescence to the order of things.

The selection of species in early modern menageries spoke to the tastes, the delights, and the curiosity of their owners, but it also followed the geopolitical logic of Western colonization. The virtual menagerie extends the logic of colonial desire to possess things at a distance but extends it beyond the limit of geography, and so turns it inside out. As Malamud remarks, "Contemporary culture resituates animals by positing that they belong anywhere, which is to say, they belong nowhere."[22] A stroll past computing products and devices brings you into contact with gophers, snakes, penguins, and lions, placed randomly side by side. These avatars of faraway lands reappear here in the context of an increasingly image-saturated landscape that these carefully chosen specimens are inviting us to inhabit. Their agency in this process is not just a consequence of history; it is also the outcome of a number of specific social dynamics. These include a shift from the indexical illustration of products (a picture of a car to advertise a car, for instance, with a sexy female model standing next to it) to the indirect, quasi-fetishistic branding of companies and individuals. New techniques of image production, a quasi-religious investment in the utopian possibilities of new technology, and the reinvigoration of the nineteenth-century optimism about "harnessing" nature among computer scientists influenced by neo-Darwinism[23] all contribute to a growing popular preoccupation with depictions of nonhuman life. These cultural dynamics have been constellated into the imagery of the virtual menagerie through a force field of literal and yet oblique meaning. From film and animation to corporate icons and social media, from virtual pets to lolcats and YouTube videos, new styles of animal depiction and new social technologies of image production have emerged together in a rush of intertextual proliferation.

In his essay on the technological reproducibility of the work of art, mentioned in chapter 1, Walter Benjamin notes that many early photographs were portraits that were simultaneously a reification of immediacy and a conduit for nostalgia. They seemed to look backward, by trying to preserve a memory, a moment lost in time, and to look forward, by creating something that had not existed before, a material object, a visual surface: in other words, a photograph.[24] Perhaps it was something like this ambivalence that caused the first geek generation to fixate on depictions of animals. They felt some kinship with a moment of transition that the animal, evoking both the pleasure of looking and the pain of displacement, helps to express. The predominance of animal images conveys excitement about the vitality of invention and change, combined with anxiety about the instability of the past which is reconfigured as a state of nature. In the context of animal representation, the hint of better human-animal-machine relations is not (simply) nostalgic, but also a potentially significant ethical component in the chaos of becoming. These dynamics comprise a genealogy of the virtual menagerie, while the concept of virtuality enables us to consider how human and animal potentiality are awakened or stifled through the consolidation of this same emergent apparatus.

The Conditions of the Event

This book begins with Debray's concept of mediation as "the dynamic combination of intermediary procedures and bodies that interpose themselves between a producing of signs and a producing of events."[25] Deleuze explains the trope of the event as a way of asking what concepts are being transformed into what subjects. "Events are produced in a chaos," he writes, "in a chaotic multiplicity, but only under the condition that a sort of screen intervenes. Chaos does not exist; it is an abstraction because it is inseparable from a screen that makes something—something rather than nothing—emerge from it."[26] Deleuze does not mean a "screen" literally, in terms of the monitors on which virtual menageries often appear, but rather that something—or a multiplicity of things in interaction with one another—mediates the object or the event: the animal, or its icon, and its appearance. Debray echoes this idea when he describes the "combination of intermediary procedures and bodies that interpose themselves" between us and what he describes as "the first appearance of nodes and networks of sociability, interfaces bearing new rituals and exercises, proving worthy as means of producing opinion."[27]

The concept of the event helps to make sense of the reorganization of life and image that has arisen with the material and social potentialities of the digitally ordered society. Only some of these "virtual" potentialities will be actualized, and this process will alter in some ways how people understand the world. Just as animal lives are changed by altered relationships between habitat and geopolitics, so animal images are changed by new relations between the force of images and the relational functions (social, economic, spatial, biopolitical) of information processing. To what possible futures does the virtual menagerie now point?

An ecological politics suggests that the virtual menagerie augurs and delights in the decentering of humans within the scheme of things, however that might occur. But holding out an ecological perspective does not describe a clear evolutionary path; as every reader of Darwin knows, evolution is not necessarily a progressive process. Exploring new ideas about a virtual future, two powerful but singularly different cyber-advocacy manifestos were published in 1985. This was the year Donna Haraway's "Cyborg Manifesto" first appeared, while Richard Stallmen, founder of the Free Software Foundation, published the "GNU Manifesto." The Free Software Foundation advocated open software development because of its author's growing disaffection with the capitalist control exercised over software by private enterprises like O'Reilly.[28] Haraway's "Cyborg Manifesto" advocates for technologically hybrid bodies because of its author's disenchantment with essentialist second wave feminism. These two 1985 texts share a strong declarative impulse for liberating the human-technology matrix from restrictive discursive and economic structures.[29] Both manifestos define the release of this potential force as a revolt against the reader's customary loyalties and actions. Both authors advocate for more reflexive attention to new technologies and particularly their revolutionary possibilities for creating more democratic and more connective forms of enlightenment. Both associate personal freedom with collectivized identities and enhanced technological capacities. Stallmen expresses a somewhat masculinist libertarianism dedicated to the freeing of information as a resource, a principle he describes as a drive compelled by nature. Haraway, on the other hand, calls into question the very concept of an originary all-determinant nature. It is not nature that compels humans and other forms of life to evolve or act the way they do, Haraway argues; rather, we (and our genders) are symbiotic nature-culture hybrids formed through social and environmental interaction.

These manifestos emerged from a rebellious counterculture that was percolating in the midst of an increasingly cybernetic scientific-technical *dispositif*, to borrow Foucault's term. The interest in generating organically modeled cybernetic systems was not limited to the military but was expanding into diverse scientific and commercial contexts.[30] Building on their growing awareness of potential associations between biological and technological information structures and their evolutionary trajectories, groups of scientists set out to design postbiological self-organizing technical systems that would have the capacity to administer the new processing needs of the information age. A number of conferences and publications from the end of World War II to the early 1960s were dedicated to learning how to solve complex technical problems by modeling information architectures on natural systems and complex living organisms. These technical problems related internally generated biological structures to the mounting needs of information management and political security. In describing this endeavor, Evelyn Fox Keller refers to the Bionics Symposia as illustrative of the new interest in biology "as a source of principles applicable to engineering":[31]

> Like the wartime architects of "command, control, and communication" systems, a chronic slippage is evident in these discussions between control and self-control. What distinguished them was, paradoxically, their greater emphasis on autonomy, and at the same time, their explicit acknowledgment of the meaninglessness of autonomy. … First-order cybernetics, born of concrete military needs, gave rise to

command-control systems; second-order cybernetics, bred from the new alliances of the Cold War, fostered a new preoccupation with self-organizing systems. For both, systems of control (with all the ambiguities of the term in place) were the primary preoccupation.[32]

Virtual menageries can be seen to index the potentialities unleashed by these scientific and technological changes. A semiotic and informational swarm of autonomous animals and systems emerged from and helped (mediologically) to actualize a multiplicity of developments. The currents of change included an escalation of scientific ambition tied to the Cold War, evangelical fervor for information flowing free from matter, and the captivating idea that liberation could provide a detour around corporate and government control through the spaces of personal computing. The event that brought these currents to actualization in the form of animal imagery was also shaped by the emergence of a potentially limitless global market for mobile technologies. This commerce precipitated the design, marketing, and obsolescence of ever-smaller digital devices, the appearance of attractive new brands and logos, the emergence of postbiological hybrids and animal avatars, the acquisition of instruments for observing wild animals in their natural habitats, the destruction of these same habitats, the dissemination of surreptitious surveillance of factory farms, and the posting of pet photographs on cell phones across the planet. These are tangible actualizations of a panoply of virtual possibilities signaled, enabled, and constrained by the virtual cages of the virtual menagerie. In an implicit gesture toward risk, the virtual menagerie morphs from a symbol to a fetish of biopolitical transformation, rousing small intensities of desire by mimicking what it damages or hides, and what it promises to repair.

What is produced by animal-human digital information processing is not just textual. The information extracted or "rendered"[33] from animal bodies can take many forms. Consider Dolly the sheep, born in 1996, the first mammal to be cloned from adult cells. Dolly is simultaneously a triumph of information, a subject, a specimen, and a fragment of the animal-machine-media event I am describing, which did not positively transform the lives of sheep. During the brief time that Dolly was conceived and lived, Stewart Brand, cited earlier as the first proponent of free information, published a further edition of the *Whole Earth Catalog*; the CD-ROM, ThinkPad, Zip drive, and IBM clones all reached the consumer market; the Pentagon initiated its cybernetic "revolution in military affairs" and began to invest heavily in software, wetware, and telecommunications; Disney acquired Pixar; Microsoft released Windows 95,[34] with Rover added to its XP system to help users dig for data; Linux's penguin became a prominent symbol

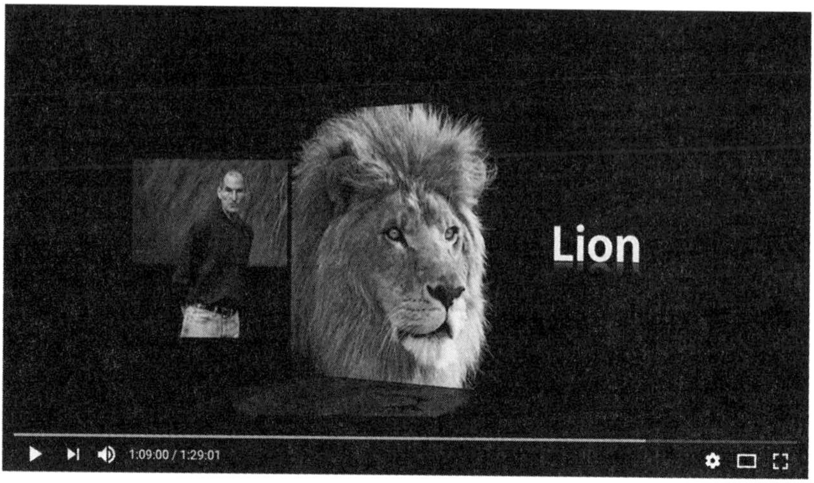

Figure 4.6
Steve Jobs releases Mac OS lion (projection), 2010, screenshot.

for data management; and the computer-animated film *Babe*[35] brought the animal's point of view into the purview of mainstream cinema. This constellation of developments emerged in the 1990s when the virtual menagerie became a prominent mediator of virtual space and information and a leading content provider for personal computing, whose database might otherwise be perceived as a frightening and chaotic aggregation of bits.

The clever monkey or panda teaches us how to speak on the telephone; the majestic lion leads us into the kingdom of Apple. That these animals are fetishes is made clear by Jodi Dean in her critique of "communicative capitalism."[36] What matters in this scenario, she argues, is that communication occurs in a way that is productive for the accumulation of capital. In that sense it is communication itself that is celebrated, rather than what is being communicated. Since the animal lacks an environment, or an *Umwelt*, as von Uexküll explained, it has nothing meaningful to communicate.[37] Thus virtual animals cannot advocate on their own behalf. They bear witness to the brief lifespans of gadgets that are brought to life in their stead. Acknowledging that the "information society" fetishizes communication helps us to confront the logic of disappearance that reshapes not only the physical environments of real and virtual animals but also, once again and continuously, the kind of agency through which these subjects can enact their being. These animals are, indeed, vanishing mediators.

The idea of communication conveyed in these affect enhancers, exemplified by the Telus ad campaign ("New Means to Communicate"—but communicate what?), is as much a fetish in relation to the body politic as the image or fur of the animal is a fetish in relation to the animal's body. A fetish is a deep attachment to a piece or token of something larger that makes it possible to experience that whole, which due to absence, wound, or trauma cannot be faced. A fetish only works to the extent that the worshiper believes that having it permits (and contains) the same level of intensity that would be provided by access to the whole. The prospect of a realm of limitless communication similarly produces "a counter-need, to use technology as a protective shield against the 'colder order' that it creates."[38] These virtual menageries protect against the deluge of information of which they form a smaller part. They work not despite but because of the fact that they have nothing to say.

Noncommunication

Lorraine Daston suggests that animals become subjects through prolonged human observation or through "the narrative form of the anecdote or story."[39] That is to say, we can only access the subjectivity of animals through human practices. The menageries of the information economy resist prolonged observation and do not participate in narrative forms. If a subject is defined as such through close involvement within a space or within the structure of a narrative, then these didactic animal figures do not seem to want to be subjects any more than they want users to be subjects. Modern literary and film theories emphasize narration and the construction of the subject, Lev Manovich argues in *The Language of New Media*, while the information age privileges information, so that "narration and description have changed roles."[40] Thus, "many new media objects do not tell stories; they do not have a beginning or end; in fact, they do not have any development, thematically, formally, or otherwise that would organize their elements into a sequence. Instead, they are collections of individual items, with every item possessing the same significance as any other."[41]

Whether or not this is the case with all new media "objects," this argument does offer some insight into the aesthetic or structural contexts in which these animals appear. There is a kinship in this respect between the promotional characters found in the virtual menageries created for digital branding and the animal characters Azuma describes in *Otaku: Japan's Database Animals*. For Azuma, the Otaku's famously compulsive pleasure of looking at graphic animal figures featured in anime, manga, gaming, computer graphics, and other story modes is created not by narrative but by modes of classification. Their pleasure derives from the spectacle of multiple objects (characters) undergoing only slight variations in time. Azuma describes this as a "dual structure of settings and small narratives represent[ing] the double-layer structure of information and appearance."[42] This "double layer" evokes the spatial relationship between the dog and the gopher described earlier, but this is not what he has in mind. These images comprise a database or collection of entities in multiple small variations. Azuma critiques this "data-ization" of Otaku as a retreat from meaning, which he describes as a form of animalization. While Deleuze acknowledges that "images can be rendered non-narrative, even non-representational,"[43] his discussion of cinema seeks to overcome the tension between narrative and sensation. Thus, a viewer can be deeply affected by her encounter with an entity or image even if it does not act or continue to act within a temporally based narrative. Deleuze writes: "At one and the same time I become in the sensation and something happens through the sensation, one through the other, one in the other."[44] This emphasis on sensation, like the trope of "becoming-animal," is intended to narrow the gap between human affect and that of other species. For Deleuze and Guattari, "becoming-animal" moves the human subject toward a different subjectivity or affect through modes of experience that are not predicated on cognition. Azuma is interested in the grammar and affect of intensive interaction with digital animals, while Deleuze and Guattari are more concerned with interrogating human ontology as a whole. Thus, Azuma and Deleuze assign completely different values to "becoming-animal," figuring the movement from human to animal in respectively negative and positive terms.

What "happens" through the embodied sensation these theorists describe depends not only on whether images or experiences are narrative or representational, however, but also on what kinds of agency they permit for animals. If pictures want something, as W. J. T. Mitchell suggests,[45] the virtual animals inviting viewers into the digital mediascape seem to want nothing other than our attention. They are studiously indifferent to questions of meaning. Azuma and Deleuze agree on this point but not on its implications. Azuma argues that the animals have become so much like a database that they have lost the drive to exceed their status as inanimate objects. That is to say, following Dean's critique of the fetish, they are animals acquired without animal spirits; they just want (us) to connect. Here the colonial menagerie's embodiment of the idea of a distant, exotic, and unexplored globe ready to be transformed has given way to an ever-present, highly financialized globe in which everything and everyone are connected. The idea of further exploration has a different meaning in this context. This digital heterotopia promises to release human subjects from one set of obligations—the Enlightenment, say, or spouse and home, or nation building, or the biosphere, or normative regulation, or the future—into a new, intensely affective biopolitical order.

In *Knowing Capitalism*, Nigel Thrift asks, "Is software's address now somewhere between the artificial and a new kind of natural, the dead and a new kind of living, or the material and a new kind of material semiotics?"[46] In this scenario, software occupies the mediating role between the biological and the social. Between the artificial and a new kind of natural—that could describe an animation or a clone. Between the dead and a new kind of living—that could describe animal life in a lab or a zoo. Between the material and a new kind of material semiotics—that could be the digital animal abstracted from the very idea of an environment, so that its life is no more tangible than a green screen or a dream. These digital creatures populate and proselytize for hybrid in-between spaces. They are loved to death, but they don't have much investment in the relationship.

And what is users' investment in them? Critics define the contemporary scopic regime as one in which viewers scan images but do not read them.[47] These digital animals rely on the fulfillment of this logic, and yet they challenge it at the same time, for however virtual they might be, and however oblique their disposition, they offer a glimpse of an enmeshed and animated life. They arrest the gaze, if only for a moment, and they promise to look back. Just try to imagine a world without me, they seem to say. Perhaps that is why we "share" them. "Despite a general awareness of the contrivances of the medium," Jonathan Burt writes in *Animals in Film*, "audiences often respond differently to animals or animal-related practices than they do to other forms of imagery."[48] It is no accident then that (as described in chapter 1) the first moving images and the first postings on YouTube all featured images of animals.[49]

While the Internet does not commonly situate animals in a narrative structure the way film does, or provide a personal and up-close encounter with exotic animals as menageries and zoos have done, the flourishing of animal presences in the global mediascape nonetheless performs important functions.[50] Such images promote the diversity of life, while through their intimate attachment to new technical commodities they indicate (or counterindicate) what this living is about. They might also remind us that this is a partial story, that innocent images collude in concealment, that industrial violence has hold of the lives of animals just as it does of us. To mark their difference from these themes, these animals keep their distance, not just from their zoological features and nominal habitats but also from the emotions that leak out when their stories are told.

In *The Laws of Cool*, Liu defines "cool" as "information designed to resist information" or "the incest of information."[51] What is the information these images resist? A style emptied of agency is not unlike a picture of an animal emptied of animality. Each is formed around what Carol Adams calls the "absent referent" through which animals are made "absent *as* animals."[52] Notwithstanding the romance that clings to the idea of working outside the knowledge economy, Liu argues, the reality is different: creative workers in the knowledge economy are not supposed to be too creative, autonomous workers are not supposed to be too autonomous. Caught in this contradictory set of expectations, designers develop an ironic aesthetic, an aesthetic of cool. Cool is ironic, inarticulate, self-centered, cruel, and private. By generating a cool aesthetic, digital imaging culture contributes to a crisis of attachment as well as a dissolution of narrative. Animal images can evoke affect in general without promoting attachment to any animal in particular. For this reason, the emptying out of meaning perceptible in these animal symbols can be linked to an implied loss of interpretive capacities assigned to humans.

It is not uncommon to attribute the diminishment of interpretive depth to new communication technologies, as Walter Benjamin does in his diagnosis of the end of storytelling.[53] In the research Liu cites, however, cool appears to be a logical emotional style for consumer societies, which thrive on the impulsiveness or "animal spirits" of its members and the rapid obsolescence of its objects. Consumer culture requires consumers to react, desire, withdraw their desire, and reinvest it by becoming attracted to new things as quickly as they take hold. Despite the appearance of being innovative, rebellious, and independent, the cool attitude propelling these images, Liu suggests, bolsters "an atomized and novelty-oriented construction of the self that is a prime target for consumer products that quickly become obsolete and call for regular replacement."[54] If the supremacy of cool risks making consumers grow indifferent to this routine and to the plethora of devices on offer, this risk is balanced by the pragmatism that is entrained into their users. They know the promises aren't real and the devices aren't essential just as children know the robot monkeys aren't real, according to Sherry Turkle, and yet they pragmatically act "as if" they are. It is not hard to see the biopolitical investment in this aspect of the event.[55]

If the virtual animal hovers between subject and machine, so do the people entangled with it. The feelings generated by looking at these iconic virtual menageries are pleasurable, reserved, childlike, cynical, hopeful, pragmatic, repressive, distracted. These animals invite their viewers to develop the capacity to feel for what they see without any disruption of assigned duties—as Carol Adams puts it, the incentive to feel, but not too much. If the animal image stands in for this injunction, all the more is this true for the idea of connection for which it advocates. The pleasurable sense of connection gained by sharing in the awesome mesh of Internet cats or splashing elephants can be fetishized as an engagement with animals, just as an animal body or body part is said to be fetishized in "primitive" cultures or as communication comes to function as a fetish of democracy in communicative capitalism. The tension between animality and information that gives rise to the virtual menagerie, like the tension between freedom and commodification, can inhibit the ecological transformation that springs from a shared concern for the well-being of animals, in much the same way (and for some of the same reasons) that the ideal of network democracy can colonize or consume—take the place of, in the name of—other political actualizations of the democratic ideal.[56]

The subject of animality might not have any bearing on the matter. But then again, it might. Liu's idea that an image can resist what it evokes, and that it can evoke what it resists, seems to have a direct bearing on the question of digital animality. If these images are resisting the direction in which they point, what is it exactly that they resist? Is it perhaps the exploitative materiality of their being, and of ours? Virtual menageries remind us of how closely we are intertwined with technologies and animals, and how much we are in their power; they also permit viewers to experience and extend the affect of ironic cool and thus to maintain a distance from the implications of this understanding.

Randy Malamud recommends that we think about "where people will be when the dust has cleared, and we would be wise, in this assessment, to look carefully at animals; to look at people and animals; to look at people *as* animals."[57] Or to look at people as hybrid lives, as human bodies variously attached to animals, technologies, places, practices, and chemicals of all sorts.

Advocating what he calls "a truly ecological reading practice," Timothy Morton writes that "ecocriticism has overlooked the way in which all art—not just explicitly ecological art—hardwires the environment into its *form*. Ecological art, and the ecological-ness of all art, isn't just *about* something (trees, mountains, animals, pollution, and so forth). Ecological art *is* something, or maybe it *does* something."[58] That is to say, art that opposes the fetishism of the animal or the cooling of the interaction does not necessarily proffer more or better images of animals while confining them to their reduced status as visual objects, in or out of collections, summoned golem-like to life by resource-gobbling computers that light up on command in various contexts of display. Nor does it simply transfer the digital recording device from the human hand to the body of the animal, as though this technological extension of the human gaze automatically decenters the human eye—although this experiment has some interesting trajectories beyond the scope of this discussion. Nor does it reject all animal images circulated in social media because they do not meet the requirements or command the values or abandon the machines or fill the apparatuses of the creative arts. Rather, artists need to challenge their viewers to resituate and rebuild human-animal-machine relations, while recognizing and respecting the embedded agency of each entity and the potential transformations of their assemblage. To recognize the interconnectedness of the world is to retrieve the strangeness of the animal, the screen, the mediation, ourselves.

5 Fur and Feathers: Ecologies of Telecommunication

At the end of a powerful investigative series on global warming, first published in the *New Yorker* and later as the book *The Sixth Extinction*, Elizabeth Kolbert throws up her hands trying to explain the cause of this looming disaster. She writes, "It may seem impossible to imagine that a technological society could choose, in essence, to destroy itself, but that is what we are now in the process of doing."[1] It's not clear whether it is the technological orientation of the society that makes self-destruction hard to believe, since technology appears at least to itself to be rational and useful; or the idea that an evolved culture could so dramatically lose the qualities of reflection and judgment thought to be unique to the human species; or the idea that a society could reach consensus on anything, even self-destruction. Or perhaps it is the actual process of self-destruction that is hard to imagine, even when you see the planet in flames and wonder how what caused it can still be allowed to happen.

The premise of a civilization at war with itself is not new. Thinkers engaged with the social and philosophical critique of capitalist modernity and many authors of contemporary science fiction place science and technology at the center of their concern. Critics of modernity perceive the unchecked power of science and technology to be responsible for the instrumental transformation of natural and social worlds and the distortion of both nature and human potentiality.[2] The desire to unmask the dangers of Faustian science has combusted most visibly in times of war, when unlimited resources are shown to be dedicated to researching, financing, and developing updated weaponry that will locate and annihilate the less technologically enhanced enemy. Afterward, these machinic resources are frequently appropriated for public and commercial use. This critical charge has been leveled most often at computing technologies.

The quandaries of human-induced climate change that Kolbert confronts evoke issues that extend beyond these particular events, and beyond the mandates of science and technology as well. Climate change implicates the wants and assumptions of every privileged person living in the technologically innovative, environmentally unsustainable society of the modern world. In the face of this aporia, the technology one most desires presents as both the enemy of the natural world and the necessary condition of its survival.

Whether through the entrenchment of everyday habits or the creation of new cultural myths, our ordinary tendency is to find tidbits of reconciliation between these opposing prospects. That is how I interpret the images of animals used from the late 1990s to the late 2000s to market mobile phones in many, but not all, parts of the world. No one can fail to notice the increasing visibility of these animals or how intimately they are made to pertain to the hardwares and softwares of human connection. As Lisa Nakamura observes, "In this post-Internet culture of simulation in which we live, it is increasingly necessary for stable, iconic images of Nature and the Other to be evoked in the world of technology advertising."[3] The images she describes beckon the viewer to travel to beautiful and exotic places where nature thrives and the other resides. The exotic beauty of this colonial imagery clearly associates the other with a closer affinity with nature and suggests that even virtual travel to those exotic shores can help restore the viewer's broken harmony with the world. The images created to promote mobile digital devices also promise a technological reconciliation between near and distant, urban and exotic, but the imaginary horizon is considerably reduced in their visual vocabulary in comparison to the travel ads analyzed by Nakamura. While the animals shown in the cell phone ad campaigns are often exotic species, you will not see the scenic and inviting habitus-appropriate beaches, forests, or landscapes surrounding them. This newer iconography is not celebrating your mobility but the mobility of the phone. The animals portrayed in these series bear no relationship to any physical site, exotic or otherwise; their habitat is the interface.

Starting in the 1990s, images of animals have been attached to cell phones and to ads, charms, stickers, and cases for cell phones in many parts of the world, especially Asia. Hello Kitty probably launched this trend; in Japan it became popular in the mid 90s to buy little Hello Kitty charms to hang from mobile phones. Hello Kitty does spring from a unique cultural history: "In countries such as Japan, cell phone charms are not just a mere decoration. They are symbols of personal expression and the times, and some, such as the Omamori and knot charms, are examples of ancient culture being brought into our modern world for the same purposes they've served for many centuries."[4] Originally these small fabric and knot charms served as religious amulets with specifically targeted protective properties. Attaching amulets to a phone reinforces the sense of the phone as an extension of the owner's body. While cell phones were initially marketed as protective devices favored by parents, they apparently did not offer as much protection as a young person might need out and about in her newly mobile, increasingly precarious universe. The popular Hello Kitty phone attachments became a global commercial phenomenon after the 1997 financial crisis.[5]

The trend of associating cute animals with mobile phones has encouraged their adoption (we use the same term, "adoption," to describe the acquisition of either a pet or a phone) among young people. The birth of Twitter with a bird logo and tweet vocabulary signaled once again that the association between animals and digital communication was more than a temporary trend. Marketing gurus seemed satisfied that the fusion of animals and digital devices at the promotional stage would increase the likelihood that they would be adopted. What was of not mentioned was that these animals and the digital devices that temporarily embodied them would meet up in a different way at the end of the cell phone's life cycle. Millions of cell phones are tossed every year. E-waste poisons the ground, people, and habitats in the regions from which many of the exotic animals used to advertise these phones actually originate, and thus, despite the promotional vocabulary of technological liberation, reinforces the colonial ordering of world regions and economies. The cell phone animated by an animal icon or amulet emits a protective vibration to ameliorate the risk of being on the move, but by simulating the desire for multiple versions it intensifies the dangers that follow in the wake of this small, adoptable, mobile device.

These dispersed zoological profiles animated a comprehensive campaign to "naturalize" the impulse to connect to others through digital technology. Just as in the industrial age factory technology simultaneously empowered and alienated its human subjects by redefining the concept and practice of work and enforcing a new work discipline, so these telecommunication technologies advance and diminish the human capacity to connect by redefining the concept and practice of communication. The way these fresh-faced animal entities arrived in tandem with new technologies partially reiterated the history of animal migration from which they arose. These animal images were designed to incite and legitimate radical changes in the ways people communicated with one another, while metaphorizing the new mode of communication as like that you might have with a pet:

briefer, more instrumental, more instinctive, more akin in fact to communication in the animal world itself. In short, "animal spirits" were no longer dangerous, they were fun! The conjunction of mobile phone and (exotic or other) cute animals served to manage their users' possibly anxious perceptions of technological and environmental risk.[6] My analysis of this mobilization proceeds by disassembling its parts and examining how they have been strategically recombined.

The now inescapable association between animal species and digital technologies reveals a historic shift that is percolating behind the scenes. The animals providing the visible face of technological connectivity in this era of anxiety are innocent, savvy, and cheerful, like animals in children's books. They carry no sign of the savagery associated with jungles or urban streets. There are never more than two or three little animals clustered in a frame, and they have as little as possible of fur or feathers. The design encapsulates the idea that it is comforting and fun to have some insignia of animal life nearby, but there is no meaningful comprehension to be drawn from it. What is important is not their life or their life worlds but only the use values they encapsulate: portability and immediacy, what we might call the remainder of animal spirits, and staying in touch. This is the grammar of animal representation in the age of risk. Thinking about these media events in relation to risk management enriches our understanding of the role of cultural negotiation in the capitalist Anthropocene. There is no boundary, only a series of layers between the appearance of an animal of whatever species and the more or less deliberate destruction of its meaning (at least as known to itself) in the act of appropriating it. This particular syntax recurs throughout this analysis of animals, humans, and digital communication devices in contemporary culture.

Proliferation

There is no more familiar and eclectic a universe of symbols than the graphic representation of animals. They are an established part of the pedagogical mainstream of childhood in many cultures. To follow their trail into advertising is to enter a different vortex, one that is, according to Andrew Wernick, "evolving towards a decorative eclecticism whose signifying gestures refer us only to the universe of symbols from which they are drawn."[7] These animal depictions do refer back to a trail of symbolic gestures following them. Where these trails are most clearly marked, they point toward children's literature and toys, to Disney and Mickey Mouse, and then to

TELUS
the future is friendly

Figure 5.1
Telus Ad Campaign—Lion, 2013. Image courtesy of Telus Corporation.

National Geographic photography and exotic tourist motifs, all of which have left visual traces in contemporary commercial aesthetics. The memories triggered by these associations are comfortable ones. The images refer to phantasms rather than to living animals. They remind you of nature but encourage a childlike narcissism by seductively transforming that nature into a more accessible technoculture that you can use without the challenge of encountering a real animal looking back at you.

These images promise affect, but they don't deliver on it. They gesture at the possibility of a shock in the encounter between alterity and innocence, but their dominant achievement is to offer a homeopathic intervention into the state of embodiment known as attachment. It is "as if" the user will become attached to the animal, but (the images tell you this as though it's an open secret) that is not really the point of the exercise. In her research on children who play with virtual and robot pets, Sherry Turkle found that the children know very well that they are not real animals (just as pet owners, to anticipate a later chapter, know that pets are not their children). But their capacity to interact with the voices and animation-like movements of these robotic animals cultivate an "as-if" response that teaches the children to be pragmatic. They can go along with this.[8] The images of animals attached to cell phones echo this pragmatic agenda. They present a continuing as-if experience to viewers, not only in their rhetoric of pseudo-animality but also in terms of the truncated communication that these images embody.

I refer the reader to Dean's discussion of the fetish of communication in capitalist media culture.[9] In this analysis, the technologies and uses of communication come to stand in for and even to supplant larger questions of democracy or justice. In this case, the fetishization extends to animality. Animals stand in for a state of nature; the technologies for which they advocate stand in for communication; communication stands in for democracy or saving the world. These representations of technological devices rely on pictures of animals that are so de-animalized that there is no significance to what they might mean or have to say. These pictures of animals promise a sense of attachment and near-security that can evoke the idea of a "natural" connection between animals and humans but that in fact relies entirely on the digital device. This sense of a natural connection is waiting to be fulfilled the way a love-struck teenager waits for a phone call. This promise has been extremely effective in the campaign to mobilize consumers in the development of the global telecommunications network.

Consider the excitement with which mobile digital technologies have been embraced by consumers, journalists, entrepreneurs, consultants, academics, artists, and funding agencies. Announcing Apple's iPhone as recipient of the *Time* magazine 2007 Invention of the Year award, for instance, *Time*'s Lev Grossman wrote: "One of the big trends of 2007 was the idea that computing doesn't belong just in cyberspace, it needs to happen here, in the real world, where actual stuff happens. This is just the beginning."[10] Since computing and the invention of cell phones actually began "here, in the real world," Grossman's statement calls for translation. The "trend" he is referring to is not that cyberspace isn't real; it is the idea that your interaction with that already familiar virtual space needs to happen *here*, in your hands, as you walk down the street or eat a meal or occupy yourself in a classroom. A cell phone can travel with you, like a pet or perhaps the menagerie of a circus. The needs of this new reality are conveyed rhetorically through the visual fusion between mobile technologies and animals. This fusion had already occurred when images of animals were used to advertise the earliest platforms and potentialities of cyberspace (see chapter 4) with their capacity to fetch data from anywhere. Here the cellphone-pet represents the potential freedom we associate with our own physical mobility, so that our bodies can travel with our data and apps to any part of the city or planet. Like the solitary cars seen cruising the countryside in auto advertisements that allow drivers to experience "real" nature, this text invites technologically alienated/equipped humans to rediscover the pleasures of living in the "real" world. Humans can reclaim their embodied selves by projecting themselves onto these digital pets/images, where they can confirm Akira Lippit's idea that "the combination of the animal subject and the photographic image alters in some essential fashion the dialectical flow of subjectivity ... one that allows for an economy of the gaze, identification, and becoming."[11] Of course the needs these animal-branded iPhones promise to fulfill are far more pragmatic. They concern how much information you can put in your pocket, how quickly you can access anything or anyone, and how this little data-guide companion can lead you through the jungle you know is out there.

These digital animals appear to be happy with their prospective emigration to your pocket or purse. They are eager to be reconciled with the humans who might pick them up and carry them into the new world. The animal's visual pliability gestures toward "a more general telematic trend towards wearable, handheld and pocket communications and entertainment media ... in which individuals are being microtargeted."[12] As a contemporary version of witches' familiars, they promise that something compelling is now emerging, something magical, a digital sprite-medium you can pick up and hold in your hand. This narrative emphasizes the discovery and satisfaction of individual desires and as a form of liberal pedagogy promises the fulfillment of these desires through the enjoyment of rapidly changing technological updates. Perhaps the online world has been guilty of distracting users from their important goals, but mobile digital technologies can help them once again occupy the center of the universe. It doesn't matter that you are now always findable inside this digital matrix, wherever you go, and that the freedom promised might be illusory. The device will help you find your way to where you want to go. By communicating this promise, telephone companies "exploit a social need for connectedness in times of social fragmentation" while manufacturing expensive consumer needs, inferior services, toxic byproducts, and increased corporate "freedom" from public policy.[13]

While the animal images used in these ads convey such ideas effortlessly, the language with which mobile devices are celebrated also promotes the idea of greater affinity between animal and machine. It is no accident that in Grossman's hymn to the iPhone, it is the device that communicates and converges, not the person. Since everyone is now connected through their devices, there is no outside to that virtual space, no fear of getting lost or left behind in this new beginning. "Just the beginning" happens again and again, as though there is no residue or waste in what is left behind, no need to remember what has been left behind. The world of computing must be "progressively experienced." By advocating for a progress that has no human or social content, these commentaries demonstrate the victory of neoliberal thought in the contemporary academy.[14] This discourse renders communication a function of the speaker's tools. The cell phone constitutes an intimate bond between the user and her medium in which a dialogic other is optional. It could be a monkey or a fish. In some important respects, it is the same old technoculture.

We do not need to know where this "new mode of thinking" is taking us; we just need to believe that it is fundamentally progressive, which means, implicitly, without evidence, that adoption of these newer tools will make people smarter and more competitive with their peers and thus equalize an otherwise unjust world. But the more people throw away their old technologies, the more unjust the world becomes. The claim that digital media offer a successful reconciliation between individual and planet disguises a global trajectory of unprecedented destruction in which researchers' role as progressive knowledge workers is far from certain. If defining ideal communication as reciprocal understanding is perceived as obsolete, advocates of these new technologies nonetheless emphasize the capacities of enhanced technical interconnection as though they can advance the cause of individual mobility and freedom without the agency of humans who might be in search of freedom. This discourse renders communication a function of the speaker's tools, a fetishization of technology that has little to do with freedom as we have come to understand it.

There are things "which professionals are almost trained to ignore," writes Arnold Pacey.[15] These "things" include "the continued onslaught of computer trash and the ongoing manufacture of obsolescence by the hardware industry," which, as Jonathan Sterne observes, "inadvertently support the global trade in toxic materials."[16] According to Elizabeth Grossman,

> Virtually none of the books chronicling the rise of high technology or high tech's social and cultural influences consider the industry's impacts on human health or the environment. ... An enormous gap remains between what professionals and general high-tech consumers know about the hazards posed by e-waste and the environmental impacts of high-tech manufacturing, let alone the importance of solving these problems. ... It seems to me that without this understanding we will continue to behave as if high-tech products exist in some kind of cyberuniverse, one that has little to do with the air we actually breathe, the water we drink, the food we eat, or our children's health.[17]

Just as the animals appear in these images with no space but the interface, the miniaturization of these devices permits users to imagine their own technological practices as occurring without physical context or limits. The animal as promotional avatar of the device suggests that the smaller the device gets, the more the digital media can offer a sustainable reconciliation

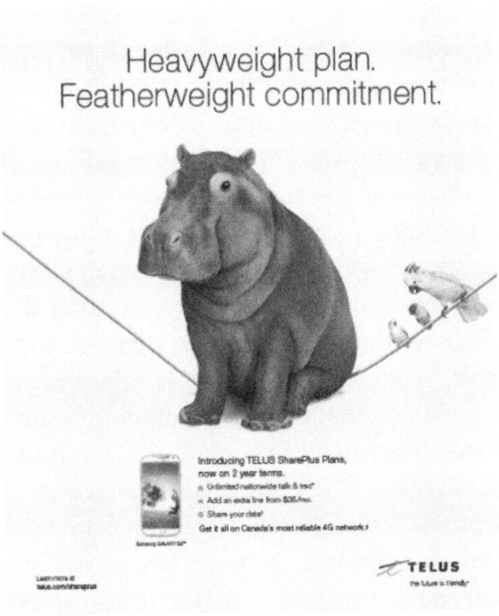
Heavyweight plan.
Featherweight commitment.
Introducing TELUS SharePlus Plans,
now on 2 year terms.
Share your data
TELUS

Figure 5.2
Telus Ad Campaign—Hippo and Birds, 2013. Image courtesy of Telus Corporation.

between the individual user and the planet. The small size and unconfined mobility of the animal image points to the same properties in the devices. As Sabine Lebel has shown, however,

> The ecological footprint of electronics becomes larger as devices get smaller. This is counterintuitive as the miniaturization of electronics seems to imply that fewer resources are needed. Although fewer materials end up in the final product, more waste products are created in the production of smaller devices and machines. These misunderstandings about the amount of resources needed to produce hi-tech devices, the by-products created in production, and the e-waste generated from these devices are endlessly repeated across scientific, mainstream, and academic literatures.[18]

In other words, these signifying animals disguise a global trajectory of unprecedented environmental destruction in which our own role as progressive knowledge workers is more elusive. As Maxwell and Miller argue, "Ecological ethics barely figures into the way media and communication researchers think about media technology. … Media studies would be profoundly disrupted were it to install an ecocentric ethics into its thinking on media technology."[19]

Instead, people celebrate the GPS capacities of their cell phones while bemoaning smart bombs, or buy the latest devices and apps for their children, or buy bottled water for seminars in which they discuss the politics of the environment. Through everyday practice, knowledge about water supplies is separated from the question of egregious toxic waste produced by the manufacture of plastic bottles and released into the water, and this issue is wrenched apart from the violent privatization of the world's water supply. Nestle famously engages in an unprecedented system of reverse recycling. The company extracts millions of tons of clean water (for which governments charge the corporation scandalously little), bottles it in plastic whose production and waste are toxic, and sells it without assuming any responsibility for the toxic waste produced in the water systems or their effects. What the bottle "represents," cold, natural springs, is substantially and strategically different from what the bottle "does": defy and undermine the right to access clean water, overwhelm the oceans, kill the birds, fish and other creatures of the sea. These two indispensable educational tools, the mobile phone and the plastic bottle, can be understood and used pedagogically as objects that separate consumers from the wisdom of spatially and ethically embodied citizenship. This fragmentation of knowledge and emotion perpetuates a largely concealed global war on animals, natural resources, land, and peoples. The irony is particularly acute given that e-waste is mainly sent to underdeveloped parts of the world in Africa and Asia from which the animals advertising them were first captured for display in colonial menageries.

In rhetorical terms, the endless campaign for the technical capacities of the iPhone echoes the utopian intent of socialist realism: to "make the viewer feel 'alive'—alive and sensually responsive. Such goals as to 'stir up,' to 'awaken,' to 'touch on the raw' take precedence over purely ideological indoctrination."[20] With this evocation of animal spirits, air and water were put to work in the Bolshevik imaginary, which in response embraced, in a stunningly self-defeating rapprochement with capitalism, a love affair with the American kitchen. Like the posters of socialist realism, the animals used in these promotional images gesture toward the promises of material improvement while doing everything possible to silence and contain the actual real, the environmental impact of climate change and particularly of electronic waste, which is despoiling sizable parts of the globe where these same animals have roamed.

In his study of the culture of risk, Joost van Loon uses the term "fable" to describe a narrative that offers an ordered representation of the world by forgetting it. The fable trumps other kinds of knowledge because it disconnects representation, signification, and value.[21] Its rhetorical effectiveness relies on what Eve Stoller describes as a "willful compartmentalization of its

Figure 5.3
Collecting Scrap Phones, 2014, photograph, Joost de Kluijver. Image courtesy of Fairphone/Closing the Loop in Accra, Ghana. Creative Commons License 2.0. https://creativecommons.org/licenses/by-nc/2.0/.

entangled parts."[22] This pattern of disconnection seems ironic in a terrain obsessed with convergence. As the fable of digitization continues to converge with animals, what matters is not actuality but the emotionally powerful image of compulsory communication as a liberating event. Letting loose the butterflies, birds, lizards, dogs, cats, fish, and monkeys across the advertising spaces of our cities is part of the process through which communication technologies converge in the fold of your hand. These technologies, like the animal spirits that promote them, succeed to the degree that their products are (unlike those same animals) well contoured to the routine practices and feelings of everyday life. Through the cell phone, the digital-animal bond helps to reconcile the opposing values of productivity and freedom. It promises to enhance consumers' social life without damaging what they already value in it. Connecting to others can happen without any limitations, for now—when so much control and risk appear to be outside your control—is the time to be flexible and free. The freer you are, and the more ambiguous your place in this hypermediated landscape, the more open you must surely be to diverse forms of experience. As with radio, you could change your ontological and social space just by hitting a different button on your dial; you change the station and, just like that, you can be somebody else.[23] The idea that mobile communication devices can solve the problems created by the coercive technologies of the everyday is a fabulation with disturbing implications. How appropriate that an animal should illustrate a fable.

Vocabularies of Connection

Note that this is an always-already-triangulated image, in which an animal embraces a cell phone, or vice versa, and looks straight at us, the viewers. The animal's readiness to look back at us functions (my informants believe) as a promise of compensation for the cold universe of machinic distance. Advertising is all about producing lack and compensation together, promising new resources for negotiating the conflicts and incongruities that arise between them as they emerge. To understand the promise of these messages is to open a Pandora's box of unresolved dilemmas. Let us examine the rhetorical achievements of these cell phone ads in this light.

First, these images contribute to a process of reification through which personal communication devices are—or at least appear to be—indispensable to the possibility of participating in an increasingly complex networked society. While the society and the network are complex, the devices appear to be simple and straightforward to use, not requiring any special technical knowledge or skill. The happy animals standing for simple use descend directly from the babies used to advertise player pianos a century ago or the tots playing with their interactive toys today.[24]

Second, an animal doesn't have a body, this graphic logic says: it *is* a body. In other words, it has nothing to learn to become what it is. Although this idea could clearly be disputed in reference to some species, the idea of the purely instinctive nonhuman body born with whatever it needs is etched in our imagination. If the animal can never be anything but what it already is, we can conscript its body or image to stand in for that part of us that will not be incorporated by the machine. With the animal-phone convergence, the body is in movement even when the image is still, for it is unconstrained by stationary media like conventional telephones ("land lines") or computers ("desktops") with their topographic baggage. The ever-convenient cell phone might keep you tethered to your work, but its animal spirit is really unconnected to anything aside from you and the network when you need it.

Third, the wider the range of resources you have at hand, the less time you have to spend choosing one over another. Do you want to summon sound or image, consume or communicate, be lost or found? It's best if you can do it all at the same time, efficiently and conveniently, as you negotiate admission to the new communities being formed in the kinship structure of equivalent technological capacity. This pursuit of diversification challenges established practices of identity. The mobius-shaped homology between animal, device, and belonging might be a form of postmodern totemism. Totemism was an important subject for early modern anthropologists excited by the logics of primitive societies under their gaze, as brilliantly summarized in Lévi-Strauss's book *Totemism*. Their debates concerned the role of animal imagery in organizing parallel and commensurate social differences within distinct clans or groups. In a clan structure, a raven and a whale are simultaneously different and equivalent, having been put in place by the taxonomy of meanings and practices through which parallel clans are formed. I am not suggesting that contemporary culture is comprised of clans organized by association with chosen animals—there is no evidence that people buy phones from specific phone companies because they like one animal more than another, although the passion evoked by sport teams worldwide and their ascension in postsecondary education in the United States are very worrisome. Rather, these animal figures evoke the idea that cell phone users can create their own tribes to fill the need for belonging.

Like human-animal interfaces in primitive societies, these associations exceed the symbolic. In addition to dispensing with substantive distinction between text and referent, the body and the image, the animal and the machine, their purpose is to transform both symbolically and practically the links between human bodies and their modes of communication.[25] If the monkey "means" anything here, it is that learning to use mobile communication technologies can help you remobilize your social identity. Modern Western subjects might be formed in the selection, possession, and display of their chosen objects of desire, but they also need to be flexible, adaptive, mobile, even disloyal. There is built-in obsolescence attached to their modes of becoming. Their attachment to the object involves cumulative detachment from meaning, a loss that parallels the detachment of animals from their habitat. This loss is potentially ameliorated by the presence of friendly animals that can roam across tropical zones without our having to worry about them. The world's a jungle out there.

Fourth, if a single body cannot make the sound of a hundred instruments playing simultaneously, a computer can; if a body cannot be in three places at once, or feel connected to others in just one place, telecommunications can help. These digital devices resemble biotechnologies in that

We give where we live.

We're committed to inspiring youth.

By inspiring young people to follow their dreams and experience the wonder of childhood the Children's Aid Foundation strives to ensure that all Canadian children have the opportunity to shine. TELUS is proud to support Spark and the Children's Aid Foundation in ensuring that all children have the opportunity to achieve their dreams. Just another way we give where we live.

telus.com/community

TELUS, the TELUS logo and the future is friendly are trademarks of TELUS Corporation, used under licence. © 2011 TELUS. 11_00165.

Figure 5.4
Telus Ad Campaign—Monkeys, 2013. Image courtesy of Telus Corporation.

they are "concerned in more or less sophisticated ways with diversifying those limited things of which bodies seem capable."[26] Thanks to Photoshop, the animal figures are infinitely adaptable to machinic environments. They talk, they invest, they rap, they gamble. We don't have to worry about other kinds of environments, because we don't see them. Being transparently artificial, the image occupies a completely abstract digital space and suggests that we can harmlessly do the same. Indeed, cell phone users are oblivious of the space they're in, but they talk of little else: "I'm coming out of class"; "I'm just leaving home"; "The bus is at Yonge Street"; "We've landed and I'll see you in a bit." In putting her phone to use, the speaker establishers her location and reconfirms her agency. The proposed human-animal mimesis can be seen as symbolic and practical armor against the leaking of meaning from the body in a culture that is obsessed with the body but has no time for embodiment.

Fifth, these images speak to and reinforce young people's awareness of the currency of their personal technologies. The display of communication

Figure 5.5
How Cute! Panda Selfie Amuses Net Users, 2017, photograph, People's Daily Online. Image courtesy of People's Daily Online.

technologies is part of the presentation of self to others, and cultural competence in the uses of these technologies is highly coded, especially in terms of gender.[27] Mobile digital convergence acquires precedence over prior modes of interaction, knowledge, and skill. Multifeatured cell phones enhance their owner's social capital; they privilege mobility, currency, and connection, and they valorize speed and convenience, all important aspects of contemporary technoculture.

The social consolidation of a technology like the cell shapes the habits, the expectations, and the nervous systems of the people who use these devices. As we learn to depend upon them, we become human extensions of their technosocial forms.

This cumulative interaction is part of the increasingly complex management of risk society. The paradox of risk society is that by using technologies to manage risk, the entrepreneurs of risk create further dangers that are less subject to conventional management. The technologies that solve problems of security and safety in one place, or for one group of people, can create destruction and dissent in and for another. Such hazards are permissible as long as they are profitable and preferably distant. The theory of risk society permits us to understand the diverse hazards of consumer technologies while empathizing with the needs and feelings of young people who consider their personal digital media to be a lifeboat in the face of unmanageable uncertainty and danger. The animals remind them of their freedom and innocence, which they hastily abandon on their own behalf. It is not just animals who fail to benefit in the balance of things.

Sixth, and last: these images are not just communications dedicated to interaction, as totems are said to be; they are blatant invitations *to* communicate. Ironically, these animal images are inviting us to communicate 24/7 in the same cultural moment that philosophers are debating species incommensurability and the perceived impossibility of communicating with animals. The overcoming of any imagined impossibility of communication is one "meaning" we can attribute to these images.

But "communication" is a problematic term, not least because there is a significant gap between how we depict our relations with the animals and how we actualize them. These wired animals are cheerful. They appear to like us. They do not appear to be threatened or burdened with impending extinction. Their habitats are not destroyed, because they have no habitats. Their habitats are irrelevant, just as ours are. It's okay if we exploit them. In other words, what is not visible may be as significant as what is visible, but it doesn't matter. This dilemma requires that we detour around the question of communication that so persuasively occupies the center of this image event and acknowledge what is being actualized in the convergence of animals and digital communication devices.

Triangulating Risk

With triangulation, as with network theory, the meaning of each part is determined by its relationship to other parts of the constellation. As I argue in chapter 6, the representation of cats was historically inseparable from their importance as sacrificial bodies within an emergent biopower apparatus. The cat was necessary to the identification of women as witches whose ostensible cat-mediated union with Satan made them subject to discipline and death by religious inquisitors. A similar principle of triangulation animates the powerful semiotic interdependency among mobile digital devices, small animals, and consumers that pervaded commercial image culture in the first decade of the twenty-first century. Through this interdependency, phones become pets and animals become media of communication cajoling young consumers to connect better, more often, everywhere they go. These properties determine certain practices. As vital elements of self-presentation, phones redefine the context of social encounter; phones placed on the table while friends eat or drink together signal that participants are ready to leave their face-to-face conversation to engage in a mediated conversation with someone else without leaving the table. As media researchers Caron and Caronia show, social context is redefined by techno-objects that introduce a new pattern of meaning: the *absent presence* of human subjects.[28] The person who is abandoned by her friend's phone call is on standby and must learn to interact with ghosts. The phones introduce "new cultural models for the context and the participants' behaviour,"[29] and as Caron and Caronia suggest, youth function as adept translators of technologies "into the terms of their specific cultures."[30] The person who has abandoned her friend is not rude; she is cool. Where these friends are having lunch is now a launching site for personal encounters and social differences that are justified and normalized by the technology. The minimum obligation is "to be always, at all times, and everywhere at least available for communication."[31] Two things are lost in this new regime of compulsory communication: freedom and silence.

In French sociologist Bruno Latour's actor network theory, reality is produced through interaction among multiple agents: human, technical, animal, and others. Water can be an agent, or a microscope, or radiation, or wolves. To say that each is an agent in the translation of virtuality to actuality is not to say that they are equally empowered, or that they fare equally well in the shifting constellations of instruments and purposes that constitute such networks. Animals are obviously not the authors of the current advertising campaign, for instance, despite their clever representation as neoliberal subjects. These digital animals and the connections of which they speak are part of a management strategy directed to the growing risks and fears of technological growth. Understanding this campaign as both risk formation and risk management allows us to emphasize what Latour's work does not: the significance of what is concealed.[32] The animal confidently displaying its device draws carefully on undercurrents of the unseen to restore a sense of equilibrium to anxious consumers who confront the risks that neoliberal governance has downloaded onto their bodies, their routines, and their futures. The simulated, despatialized embodiment of the animal communicates the idea that information can be liberated from time, space, and materiality in general. The more strongly you feel the effects of compulsory connectivity, the less likely you are to acknowledge its effects on distant bodies and natural spaces.

Mobile digital communication devices help users to manage contemporary insecurity and risk, but, as hinted in their didactic link to animals, they are also part of the production of risk that threatens the wellbeing of the planetary body. This paradox is the underlying logic of the media event. Theorists of the "event" describe it as an eruption of meaning that both disrupts and extends the political logic from which it emerges. If violence is an outcome of the production of abstract space through which capital is accumulated, as Marxist theorists Henri Lefebvre and David Harvey argue, the event has a "disarticulating" force that can be released to unpredictable effects by the actualization of the material properties of the media.[33] This "event" is part of a major discursive shift in which political and military certainties are giving way to a new kind of "re-enchanted" war, as Christopher Coker calls it, through which human armies are being supplanted by information, and conventional military power by the assemblage of organic and nonorganic matter in a cybernetic grid.[34] "Our former belief in the survival of the fittest has been replaced by a belief in the survival of the best informed," Coker suggests.[35] Just as the mystique of military sacrifice through death gives way to informatics, so too the concept of survival of the fittest gives way to adaptation to insecure environments through information processing.[36] These trends are brought together in the rhetorical triangulation of communications and animals, with obvious resonance in popular culture.

Perhaps the authors of this campaign have feelings about the rain forest or experiments on animals, perhaps not. They may have chosen animal images because they wanted to avoid associating their products with specific human faces or bodies with all their contentious races and ethnicities. They may have been drawing on more esoteric connections between software platforms and species like birds and snakes that have circulated for decades in the digital background of the public networks. Whatever their intent, these animals' cuteness evokes and dissimulates the violence through which animal bodies, human bodies, and technological systems "converge" in the telematic network in whose name they appear. The semiotic mobilization of animals as subjects and objects in this connective network silences and displaces the real suffering encountered by animal species, manufacturers, and toxic waste dispensers in third world countries, and the rapidly depleting biosphere on which they depend. Through the animal body, violence is enacted, dematerialized, and repackaged in the name of love.

Theorists define technological society as one in which "people think of the world around them as mere indifferent stuff which they are absolutely free to control any way they want through technology." In this configuration, liberalism forms "the political corollary of technology"; both proceed from the assumption that "man's essence is his freedom [and that] liberty is achieved by overcoming or defying necessity, not by living within it. [Thus] the human good is what we choose for our good."[37] If technology is the means by which freedom is achieved, at least freedom as conceived by liberalism, any Faustian harm is justified if it enhances "human good." By excluding the rights of nonhumans and of course some humans, technological achievement becomes an end rather than a means, and political judgment disappears.[38] It is not surprising, given how long "man" has been the "we" in such philosophies, that the world is running into difficulties. "In societies where 'man' is seen as the measure of things," writes Joost van Loon, "risks cannot but become more prominent."[39]

As historian Erica Fudge reminds us, Western culture doesn't just instrumentalize technology to achieve its goals; it also instrumentalizes the figure and body of the animal. "Animals are present in most Western cultures for practical use, and it is in *use*—in the material relation with the animal—that representations must be grounded."[40] The campaign to expand the market for rapidly obsolescing consumer electronics through association with animals is part of a strategy to engender support for the development of military communication hardware on which the American economy, in particular, so strongly depends.

In countries in Africa and Asia, the peoples, landscapes, and nonhuman species *not* included in the modern "voice implied by we" in books like this one bear the destructive weight of a rapidly growing volume of toxic trash that completes the cycle of production and consumption of these rapidly obsolete telecommunication technologies. So drastic are these conditions that new paramilitary security forces are being formed to control the workers whose job it is to dispose of the toxic trash that "we" are exporting to their countries. This is part of a larger redefinition of security (happening now reputedly without Trump's participation) in which climate change, not terrorism, is defined as "the greatest threat the United States faces, more dangerous than terrorism, Chinese hackers, and North Korean nuclear missiles."[41] The political and military machinery might define environmentalists as the new insurgents, but the struggle over the future of the planet is not at this point a military one. In fact, "our greatest treasure and most potent adaptive technology, the only thing that might save us in the Anthropocene, because it is the only thing that can save those who are already dead [is] memory."[42]

Extinction of the Dinosaurs

Earlier I asked: If an animal is mediating, what is it mediating? Invariably the investigation extends beyond the interspersed animals, users, and particular transport or communication technologies that can be interpreted through ecological metaphors. These assemblages are material practices with larger economic and political contexts and trajectories. The semiotic association of phones and small animals emerged, as we have seen, in a context dominated by the naturalization of communication technologies and the denaturalization of natural entities. Just as colonialism shaped the movement and meanings of live animals, so the infrastructure of global culture has shaped the collapse of currency and information into one another, the rearticulation of these in a global communication-security network, and the reiteration of the animal image from the debris of this collapse.

These developments are the underpinning of an ongoing military research project variously entitled "Project Thor," "Rods from God," or "kinetic energy projectiles." Rods from God is an outer space weapon initially developed by Boeing and the Rand Corporation, who named it "Project Thor." It was shelved initially as being prohibitively expensive.[43] Boeing researcher and military veteran Jerry Pournelle, who originally conceived of this weapon in the 1950s, "imagined the military equivalent of the extinction of the dinosaurs."[44] It deploys digital information processing and search capabilities that can guide lethally projected tungsten rods to targets on or beneath the earth's surface. Navigated by satellite and driven by its own kinetic energy, the Rods from God has been heralded as an unprecedentedly powerful, fearsomely expensive innovation in the corporate-military research-and-development infrastructure.

The Pentagon's Revolution in Military Affairs was instituted in order to establish what Brian Murphy describes as a "continuous four dimensional physical and cyberspace grid through which all warfighting relationships are linked."[45] This "revolution" replaces earthbound technologies of the military arsenal by shifting communication from a tactical to a strategic role.[46] Moving with unprecedented power at unimaginable speed, tungsten rods can burn and destroy targeted matter far below the earth's surface. According to recent online comments by military personnel, this technology is already in place notwithstanding denial from the military itself. This "kinetic energy projectile" is the logical extension of a U.S. military partnership with telecommunication companies that is redefining both war and communication by focusing on the relationship between them. Between 1992 and 2004, the time period in which the market for cell phones and social media emerged, the Pentagon was strategically transformed into C4ISR: Command, Control, Computers, Communications, Intelligence gathering, Surveillance, Reconnaissance. According to Murphy, 25 percent of its contractors specialize in information technology and have not held previous military contracts.

As an invention, Rods from God is far more destructive of life than the iPhone. But it would be neither thinkable nor economically feasible without the growing market for digital and satellite communication technologies and their contribution to the resources and research facilities of the major telecommunications companies. Canadians are not untouched by this trend. In 2006, at the height of its cell phone campaign with its lovely goats, birds, monkeys, and rhinos, Telus reduced its staff by a cruel 25 percent and won a contract to supply Canada's Department of National Defence with "global telecommunication services."[47] Today Telus generates about half of its revenues from wireless communications that are being lavishly marketed to consumers in both developed and "developing" countries. Over time, the most advanced militaries, led by the United States, are replacing human soldiers with cybernetic avatars, including robotic insects and birds, so that human skill is displaced onto cybernetic weaponry.[48] Once again, portions and replications of animals serve as emissaries for new regimes, but this time they have a deadlier function. These robotic weapons, increasingly housed inside real or simulated animal bodies, obviate the need for soldiers to enact human skill, presence, consent, sacrifice, or ethics.[49] DARPA (America's longtime Defense Advanced Research Projects Agency) has created robotic hummingbirds with a promising future of spying on the "bad guys."[50]

Media events mobilize diverse agents, some of which will slide back into oblivion. Risk management encompasses and mobilizes very agile tactics for averting and diverting the subjects of risk culture. With this in mind, let us revisit the face of this telematic grid and its assemblage of small animals and small machines in the fabulating universe of total communication. These animals look at us and say: You are not alone. Whether you are living or dead, you can reach out across any distance and touch someone. Companion animals confirm our humanity, and you will find such telecompanions in the midst of endless space. The animal species conveying this message are all movable; one can imagine picking up and carrying any one of them just like a phone, except for the chimp and the butterfly.[51] As the exception that proves the rule, Google puts Moose Internet Services and moose-hunting licenses next to one another, constellating a single species menagerie that advertises its own murder the way simulated cows sometimes appear in food ads inviting us to eat manly beef. How easily companionship flips into violence when the animal begins to grow. But this is a deeper truth of all the images. Let us consider their rhetorical achievements.

Talking to Animals

In the "aesthetics of livingness," Burt comments, there are two possible responses to the animal in art: "something to say and nothing to say."[52] In his 1995 study of angelology, Michel Serres observes that media establish human-machine intercommunication but do not enable us to talk to animals.[53] In contemplating the question of communication with animals, John Durham Peters makes a similar point: "That we can never communicate with the angels is a tragic fact, but also a blessed one. A sounder vision is of the felicitous impossibility of contact."[54] In his review of Peters's book, Donald Theall adds that "the problem of communication is not that we think of animals, aliens, and machines as exotic, but that we fail to recognize that it is we who are exotic."[55]

Projecting exoticism into the animal reinforces the assumption that humans can reason and understand while animals lack such capabilities. It is because Western civilization relies so heavily on this presumptuous distinction that cruelty to animals has been condoned throughout its history.[56] Philosophers, scientists, and animal rights activists have all contributed to showing how wrong this allegation is, helping to animate a major ontological shift in the West that finally makes it possible to imagine the act of looking in both directions.[57] If you place yourself in the hypothetical position of most animals, and imagine staring at us exotic humans, you are unlikely to like what you see. The commercial animal imagery illustrated here bypasses such issues and plays lightheartedly with the assumption that animals lack thought or perception by associating them with acts of mediated communication.

The irony of the "dumb" animal speaking on the phone hints that reason and intelligence are extraneous to the prospect of a chat. The joke is that the animals want to communicate with us. The joke is on us, because we are more like "animals" than we think. We are willing to abandon security and ethics if we can buy a new phone like this one. We are willing to sacrifice the land and water, the safety of others, and the future of the planet for the pleasure of sharing in the products of technological prowess. While we humans believe ourselves to be unique in grasping concepts and moral relations, something has apparently happened to our brains. We

Figure 5.6
Japanese macaque holding an iPhone, 2014, photograph. Image © Marsel van Oosten | squiver.com.

permit these objects of possession to undergo constant slippage, one thing constantly substituted for another as though nothing is unique or precious or indispensable. The way this process seems to be carrying us slowly and inexorably toward the extinction of life might be considered one of the ways we are exotic.

To resituate the concept of the media event in the context of risk is to realize that actualizing a technological potential is not always an affirmative process. This can be illustrated with the nature of risk associated with mobile communication and the specific strategies of risk management that arise in relation to it. Consider five points of actualization in the unfolding connection between cell phones and animals.

First, at the end of a course called "Nature in Narrative," I met with five fourth-year undergraduate women over a beer. In response to my queries, all of them had cell phones, and all had pet photos displayed on them, including the phone belonging to one student who doesn't own a pet. Viewed together, these snapshots draw our attention toward the ordinarily unrevealed networks of human-animal-technological interfaces in which compliance is translated as love. If possession of the phone starts to feel compulsory or invasive, the pet photograph provides evidence of good nature. Freedom so quickly turns into its opposite where love and technology are concerned.

Second, cell phones are physically harmful to animals through each stage of their cycle of production. They contain an ore called coltan that is mined in Africa. While many animals are in wildlife reserves or "protected" parks, illegal miners continue to invade these areas because demand for the ore is so high. Cell phones and their accessories also contain arsenic, cobalt, copper, lead, and zinc. "Animals are not only put in danger while we mine the necessary products to produce the phone, they are put in jeopardy when we throw them away too."[58] A 2007 study conducted by three departments of Panjab University in India reveals that cell phone towers are the "dominating source of electromagnetic radiations in environment in the city" and can lead to disease in plants and animals. "Ever wondered where the butterflies, some insects and birds like sparrows have vanished?" one newspaper write-up begins. "Well, your constantly ringing cell phones could be responsible for this."[59] Chemical compounds used in batteries and chip production and crowding the recycling sites spreading across the developing world are known to cause neurological and environmental damage.[60] Americans discard an average of 130 million cell phones per year,[61] each one of which contains more than two hundred chemical compounds.[62] American researchers have announced a plan to equip cell phones with monitoring devices that will alert users to toxic materials in their environments. They don't explain how to manage the millions of cell phones discarded across the country, most of which end up in poisonous recycling plants processed by poor laborers in distant countries. An uneasiness about the issue haunts the landscape. The central object of concern for military research today is not foreign terrorists; it is environmentalists.

Third, there is always an upside: you can donate your cell phones to zoos, humane societies, and animal rights organizations, which will use the proceeds to help animals, including endangered species.[63] You will feel pleased with yourself and are unlikely to trace the exact details of the recycling process. If you aren't ready to lose your phone, or you have purchased a new one, you can buy a purple paw to hang on it, and Purple Paw will donate funds to the Animal Rescue Site.[64] Zoos might be losing their credibility as contributors to conservation and animal welfare, but they are working hard to regain it by taking in the e-waste generated by young adults with fond memories of days at the zoo.

Fourth, if information overload or planetary depletion are stressing you out, medical research confirms that companion animals are good for your health; owning a pet shows direct benefits for blood pressure and other stress-related physical indicators, as the lucrative pet food industry is only too happy to point out. If you are worried about losing your pet, you can equip her with a microchip, a digital communication device, or even a cell phone; you can always know where she is, just as someone somewhere can always know where you are.

Fifth, during Hurricane Katrina in 2005, some people were rescued because they had access to cell phones. Unfortunately many others did not survive, whether or not they had phones in their possession. Thousands of animals did not survive the floods. They were expendable, just like the African-American population of New Orleans, as Carolyn Ellis writes in an eloquent account of reliving Katrina at the sight of a half-dead cat.[65] More recently, a young man who rescued a rabbit in a 2017 California wildfire was celebrated and excoriated across the globe. A *rabbit?* No such response accompanied an even more recent photograph of a rescued bear cub with burned paws. In the wake of global climate change, racialized and poor communities and animals are losing their habitats. Some populations, like cats and mosquitoes, are exploding; others are being cornered or decimated by the destruction of their habitats, and by the mining, manufacture, and disposal of the digital communication devices upon which we knowledge workers so strongly rely.

Conclusion

As feminist cultural theorists have emphasized, affect and emotion are central categories of experience that are increasingly implicated in power relations and constantly negotiated in the relationship between public and private spheres. We need to approach these ads for telecommunications products in terms of affect, rather than meaning as conventionally understood. Virtual animals don't "mean" animal bodies or the dynamics of nature here, in any literal sense; they mean the desire to connect in a context in which nature is so remote as to be reducible to a fetish. These ads excel because they are successful in manipulating real emotions. They produce lack (lack of embodiment, connection, relations to nature, affect) together with compensation for it, and promise something magical in the spaces between them. This promotional logic, in concert with the technology being promoted, is spreading into all domains of personal and social experience, including nature.[66] They make tangible the degree to which the images, along with the devices they promote, are products of highly integrated corporate industries that promote and manage the uses of newer consumer-friendly technological innovations. The history of cell phones and of their semiotic and material dimensions is thus an instance of capitalism's biopolitical "subsumption of life," an idea introduced in chapter 1. Also materialized in this mobilizing event is a greater presence for and awareness of the animal world in the spaces of image culture. These images have the capacity to challenge the carefully cultivated indifference to that animal world.

The virtual animal fuses one discourse (animal spirits, instinct, nature, and the welfare of the planet) with another (communication, technology, connection, and security), making it impossible to consider one without reference to the other. While the popularity of animal imagery suggests a growing public awareness of environmental problems, it also reveals the degree to which this awareness is subject to the social and psychological machinery of capitalist technoscience, which explores the affective responses of prospective viewers with the same fierce focus that it employs to explore the surfaces of Mars. This rearticulation works at the level of persuasion because it is true at a profound level. While risk management assuages the unpredictable problems that arise from cumulative technological growth, the animal reminds viewers of immanent "natural" disasters through which our interests merge with those of the nonhuman animal world.

Writing before the turn of the millennium, environmental philosopher Neil Evernden had this to say about technological modernity:

> The fact that we are content to construe nature as an object of the moment is symptomatic of our desire to avoid any constraints and to have a free hand to manipulate the world into the forms suited to the exchanges of modern technocracy. The investment we have in the maintenance of this understanding of nature is enormous. And yet, it is not secure. Nature-as-self is also a contemporary reality. It is certainly not the norm, but it is credible enough to generate widespread discussion. And if we ever find that nature-as-miracle has found its way into the columns of Time Magazine, we may begin to wonder whether nature, whatever it may be, is about to slip its leash.[67]

What distinguishes the present from the premillennial moment in which Evernden was writing is the degree to which nature *has* "slipped its leash." My esteemed former colleague could never have anticipated the ferocity of its unleashing. In a society of compulsory communication bruised by the extent of "natural" disasters, looking at animals assuages the emotional needs for connection and security for people who are struggling to adapt to both new technologies and a threatened planet. The need to fulfill such needs is stimulated but also diverted by the forests of animals, both the digital ones and the ones being destroyed by forest fires and toxic waste. These images naturalize and obscure a new order of things. We look at the animals and the animals look back. They are not speaking, but they are not silent, either.

6 Cat and Mouse, Symbiotics of Social Media

I find myself indebted to the net for its provisions. It is a steadfast benefactor, always there. I caress it with my fidgety fingers; it yields to my desires, like a lover. Secret knowledge? Here. Predictions of what is to come? Here. ... The net's daydreams have touched my own, and stirred my heart. If you can honestly love a cat, which can't give you directions to a stranger's house, why can't you love the web?

Kevin Kelly, *What Technology Wants*[1]

Nobody wants ads any more. They want cat videos.

Tim Nudd, *Adweek*, November 17, 2011 (citing John St. Advertising, Toronto)

Currency

These pundits are right. Midway through 2018, there are more than eighty-six million posts on #Cats_Of_Instagram, and that is just scratching the surface of the Internet cat population. A single YouTube video compilation, "Cats Will Make You Laugh" had 76 million viewers by 2017. According to Google, people search for the word "cats" 30 million times per month, nearly three times the number of searches for "Kim Kardashian" and five times that for "bacon." Photographs, videos, and graphics of cats provide the most prolific visual content (second to pornography) in the ever-expanding spaces of the Internet. Dogs might appear more frequently in the news and in conventional entertainment, but cats go viral.[2] So foundational have cats become to online communication that pictures of cats are widely used as metonyms for the state of being online. Millions of visual memes and metacommentaries have been built from cat pictures and posts.

The cat-Internet phenomenon is one of the most celebrated outcomes of the technotopianism of the 1970s. Cats appeared online as soon as there was online space open to the public, and quickly became a truly global Internet phenomenon. Putting aside advocacy and rescue sites, the background for these snapshots and videos (if any is provided) is an interior setting in an unexceptional domestic landscape, indoors or perhaps on a patio just outside the door. Sometimes the cat cuddles or plays with another species, perhaps a rabbit, turtle, or dog, or is dressed up as another species, or as something unfathomable. No matter that many memes and jokes emerge to mock and punctuate the online pet population; this trope is invulnerable. Regardless of their orientation to gender, race, meat, or wildlife, people are entranced by the images. This is not hard to understand. These cats occupy the center of a universe, and they are lovable, furry, and full of personality. They do not appear to be vulnerable or distressed. There is no display of violent or predatory behavior. You probably won't see the cats kill anything; their animal spirits are almost (but never completely) domesticated, and no trainer or captor is needed to display them. Like the producers of porn or documentary, the photographers are mainly absent from the visual field.[3] The photographs foreground the comfortable sensuality of the cats and their interactions with the domestic worlds they inhabit. Fluffy bodies are a strong contrast to the digital graphic interface in which they appear.[4] By the time these images have been reframed, photoshopped, touched up, or captioned, however, this contrast has turned into something far more complicated.

This chapter revisits my first foray into animal representations to explore the symbiosis between cats and social media in the context of this book's central concerns. Joining together affect and monetization, personal and "public" (virtual) space, ardor and diffidence, reference and meaninglessness, the cat-Internet phenomenon resembles the symbiotic configurations formed by giraffes and ships, beavers and canoes, software and menageries. Each configuration extends and relies on the affordances and meanings of earlier ones. The appearance of the cats announced the arrival of a changed affective regime marshaled to refurbish the human resilience damaged by neoliberalism, economic austerity, and climate change. Cats have played a major role in this enterprise. They help people feel cozy and connected, and the inventive ways these images and feelings are conveyed encourages people to expand their reach into the diverse platforms and activities of social media. The insanely large multitude of furry bodies online is generated by many forces. I begin with notable highlights of the history of cats that preceded their ascendancy in the *Umwelt* of the Internet. To help understand their mediological role in generating this new *Umwelt*, I also revisit an influential philosophical debate about cats.

Disclosure: I love cats myself. I have lived with them all my life, even as a university student and nomadic contract teacher with little control over my life and time. They ground me, they make me come home, they suggest I sit down and share some love. I can think about things while in their company; feeling connected to them makes me feel more like myself and more in touch with others. Losing a cat (or dog) tears me apart in some part of my psyche that can't be explained with reference to the usual anatomies of feeling but is only explicable to others who share the experience. The discovery that people grieve when they lose their pets seems to be relatively new, but a close connection with a domestic cat is not new or idiosyncratic. Records, photographs, journals, and biographies reveal hundreds of pictures and testimonials of writers and artists living with cats. Cats might have become acceptable domestic companions after being embraced by writers and artists, but that population is tiny compared to the human-cat-screen assemblages now spanning the globe. This sharing extends the envelope of intimacy we share with them into cyberspace.

Unlike giraffes, beavers, and lions, cats are not specific to any continent or bioregion. The enjoyment of them crosses continents, languages, races, temperaments, and genders. A cat living in Japan and a cat living in Florida could have different histories but look identical in a photograph. Pictures of cats are mainly photographed by and associated with their owners, who display their lovable cats as evidence of their compassionate and fun domestic life. The owners' cats are not totemic in any conventional sense, in that they do not postulate or invite a stable exchange of qualities between animal and owner, or between species and any social group or place. Rather, they are ideal subjects of a neoliberal economy, mobile, free-floating, agreeable, and sporadic. The photographers play with the conventions of animal portraiture just as cats themselves, according to folklore, play with human expectations. These pictures are created for exchange, not information; in this respect, they mimic everyday encounters between neighbors or strangers who find a route to communication through their pet. The proliferation of these images is surely related to the growing ambivalence and stress people feel when confronted by dubious futures. It indicates their drive to intervene however gently in those futures, to turn the unpredictability back upon itself, to temper the impact of that unpredictability, to mean and not mean, care and not care at the same time. These meanings tease one another in the virtual circulation of cats the way a cat teases a mouse.

Internet cat sites offer communion with a group of like-minded people, a cat nation if you will, with shared sites and communication practices and a range of unstated codes and beliefs. Some sites, like Internet Kitteh Studies, Toronto Cat Rescue, or Cats Against Capitalism, offer a specific mandate

Figure 6.1
IM IN UR FOLDUR KERUPTIN YR FYLZ, 2007, digital image, Clancy Ratliff. Licensed through Creative Commons 2.0, https://creativecommons.org/licenses/by-sa/2.0/.

for participation, a kind of cats+ for academics, advocates, and socialists, respectively, while on the other hand Stuff on Cats, Kitten Competition, Cats in Sinks, and innumerable other sites are deliciously ostentatious about their rejection of purpose. Memes abound in a register that is both sweet and sarcastic. The millions of cats roaming the Internet pathways greet viewers who want nothing more than distraction and a more pleasurable passage of time, insisting that "nothing more" is not nothing. As Jodi Dean, author of the critique of communicative capitalism and source of regular Facebook updates featuring photographs of her cat, has written: "I can't help but think of the cute cat photos and funny animal videos that circulate on the net. Why do people upload, forward, and link to these? It's not only because cats are cute or even because one's own cat is completely interesting. It's the feeling that cuteness accesses, the feeling that moves it, opens to something more, to a kind of beyond."

"Opens to a kind of beyond": this theme appears again and again in these texts on menageries, and yet again in the next chapter as a description of birdsong. "I can't help but think of the cute cat photos" registers a different mood, not so much longing as compulsion, a gentler version of the compulsion we saw among the viewers of April the Giraffe's great expectations. Circulating in the peculiar time-space of social media, these images of cats are created and circulated through posts that function as postcards between friends. They are icons of a nascent epistemology, monetizations of animal and domestic life, comfortably empty or phatic utterances, links with childhood or childlike feeling, extensions of hominess and neighborliness, mockeries of gender and animal taxonomies, and implicit or explicit resistance to work disciplines that, unlike the rebellious animal spirits evoked by Virilio or Pasquinelli, keep us at our desks or phones. Sometimes these posts are accompanied by requests to help name a kitten, or contribute to funds for medical treatment, or find cats places to live, echoing virtual handheld pets like Tamagotchi (which hit the market in 1996, nine years before YouTube) that would buzz their child caretakers for food and attention until inevitably they died. Cats on the Internet are better-looking than these robotic counterparts. Cat pictures and commentaries are easier to share, and they are windows onto real animals, not electronic ones.

These cat posts can be thought of as a form of currency. In early agricultural societies, in early Roman times, and in the fur trade, coins replaced or were traded for animals. These coins were often inscribed with images of these same animals, becoming mimetic objects that could supplement the capacity of new middlemen to link buyers and sellers in the routines of material exchange. Cat snapshots are analogous to these coins in that they are portable and meaningful tokens exchanged between people to confirm, measure, and extend their shared values. Their value isn't based on their monetary worth, although millions can be made from owning the right Internet cat, as the owner of Grumpy Cat recently demonstrated in a lawsuit against unauthorized use of her cat's image. Owners of celebrity cats can profit handsomely from their pets, as do search engines and platforms, but these successes are rare. The value of online cats is mainly determined by how they make people feel. As digital objects they are exchanged for what are ideally still immaterial values such as company, distraction, satire, protest, laughter, and cross-species friendship.

Figure 6.2
I MUST FLY MY PEOPLE NEED ME, digital image, Maru&Hana.

Each strand of the history of human-cat relations bears the marks of radical transformations in social attitudes toward these animals. As people sharing cat images today, we are not required to remember such history; online cats expel traces of conflict or suffering from the visual field, except when there is evidence of human cruelty, when the narrative moves from lost to saved. The feline interface draws people to the cat's outstanding characteristics, as depicted therein: their captivating sensuality, strong sense of personal space, quick responsive bodies, oblique expressions, and wily capacity to feign indifference. Their presence invites viewers to enjoy the soft but intransitive responses people experience sitting with cuddly fur babies that they cannot touch doing untranslatably catlike things.

As the intense industrial organization of space and time recedes, people's work and home situations have become more precarious, and privacy and individuality require extra supplementation to feel like genuine attributes. The cat, the personal page, and the selfie appeared together on the online horizon, extending the modern fusion of single-family dwellings and pet ownership. As Erica Fudge writes in *Animal*, "Increased privacy—a new human individuality—occurs at the moment when the increased individualism of the pet is also being established."[5] The cat is not only a family pet seen through the digital screen or window; the cat and the screen are the window onto everything. The performance of private life online might open the individual user to an unimaginably spacious global network, but it also helps the individual name and resist its scope and power. The cat avatar declares the user's presence, it grounds her existence in a particular place, and it enhances her mood. Changes in the regulation of work and time, combined with the generative syntax of the Internet, make it possible to put currency and affect together in a single thought. In this fractious social milieu, cats are, not for the first time, the perfect medium.

Parallel Histories

In the popular genealogies filling the bookstores and documentary channels, the earliest cats were wild animals. Later, cats were worshipped as gods in Egypt, and later still they were massacred as representatives of Satan. As a result of popular mobilizations against cruelty to animals, they became household pets. Initially they were pets for artists, atheists, and prostitutes, but eventually they encountered grace and now live under the protection of the state. This narrative of transformation is as popular to cat lovers as Christmas and Easter are to Christians, and it follows a somewhat similar trajectory. Cats came from (or were) gods, they were suspected of having unnatural powers, they were massacred, they came back, they always come back. Contemporary cats may live as domestic pets, these histories remind us, but they can never be fully domesticated. The other consistent theme across these narratives is the ambiguous nature and personality of the cat itself as a liminal animal, an animal that crosses between worlds, an animal that threatens boundaries and taxonomies, an animal onto which anything can be projected. The cat's seemingly deliberate lack of transparency accounts for both the terror that cats aroused in ancient and Christian mythology and their ambiguous status today.

According to a sassy English proverb first published in 1562, "What, a cat may look on a king, ye know!"[6] Queen Elizabeth I held the throne at the time, so the proverbial expression evidently predated its appearance in print. The revolutionary idea that inaugurated the modern age, that all living beings have rights, took hold here in the image of a cat in full possession of its eyes. The year this book was published, sixty-seven women were tortured and burned as witches following a hailstorm in Wiestensteig, Germany, which they were believed to have caused. Witches were often burned with their cats, their "familiars," who lived with them as intimates and were thought to be mediums for Satan.[7] The savage event of 1562 reignited a violent crusade against women and witchcraft, despite the fact that the crusade's hysterical tenets had already been repudiated by Church authorities. The misogynist and superstitious fury raged nonetheless across Europe until around 1630.[8] Paranoid fantasies about women as Satanic enemies were upheld by church authorities during this period despite official protestations against them, much as white supremacy is aided and abetted by the White House under the Trump presidency.

As one fabled cat gazed at the body of power and other cats were being hung or consumed by inquisitors' fires, the first religious war began in France, the first dramatic tragedy in blank verse, by Christopher Marlowe, was performed before Queen Elizabeth,[9] and Spanish Archbishop Diego de Landa burned the sacred codices of the Mayan people because he viewed them as proof of diabolical practices. Archbishop Landa wrote home saying, "We found a large number of books in these characters and, as they contained nothing in which were not to be seen as superstition and lies of the devil, we burned them all, which they (the Maya) regretted to an amazing degree, and which caused them much affliction."[10] When this travesty occurred, Mayan culture was almost a thousand years old, and the documents would have had enormous power. The "characters" that so insulted the colonial archbishop were narrativized images of animals such as dogs and jaguars.[11] The colonial impulse to interpret, reform, and subjugate other cultures through the biopolitics of the animal had begun. The world was changing, religious and political institutions were in turmoil, and cats

Figure 6.3
Francisco de Goya, *Ensayo (Trials)*, from the series *Los Caprichos*, 1799, etching, aquatint, and burin. Image courtesy of the Los Angeles County Museum of Art.

kept appearing in the middle of things. This transition from one mode of society to another raises suggestive ideas about the parallel prominence of cats today.

In *The Death of Nature*, Carolyn Merchant notes that in early modern Europe, "The goat and cat were associated with women and witchcraft because of their presumed sexual lust and slyness."[12] Etchings and woodblocks of the time show graphic images of cats lined up as sacrificial bodies next to the witches with whom they lived and died. Threatened by the traditional knowledge and healing practices of women, local authorities viewed the interdependency of women and cats as evidence of a pact between the woman and the devil mediated and effected by the cat. Eliminating the legitimacy of traditional healing practices was a crucial step in the ascendance of modern medical science, animated perhaps ironically by profoundly superstitious popular belief in a historically continuous patriarchal subjection of women. If the disenchantment of the universe had far-reaching effects, cats suffered particularly brutal consequences. It took the concentrated efforts of naturalists, animal protection societies, artists, writers, and illustrators to rehabilitate the cat as an animal deserving of compassion and rescue. Cat books, illustrations, and exhibitions, culminating in a show at the Crystal Palace in 1871, turned popular sentiment in favor of cats and spawned an outpouring of compassion for them. Cats and children were brought together in narrative and imagery through a refeminized ideology of natural innocence. Cats were so thoroughly rescued by Victorian culture that by the beginning of the twentieth century their depictions involved a sweeter, more decorous femininity allowing cats the safety of a domestic life. Illustrations and magazine covers began to feature beautiful women posed with cats.

In early and modern Europe, cat massacres were public ritual events sometimes documented by their enactors.[13] The public massacres stopped by 1905, but if an animal today is randomly tortured, it is likely to be a cat. Humane societies across North America still refuse to release black cats near Halloween, to protect them from this end.[14] You might say that the cat, like the giraffe and the beaver, was a "vanishing mediator" in the troubled transition from traditional and religious authority to modern forms of power that are now undergoing their own unsettling transformations. They are "vanishing" not because they are extinct or invisible but because, following Max Weber's analysis of the priest's role in transferring power from church to bureaucracy (see chapter 1), the social transformations facilitated by their presence have occurred and they are no longer needed in the same way. Who needs a priest in an industrial bureaucracy? Who

Figure 6.4

Harper's Magazine cover, May 1896, commercial lithograph, Edward Penfield. Image courtesy of the Detroit Institute of Arts.

needs a witch in a secular government? These vanishing mediators were crucial to bringing about these new modes of social organization. Giraffes and their keepers, beavers and Indigenous trappers, cats and questionable women became linked symbols of colonial and repressive action in times of turbulent change during which they emerged as symbolically charged and necessarily linked figures only to recede once again into the background. The charisma that placed these animals into the orbit of such disturbances was viewed positively in the giraffe, negatively in the cat. With the architectonic changes besetting modern life, cats have not disappeared, however (nor have giraffes, for that matter, not yet anyway). Cats reappeared as symbolic mediators for people experiencing the maelstrom of social, technological, and psychological tensions that have accompanied corporate globalization and increasingly precarious lives. Despite the seeming loss of history, traces of these older historical and anthropological layers of meaning are visible in recent work on human-cat relations and offer a differently angled lens onto the virtual cat.

The historical changes that mobilized greater prominence for cats in the sixteenth and twentieth centuries were accompanied by an explosion of popular image-making techniques and pointed philosophical commentaries. The cats now proliferating on T-shirts, coffee mugs, greeting cards, calendars, cartoons, websites, and personal emails are not exactly "animals"; they do not occupy wild space, they have no habitats, they are not wild. This rhetorical ambiguity draws our attention to the degree to which, as Leach argues, we are supposed to draw a singular connection between animals and the spaces they inhabit: pigs, farms; horses, fields; wolves, forests. The depiction of animals that have crossed such boundaries—horses in slaughterhouses, wolves in farms, pigs in flight—is accompanied by unease, even panic, arguably arising from the disruption of boundaries as much as from the cruel treatment of animals. Cats themselves are famous for their fascination with doors and their capacity to cross spatial boundaries of every kind. That is their nature. But that is not nature enough. Cats do not evoke powerful "otherness" for humans hungry for connection with the wilderness sublime. Where the discourse on animals has become abstract and universalizing—to the extent that Jacques Derrida famously exclaimed his dislike of that terrible word, "the animal"—the culture shared by cats and humans is intimate and particular. It continues between acquiescent agents over long periods of time. Derrida himself wrote that his own cat's eyes "provide his own *I*'s first mirror" and confessed that this glimpse opened the door to a fundamental compassion for animals and a transformation of his understanding of both philosophy and self-knowledge.[15]

Representations of animals play an important role in negotiating political and cultural tensions. At the most general scale of social belief, humans are moral beings who can reflect on their actions; animals are not. People who misbehave are acting like animals, their "animal spirits" have overtaken them and destroyed their rational capacities. "Animals!" spat the white police officer while watching African Americans protesting vehemently in Ferguson, Missouri in the famous uprising against racist police violence in 2014. Humans are obedient; animals are not. Humans have language; animals do not. Humans have hands or use tools; animals do not. Humans can pretend; animals cannot. These distinctions hardly merit belief today. Whoever proposed this last distinction could not have not known a cat, for cats are great pretenders. They pretend to bite, pretend to chase, and pretend to sleep, and they know as well as we do that they are pretending. "Who knows, when I am playing with my cat, that she is not toying with me?" Finally, a scientific study published in March 2018, four hundred and twenty years after Montaigne wrote about his cat, has confirmed that cats can pretend.[16] Not wanting to miss a beat, *Smithsonian* reports a recent finding that cloning will not restore endangered species and suggests that perhaps "we can dress up cats and just pretend."[17]

In the field of critical animal studies, there is wide consensus that categories of difference between human and nonhuman animal beings must be transformed to enable better modes of interaction between species. At the same time, some of the most profound theorizations of this shifting boundary are marked by hierarchy, anthropocentrism, and sexism.[18] These issues are all crystallized in debates about cats. This fissure in theory and practice is one of many features that make the study of online cats irresistible.

Fissures in Philosophy

The French writer Michel Eyquem de Montaigne was twenty-nine the year the proverb of the cat looking at the king was published. Twelve years later, in 1580, Montaigne published his essay "Apology for Raymond Sebond," in which he rebukes his contemporaries for their vanity in presuming superiority over nonhuman animals. "Presumption," Montaigne insists, "is our natural and original disease. The most wretched and frail of all creatures is man, and withal the proudest."[19] Elucidating the talents and gifts of various species, Montaigne castigates his fellow thinkers for their failure to ask fundamental questions about them. Montaigne asks: "When I am playing with my cat [*ma chatte*], how do I know that she is not toying with me?"[20] Derrida cites this rhetorical question about the playing cat in his own essay, "The Animal That Therefore I Am," in which he speculates about his cat's gaze on his body as he is getting out of a bath.[21] Derrida's excavation of Montaigne's pointed question is a reminder to readers that the critique of anthropocentrism began well before the twentieth century and that cats were in the middle of it even then. The playful cat bouncing from Montaigne to Derrida to YouTube illustrates the connection I am drawing between early modern and late modern cultures in terms of the use of animals to mediate upheavals in their geopolitical and epistemological foundations. The cat that toys with these philosophers demonstrates that the animals who mediated such changes were not only occupants of menageries but also other species, cats in particular. While the gaze of Derrida's cat has been discussed far more often than the mind of Montaigne's playing cat, both philosophers chose to conscript their cats to proselytize against arrogant anthropocentrism.

Derrida writes of his cat that it is not a metaphor but a specific cat, a little cat. In speaking about "his cat" he is speaking not only of a particular cat but also of a particular relationship. This aspect of companionate culture—the fact that, as Gilles Deleuze and Félix Guattari put it, one can talk about "my cat, my dog"[22]—is a point of principle that divides these thinkers. Does the relationship with an animal not change when you nominate it as "mine"? Is this not always already a grammar of domination? As Bruns observes, however, Derrida does ascribes a point of view to the cat, which means that between himself and his cat "there is a reversal of subjectivity in which Derrida is no longer himself (that is, no longer self-possessed, able to say 'I' without *malséance*)."[23] In other words his cat has supplemented "his" identity; he has gained companionship and lost normative (male) self-possession. For Deleuze and Guattari, however, the possessive pronoun attached to animals ("my" cat) evokes something pathological.[24] Their antagonism to this formulation is presented in terms of modern psychoanalytic science and classical myth, but it arguably retrieves the less august suspicions evoked by the idea of the sixteenth-century obsession with the "familiar" as a conduit for secrets and pathologies. Deleuze and Guattari prefer more abstract, more unsettling relations with wild or pack animals, even if, in secret, at least one of them did cohabit with a cat. Yet our language encourages us to refer to many relations this way. We speak for instance of "my" neighbor, "my" student, "my" father," "my" partner, "my" room, "my" office, and of course, "my" self. These phrases oscillate between kinship and possessive individualism in ways that are too complicated to summarize in a phrase or single relationship.

These critics are not interested in companion animals but something more exotic, more distant from everyday urban culture, like coyotes (a tradition initiated by Joseph Beuys), wolves and lobsters (a favorite reference for Deleuze and Guattari), sharks (featured in the work of artists Olly and Suzi and reproduced on the cover of Steve Baker's *The Postmodern Animal*), insects (mutated or metaphorical), or bears (live or stuffed). To marshal the vital energy of the "animal" in these performative tropes is to summon from inside oneself the animal spirits of those species farthest from us and least vulnerable to our way of life. They imagine untouched spaces where wildness dwells and seek to evoke an analogous space within the human. In summoning this idea of becoming, they instrumentalize nonhuman subjects as though nonrelationships are more powerful than relationships. This extends the phenomenological impulse so far into thought that it reverses itself (to borrow a trope from McLuhan's *Laws of Media*), requiring no encounter with an actual animal body and offering a narrative of animal being that is perhaps too coherent to resemble life of any kind.

Deleuze and Guattari write in *A Thousand Plateaus* that "artists 'become-animal' at the same time as the animal becomes what they willed."[25] This emphasis on the malleability of the animal subject reinforces the assumption that the meaning of this nonencounter is produced by and within the human subject. Such meetings of artist and animal can be seen as attempts to revitalize Keynes's "animal spirits" for creative purposes that are essentially humanist in scope. Deleuze and Guattari write, "How to operate other-than-in-identity—and ... how to operate as an artist—has to do with speeds. To 'make your body a beam of light moving at ever-increasing speed,' they write, is something which 'requires all the resources of art, and art of the highest kind'—the kind of art, that is to say, through which 'you become animal.'"[26] Despite his own commitment to "becoming animal," Baker concludes that "animals, for Deleuze and Guattari, seem to operate more as a device for writing—albeit a device which initiated its own forms of political practice—than as living beings whose conditions of life were of direct concern to the writers." For them, Franz Kafka's novel *The Trial*, in contrast to some of his earlier works, "liberates itself from all animal concern to the benefit of a much higher concern."[27] Deleuze and Guattari cannot swallow the idea of cross-species intimacy because that relationship defies the virile mimicry/antagonism of human and animal natures that underlies their work. While they evoke animal spirits as foundational to artistic realization, connection with these animal spirits can only be asserted through the metaphorical and spatial reaffirmation of humanist exceptionalism. As with the genre of nature films, such depiction "minimizes conflict between natural environment and human society, animals and persons, and invites viewers to forget that their view of nature is actually mediated, even as the very act of nature spectatorship underscores its distance and unfamiliarity."[28]

Wherever you stand in these debates, there is a politics at work in the encounter between human and animal—not just in terms of morality and feeling, but also with regard to the constitution of space and time within which the encounter occurs. These authors' interest in "the speed of light" echoes futurist manifestos (although it is far more indebted to surrealism) and, closer to home, reminds us of criticisms of the condensed rhythms of nature that characterize nature documentaries by Disney and *National Geographic*, among others, in which hunting, mating, family formation and aggression are sped up and foregrounded by editing.[29] No doubt you, like Olly and Suzi, would wish your encounters with wolves, spiders, and sharks to be cautious and swift. Beuys, who spent a week with his coyote, maintained that their "roles were exchanged immediately,"[30] so presumably the remainder of the week was a performance of redundancy. These writers presuppose a state of wildness that can only be found in vast natural territories that are catastrophically shrinking. Both approaches prefer virility and speed to empathy and proximity.

Critical debates about domestic pets reinforce the taxonomy through which humans across cultures have created separate categories and spaces for nonhuman species: wild animals, edible animals, working animals, pest animals, and companionate animals whose divided industrialized taxonomies are both spatial and deeply instrumental. Historically, a single animal could occupy multiple categories. One could have pet goats, pigs, or chickens in the house, while rearing others of the same litter outside for food.[31] One could have cats that lived outdoors in proximity to turkeys, coyotes, and snakes, as we did in childhood living in the country. Today, however, the category of companionate animal is more carefully regulated. The only animal that can be said to properly occupy multiple categories is the rabbit.[32] "Family" pets are restricted to domestic spaces and habits, in part to protect birds and other outdoor animals, in the case of cats, in part to protect the pets, in part to protect us. They play an important role in constituting and symbolizing these spaces and habits. The relationship with one's cat is mundane, it is sensual, and it can last for years. It is not (but also not not) the "quality" of the cat or the human that is at stake in this encounter, but rather the interaction of these two species in constructing the spaces of everyday life. Such coexistence is only possible with some animals; since the industrial revolution, urban dwellers have been widely prohibited from sharing their space with animals designated as wild or agricultural.

While the cat mediates these and other (virtual) spatial tropes in multiple directions, critics of pet ownership insist on making a clear distinction between them. Animals are in the wild; pets are in the house. Living with cats is a symptom of human neurosis located specifically in the bourgeois domestic sphere. By training animals to depend on humans for food and survival, humans transform them from free beings into enslaved beings. The slavery motif implies that if we were not intent on being masters, our slaves (pets) would be free. Yet owning or living in proximity to a cat was for centuries a major asset for marine and agricultural enterprises, and these cats helped humans to domesticate as much as the reverse. Just as animals of many species are tied to mediological change rather than the content behind which media disappear, so the human species has emerged, evolved, and been domesticated through interdependent relations with animals. "There cannot be just one companion species," Haraway observes; "there have to be at least two to make one. It is in the syntax; it is in the flesh."[33] This statement has a wider relevance.

The didactic geography I am describing sets the scene for Michel de Certeau's discussion of control strategies as "actions which, thanks to the establishment of a place of power (the property of a proper), elaborate theoretical places (systems and totalizing discourses) capable of articulating an ensemble of physical places in which forces are distributed."[34] In this definition, domination is achieved by inscribing power through struggles for property, discourse, and place, each entity seeking mastery by means of the others.[35] It is worthwhile to link de Certeau's injunction to analyze power relations in terms of property, discourse, and place to the classification of animals. Edmund Leach has documented "astonishing parallelity between the popular categorizations of space, kinship classification and the differentiated treatment of domestic, farm and wild animals."[36] In short, the classification of animals is related as much to property and kinship relations as it is to the inherent qualities of the species themselves. In this context, the cat can be understood as an animal uniquely traversed by three common binary categories: ostensibly regulated human society versus an ostensibly unregulated wilderness; companionate animals or "familiars" versus wild and edible animals; and private or domestic space versus public space. The cat's present cultural classification identifies it in each case with the first of these binary terms, no matter how unstable the classifications really are. This set of associations with domestication threatens to make any personal identification with cats lead to a subtle self-diminishing in social and professional stature. This "property of a proper" (in de Certeau's language) awakens and empowers the need for women, especially, to stare back at the gaze that so desires to diminish their own property, discourse, and place.[37]

There is another problem with the reference to kinship in this critique of pets, however. "To regard a dog as a furry child, even metaphorically, demeans dogs and children," Haraway insists."[38] Pets are often embraced precisely because the relationship is not familial in a conventional sense. Surveys of American pet owners show that millions of pet owners feel closer to their pet than to their best friends, their children, and their spouses. Pets can take the place of other supplementary or familial figures (often disadvantageously for women's reputations). These issues require us to take seriously the specific historical-political relations that situate our relations with all species, and to interrogate more reflexively the biopolitics and forms of life that shape our interactions with them.

The complicated geometry of cat-human relations is further complicated by the technologies that mediate them. An unknown person takes

Figure 6.5
Two Women with Cats, 1885, cyanotype, George Eastman Museum. Image courtesy of the George Eastman Museum.

a photograph of two women sitting in a backyard with cats. The photograph appears to be taken in the early twentieth century, judging from the women's clothing and the property of the photograph itself. Family snapshots of the time were often cyanotypes, a product akin to a blueprint that was developed in water and that was easy to produce with Kodak film (which may explain why this photograph appears in the archive of Eastman House).[39] In this domestic setting, the merits of the more accessible point-and-shoot cameras are demonstrated together with the readiness to open the door to more modern attitudes toward cats and their relations with women.

By the early twentieth century, cats, like pianos, were part of the ideology and practice of domestic life in many countries. If cats' lives were initially symbiotic with human lives because their hunting abilities helped to control pests in marine and agricultural environments, such attributes are not important to their modern function. Their role now is an affectionate one. Perhaps the public consideration of cats' capacity to hunt and kill rodents and birds would undermine the symbolic regime connecting cats with childhood that emerged in the Victorian era and has so dominated children's culture in the last century. It would also cut into the billions of dollars spent each year on feeding these pets. The acknowledgment of cats' extensive hunting capacities and their decimation of bird populations[40] is an important step toward reanimalizing them and their representation. This is an important countermeasure to the denaturing of cats (and birds, beavers, and other animals) that has become "naturalized" in our culture.

Tactics for countering such control strategies can be therapeutic for deteriorating social relations. The owning of pets whose images are disseminated across the home is an invitation to maintain interspecies connections with pets while altering the boundaries of public and private space. Such tactics are themselves subject to the constraints of established ensembles of physical and discursive power. Given the prohibition I just described, a scholar can accrue legitimacy and esteem in a professional context by talking positively about whales, wolves, horses, or lobsters, even dogs, but not cats. The intensity of negative response to this project when I began my research echoes a prejudice deeply rooted in the history of species relations in the West.

Medium, Resistance, Gender, Cats

In the modern period the cat's role switched from hybrid worker to spirit-demon to pet as a consequence of changes in the social landscape that redefined the roles of animals as violently as those of people. With the growth of industrialism in England and across Europe, city life made it impossible—that is to say, illegal—to keep many species of animals as domestic pets.[41] The pet became defined as a nonworking animal, while other animals worked like slaves in the streets and underground realms of the city and still others never left their stalls until they went to the slaughterhouse. As working and farm animals were forcibly ejected from the domestic sphere, machines replaced both people and animals. The popular embrace of dogs and cats as domestic pets was part of this rationalization process. Human and animal bodies and their meanings were reorganized together by the discursive regime of industrial capitalism. Once nature seemed comfortably under control, pets were safe for middle- and upper-class households to love and embrace. The sense of complacency engendered by this perceived taming of nature helps account for the rage of critical theorists who attack those pet owners. There is no doubt that cats occupy a special place as targets of such rage. There are even bestseller books inciting hatred for cats, albeit countered by far more books advocating love for them. As Kathleen Rogers remarks, "There are no *I Hate Dogs* on the lists."[42]

Figure 6.6
Hipster Kitty Meme, digital image.

Animal taxonomies often endow differences among species with moral, aesthetic, spatial, and political significance. If contempt for domestic pets and the kitsch that surrounds them echoes the modernist antipathy to doors, textures, and domestic interiors, affection for them upholds the home as a rich, creatively made environment. Modernist aesthetics sought to overturn sentiment, tactility, and decoration to achieve new levels of purity and bold simplicity. This was a logical reaction against Victorian culture with its preference for voluptuous enclosure.[43] It also contributed to the spread of glass, concrete, and tar that dominates the urban habitat in which a huge proportion of the world population lives today. The social architecture that designed the contours of interior space has been reconfigured in the vampiric spread of condominiums and high-rise apartment buildings. These spaces are designed to be interchangeable and well connected, presumably so that self-directed underemployed humans can launch their companies online while waiting for a job.

People living in these spaces need proximity to animals just as much as people living in other places on the planet. It is a commonplace that cats do not respect doors and windows, or rather that they are obsessed with them and insist on going in and out of them. They need to inspect and reconstitute their territories. Mirroring their humans' lives online, live cats inhabit not just interiors but also the hallways beyond the doorways, the walls over which they escape, the alleys extending the space down the block. Cats actually traverse a larger scale of exploration than we think, according to Desmond Morris, moving knowledgeably between domains and local geographies with ease.[44]

Henri Lefebvre writes of space:

> Visible boundaries, such as walls or enclosures in general, give rise for their part to an appearance of separation between spaces where in fact what exists is an ambiguous continuity. The space of a room, bedroom, house or garden may be cut off in a sense from social space by barriers and walls, by all the signs of private property, yet still remain fundamentally part of that space. Nor can such spaces be considered empty "mediums" [sic], in the sense of containers distinct from their contents.[45]

For Lefebvre, too, a space or medium means nothing apart from its mediation with other places. This passage resembles the thought practice of a cat. Just as wolves and lions survive in the wild, cats who get through the door must survive in the 'hood, expertly defying its boundaries and dangers. The jazz iconography of urban "cool cats" refers to the bravery and wiliness needed to negotiate the metropolis at night. This capacity was significant to the African American jazz musicians who embraced the term. Cool cats wander and hunt, cruising the urban wilderness while beguiling other cats and a few members of the human population, and they cannot be trained or herded. Cool cats reconcile urban life with animal spirits. Only humans can match (or suppress) the capacity of cats to master the entries and exits that constitute and divide these spaces. Rather than having to stand in for whatever fantasy of the wild animal we humans need in order to other ourselves from it, these human-cat networks represent the interconnectedness of all animality, including our own, in the digital-urban wilderness. The circulation of Internet images acquires clearer meanings in the context of new interspecies interconnectedness forced upon us by the vicissitudes of urban life.

Studies in Iconography

To the extent that they are horizontal, costumed, or flirtatious, cats online confirm through hyperbole their association with traditional perceptions of women and children. The visual aesthetic of Internet portraiture is nonetheless slightly ironic and overtly digital. By expressing a self-conscious knowledge of photographic codes, these images distance and yet reinforce the efficacy of these same codes. In disposition they stand somewhere between pink flamingos, with their archly decorative camp suburban flare, and babies, with their direct innocent gaze and floppy bodies. Cats require no decoration, for cats are decorative all by themselves, and if you add a ruffle or prop to the image of a cat—poof! You have kitsch. Semiotically, the photographs embrace and yet distance us from their subject, which makes them peculiarly appropriate for electronic messaging. Posed in various settings and enduring the occasional costume, the cats test the distance they and their owners have traversed from their animal natures. The proliferation of images suggests a sense of anxiety about this displacement, and the photographers' fetish of feline bodies tests the evidence for the coexistence of digitality and life.

In writing of the longing evoked by the photograph, Roland Barthes claims that we can know the impossibility of the real in photographic representation but nevertheless feel its presence.[46] The link between the photograph and what it represents remains intelligible, and he resolves to "make myself the measure of photographic 'knowledge.'"[47] In his analysis the photographic punctum produces a momentary chasm between the representational and the real that gives rise to moments of genuine feeling and recognition. In Barthes's writing, photographs are never interchangeable with their referent or perceived to stand in for the real. The ambiguous relation with their subject is part of their poignant affect, creating a space for a sense of remembrance and loss, as Barthes discovers by looking at a photograph of his mother as a child. In this light, photographing animals makes explicit that the token or ambiguous objecthood of representation is conjoined only momentarily with a sense of the real; it offers a bridge between the lives before and behind the screen, and even (though we do not want to make this connection too mechanical) a simultaneous experiencing of the cognitive self and the animal self.

We are animals looking at pictures of (nonhuman) animals. The denaturalized animal photograph simultaneously evokes and distances the sense of shared animal self. What is the source of this ambivalence? Sarah Kember describes photography as

> a mechanism of knowledge and power which allows the subject to compensate for a perceived loss, absence or threat in the object world and for the feelings of anxiety, fear or despair which are thereby provoked. This may include a loss of power over the object, the absence of a loved one or the threat of difference. A photograph is a small, tangible object, a trophy or token which defies the passing of time and insists on the presence of that which it depicts. It offers up a scene or event to perpetual scrutiny and immortalizes the subject's perspective.[48]

The cat photographers invite their subjects to insist on their own presence, and as these digital kitties romp their way through the Internet they convey a touch of indifference to the viewer's power of scrutiny or moment of affective investment. The failure of these pictures to fulfill the sensuous connection between "pet" as noun and "pet" as verb contributes to this on/off affect. Their photographic "performance" evokes their viewers' desire for intimate connection which is invited by the presence of the animal and blocked by its status as an interface. The cat holds out the promise of bursting through that window and achieving that intimate connection. Kevin Robins once described image technologies as modernism's defense mechanism against "the fear of being touched by the unknown."[49] Together with their photographers, these digital cats allay this fear through their symbolic connection to domestic spaces that still resist being morphed together digitally into the unknown.

Internet images free the cats photographed by the people who own them to wander and to flourish in the digital spaces of everyday life. As they travel through cyberspace, they metonymically reference their owners and even more their owners' homes. The Internet cat leaves behind but also references the conventionally circumscribed cat space running from the upholstered chair to the tabletop to the front door to the window and even (if permitted) the neighbor's back lawn. *Home* is understood as the

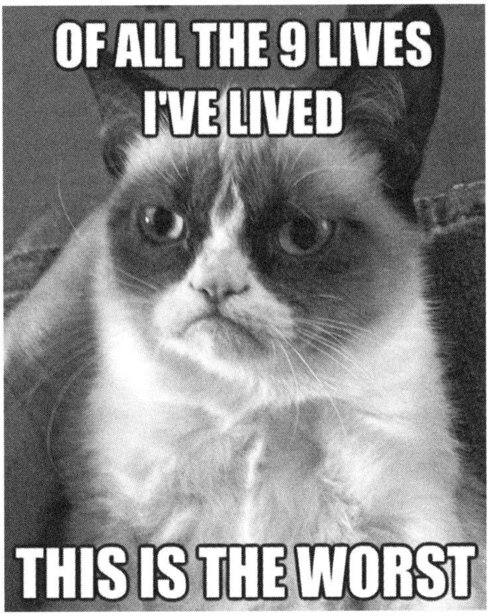

Figure 6.7
Grumpy Cat Meme, digital image.

product of people living with pets and pets living with people, forming a spatially accommodated "family unit" comprised of multiple species. They create their territory through daily practice while at the same time, if their human lives are like those of a growing number of people in the world, they prepare to depart that territory on demand. This relatively mobile co-species habitation seems increasingly indispensable to the specificity and meaning of "home"; the more unstable that meaning or place might be, the more important the presence of the cat. By their intrepid referencing of these contexts, digital cats help to constitute and connect the landscapes that surround us and flow into and through the Internet.

The formation of home as a private domestic space contributed significantly to the development of the modern human subject. The adoption of and care for domestic animals was felt to enhance the unique moral and cognitive qualities through which humans distinguished themselves from other animals. Modern humans claim a special place in the universe by denying their bestial nature; the keeping of pets is a good illustration of human compassion no matter what is happening to other animals. Those described as resembling animals (such as the aboriginal, the nonwhite, the enslaved, the lusty, the demonstrators in Ferguson, or the mentally ill) are

Comrade Jessie rejecting patriarchal rules on female decency.

Figure 6.8
Comrade Jessie Rejecting Patriarchal Rules on Female Decency, Cats Against Capitalism, June 2018.

deemed to be not human but not tame either, that is to say, not deserving of compassion, dignity, or rights. The term "posthumanist" communicates for some the recognition that speciesism has been fundamental to the formation of Western subjectivity and its own forms of violence. If the European empire was founded on a cultural taxonomy of unacknowledged racism and colonialism, as Edward Said so powerfully demonstrates,[50] Western history was also founded on categorical moral distinctions between human and nonhuman animals that has helped to orchestrate those differences and struggles. But anyone, even the nonwhite, the queer, or the disabled, can live with a cat, as long as it is permitted in the lease.

What Is at Stake?

The dominant question posed by animals throughout the West, reaching its peak with the ascendancy of industrialization, was not how to understand animals, but how to dominate and use them. A commonplace truth about cats is that they are never completely tamed; they retain traces of the wild, residues of independence and guiltlessness no matter how domestic they become. These qualities drew artists, writers, and others to live with them before they were more widely accepted as domestic pets. There may be some projection in the readiness with which women and children are associated with cats on the basis of their presumed shared qualities of animal spirits, sexuality, and guile.[51] If something as sensuous and domesticated as a cat can retain aspects of its species nature, then perhaps those of us associated with cats have not lost ours. Is this a good thing? There is a lot of violence as well as sentiment and sensuality in the history of human interactions with cats. As domesticated animals, cats allow us to feel good about ourselves, but only if our feelings and practices really are good-natured.

Urban dwellers romanticize and distance themselves from wolves and lobsters while their spaces of inhabitation rot and shrink. But cats are for better or for worse a permanent part everyday urban ecology today. Just as

Figure 6.9
Comparing phones after a meeting, Absinthe Cafe, York University, 2011, Alan Weiss. The middle phone and its cat are property of the author. Image courtesy of the photographer.

angels were imagined and designed to oscillate between the transcendental and the corporeal, so Internet cats oscillate between live and virtual, inside and outside, wild and tame, fascinating and routine, calming and disruptive, work and play, discipline and sabotage, predator and prey. These cats encourage but do not guarantee a more reflexive understanding of how we inhabit domestic and urban spaces, and of the precarious economic and environmental situations facing so many of the people who live in them. The cats being messaged across cyberspace speak to and from these charged places, and challenge the hierarchies between classes of people as well as between people and animals. I read their message, however sweet, sardonic, silly, or sentimental, as a hopeful one. Cats stop, Jean-François Lyotard suggests, "at thresholds that we do not see, where they sniff some 'present beyond.'"[52]

7 "That Old Familiar Tweet Tweet Tweet": Birdsong, Music, Affect, Extinction

Prelude and Fugues

Jordan, Ontario, is located in the midst of Canada's Niagara Peninsula, a region known for its wines and waterfalls. The countryside was quiet and bright with snow when I went to visit a hotel-spa there after my mother died. I signed up for a reviving treatment. The massage therapist put on a soothing soundtrack that featured the call of a loon mixed with piano music, sea gull cries, and the rhythmic crashing of an ocean wave against the shore. The soundscape was intended to make me calm and relaxed, but it had the opposite effect. "No," said my mother's voice, never shy of an opinion. She was always attuned to the sound of the loons at dusk calling across the lake. "Stop," she would say, "listen," and we did. "This can't be right," said her opinion. "Do loons even belong next to seagulls?" I learned later that it can happen with young loons wandering near a coastline, or when gulls raid garbage dumps located near a lake. The gull/loon duet occurs when nature veers off course, in other words, and there I was listening to a CD entitled something like "Beautiful Nature, Birds, and Music: A Soundtrack for Perfect Relaxation."

I found this listening experience distracting, not only because of the irritating blandness of the genre, but also because of the disconnection between species and spaces on which it relies. My sense of spatial anomaly disrupted a moment that was being carefully orchestrated to convey the harmony of nature. I resented this pretty sonic heterotopia for its pretense of innocence and its emotional manipulation. The realistic, cleanly digitalized sound of birds is adapted to its present purpose of helping listeners to imagine being in that space, seeing these birds, smelling the saltwater waves. If life is rushing you, the music murmurs, the birds can bring you back to yourself. For this psychic recovery to occur, though, there is a price: you will mimic the way the birds' voices have been severed from their *Umwelten*, and disconnect from the world around you and many of its meanings. To become human again you must grow closer to nature, but to do this, you must forgo any knowledge of a predigital nature. With my mother's voice in my ear, I failed to enact my part in this unwritten contract. This chapter is about that moment, and what led up to it, and all the things it might mean.

Hearing digital renditions of animal sounds is an increasingly common sonic experience. Birds can be heard singing and chirping in a range of spaces and social situations, from spas and therapeutic spaces to satellite music streams, cell phone apps, and Twitter. Rather than conveying inside life out into the wider world, like the Internet cats described in chapter 6, these soundtracks bring inside a purified version of life outdoors. My parents had a bird clock in their kitchen with twelve different birds that chirped one an hour, a mnemonic tool for identifying birdsong by attaching sounds to pictures of the species. It was a sweet concept, if ineffective. The technology seems hundreds of generations ago now, an object with poor sound quality made at the time when the aesthetic and spatial convergences of nature and digitality were just beginning. The decision to mix a loon with a seagull, a synthesizer, and a recording of ocean waves was the outcome of a longer history of sound recording developed in connection with changing ideas about nature, music, and meaning.

My analysis of this recording history is indebted to Jonathan Sterne's distinction between technology and media. To become active as media, he writes, "technologies [have] to be articulated to institutions and practices."[1] Similarly, for ethnomusicologist Steven Feld, musical sounds "communicate through and about acoustic patterns," but "they are socially organized to do far more, by modulating special categories of sentiment and action when brought forth and properly contexted by features of staging

Figure 7.1
CD covers of birdsongs, 2017, screenshot.

and performance."[2] Feld and Sterne regard the transmission of meaning through sound to be based in the articulation of diverse practices to one another in specific circumstances that are defined, expressed, and changed through musical performance. In other words, as John Shepherd puts it, all music is social text; "a viable understanding of culture requires an understanding of its articulation through music just as much as a viable understanding of music requires an understanding of its place in culture."[3] These musicological insights are important to understanding the processes being described not just in this chapter but throughout this book.

In the following pages I explore how birdsong came to be embedded in recorded music like the soundtrack I heard in Jordan, Ontario. I extend Shepherd's analysis of how culture is articulated through music, and how music is articulated through culture, to consider how human and nonhuman music are articulated throughout this process. Shaped by this history, soundtrack producers perform an expert extraction of pleasure and economic value from the bodies and voices of animals. A number of distinct paths have come together to create this cultural genre of nature or new age music. The history of Western musical thought has been sharply serrated with debates about representationalism in music. Next to this history and only sometimes intersecting it, the history of sound recording has drawn extensively on military innovations brought within the reach of musicologists and ornithologists. Following another trail, the poetic association of birdsong, flight, freedom, and loss so important to nineteenth-century poetry and aesthetics influenced Rachel Carson's transformation of "nature writing" following her experience of a poisoned silent spring. In yet another pathway, knowledge of the endangerment and extinction of species was first presented to a public audience in the early twentieth century with research on extinction in bird populations. These events have complicated the experience of listening to birdsong and the enterprise of recording it. For some notable sound-making bird species, recordings are all that is left of them.

Following this multitrack recording's multitrack genealogy allows us to identify how these strains of music, scientific research, and poetry began to merge in listening to the sounds of nature. The eloquence of Carson's writing cannot be separated from this convergence. Her book *Silent Spring*, published just months before Honeywell's launch of its menagerie with the chimp made of computer parts, was an unprecedented contribution to public science writing that combined an ode to the fragile beauty of nature, anger at her fellow scientists, and irrefutable evidence of harm. By attacking the widespread popular faith in chemicals, and more broadly science's good faith in modifying the natural world, and by expecting scientists to follow a different ethical path, Carson incited a rupture in American culture. These themes appear in a different register in the therapeutic soundtracks dedicated to self-care in the age of virtual menageries. Here, the self's primordial responsibility is to heal oneself outside of the logic of progressive and measured time that produced the need for such therapy in the first place, and animals provide an appropriately biopolitical solution.

Of all species, birds are the most common mediators between people and wildlife. There is still no habitable place on earth that does not have birds (at least at the time of writing), no place where children will not see birds waddle or fly. As symbols birds have long tested the boundaries between human and nonhuman species. In Greek mythology, they were linked to Apollo and signs of prophecy, while centuries later, in Edgar Allan Poe's famous poem, the raven's voice spells doom. In some Indigenous stories, ravens helped to create the world; in many, ravens are tricksters who turn everything inside out and challenge us to face the consequences. This wily agent has power at the beginning, the imploding middle, and the end of the world. The Cornell Institute of Ornithology recently evoked this bird's mythic power by naming their new sound recording software Raven. This Raven digital trickster captures and mixes the worlds of sound we hear on nature soundtracks such as the one I just described. Ravens are not particularly musical birds, but like their cousins the crows they are celebrities in ethology and social media, where observation of them has done a great deal to shift how people think of birds. Whatever Cartesian science said an animal cannot do—tool use, language, memory, emotion, face recognition, problem solving, sequencing, intelligent play—you can watch ravens and crows accomplish on social media. A homemade video that went viral in 2016 showed a crow sliding down a snowy rooftop on the lid of a yogurt container, carrying the lid to the top, and sliding down again. This activity displayed intention and planning as part of the bird's capacity to play. In the extended digital feedback loop in which crows can ski and ravens can make sound recordings, the lines drawn by modern epistemologies to divide humans from animals are unraveling.[4]

Human cultures have always mimicked as well as exploited animal bodies; today, it is broadly acknowledged that nonhuman animals are sentient (notwithstanding recent directives by the British government),[5] that they can be expressive and creative, that they make choices, and that they mediate our relations, not only with animals but also with each other, and not only with each other but also with our selves. As this chapter shows, birds implode our humanist presumptions and contribute to the natureculture assemblage being imagined in the work of theorists, writers, filmmakers, artists, and musicians in recent years. In its initial relationship with birds, Western science lifted them from their mythic contexts and redefined them as instinctive biological machines. This hierarchical paradigm crumbles when we begin to experience ourselves as imperfect machines imploded by the technologically enhanced speed and compulsions of everyday life. Humans are ironically now being situated as functional or not so functional machines requiring recalibration through solace from the artistry of birds.

Animal songs have been part of human music throughout the world "for at least as long as written records can tell us."[6] Humans arguably learned to speak as well as to sing from listening to birds. Scientists find that on close examination the human language "resembles the speech forms of two other animals on the planet: birds and nonhuman primates."[7] This hypothesis, published in *Frontiers in Psychology*, explains that listening to birds led to the creation of the melodic part of human language, while listening to other primates helped our human ancestors to develop and express more complex meanings. As a result, "linguists and biologists are speculating that our speech evolved with the help of chirping birds, or birdsong, and some of the alarm calls of monkeys."[8] These sounds evolved to form the syntaxes and expressive qualities of human language.[9] Learning more about bird and primate languages and their capacity for variation, expression, and meaning opens the door to different kinds of listening and reconfigures our bonds with other species.

Today, however, children are unlikely to learn the language of birds because they spend too little time outside. In the first page of his 2015 book *Thumbelina: The Culture and Technology of Millennials*, French philosopher Michel Serres names the absence of contact with live animals as the first defining feature of this generation.[10] Picture books, robotic toys and pets, and children's television supply voices for animals that only seem to speak for themselves. The more interactive toys become, the less they are likely to encourage knowledge of the richness and complexity of animal sounds and the less likely these children are to miss a particular animal or bird sound when it is gone. I am not saying that the only way to learn about animals is to have a direct encounter with them. As composer John Adams argues, it's no good telling people that ecological listening experiences can only be found outdoors. "My music is going inexorably from being about place to *becoming* place," he explains.[11] Mind you, one cannot walk through that sonic space and feel the wind or face the predator or miss the species that have disappeared. What kinds of virtual experiences do these soundscapes create? Before turning to the sound objects themselves, it is useful to this mediological project to learn more about their history.

Whose Music?

For centuries, Western art music was shaped and disciplined by the drive to expel animal sounds from musical expression. The expulsion of impure sounds was explained by the musicological premise that music should not be pictorial or representational. The drive to eliminate all imitation preoccupied musical aesthetics in the late eighteenth century. "One can hear clocks strike, ducks quack, frogs croak, and soon one will be able to hear a flea sneeze and the grass growing," complained the critic Johann Adam Hiller in 1754.[12] The anti-anthropomorphic premise Hiller is advancing is that art should not be representational or pictorial, but rather should aspire to be autonomous, and its aesthetic value measured by its success in pursuing this objective. It should bear no relation to clocks or ducks or singing birds, even to the mechanical singing birds that were then favorite possessions among the music-listening elite. As Edward Lippmann explains, "The last few decades of the century witnessed an increasing emphasis on the expressive aspect of music and the unequivocal discard of imitation as an aesthetic principal. Yet we have to think of the controversy over imitation as a perennial one that continued in some form, as issues tend to do in aesthetics, well beyond what seem to be a definitive outcome."[13] The relationship between imitation and expression has been revisited again and again, assuming new dimensions with changing musical practices, concepts of representation, and recording technologies.

If eighteenth-century critics insisted on distinguishing between expression and imitation, they could not agree on what imitation was, or even whether that was something that music actually did. When musicologist Boyé "turns to the wording of birds and to the sounds of inanimate objects, such as the wrestling of leaves ... he finds it absurd to claim that music can imitate either of these."[14] If music is nonrepresentational by its very nature, that is to say, if it cannot be engaged in imitation, then it is not possible to imitate a duck and it would be more accurate to say that music creates resemblances, analogies, or emotional experiences (what used to be called "musical pathologies," or emotional effects) in response to the idea or subject being represented. Whether imitation was something that music could not or should not do, this controversy did not challenge deeply ethnocentric and anthropocentric aesthetic principles, enabling critics to demonstrate their authority by defending their aesthetic preferences as

Figure 7.2
Automaton Movement with Two Singing Birds, 1865. Image courtesy of Reuge: The Art of Mechanical Music.

laws derived from the principles of art. As Shepherd and coauthors write in *Whose Music*, "The workings of the musical process" in this literature "tend to be conceived as absolute, permanent and ultimately discoverable beyond the vagaries of human thought and perception because such an approach aids mystification and so role-security."[15] The tradition they are addressing defined music both ethnocentrically and anthropocentrically, which describes indignant critics like Hiller in a nutshell.[16]

Little did Hiller and his fellow critics realize that in the future listeners uncommitted to such principles would pay good money to hear birds chirping and quacking in musical contexts. In the meantime, no matter how much music critics debated whether music could or should illustrate anything external to it, birds continued to sneak into its creation. In fact, bird songs remained "the most common objects of musical illustration," according to musicologist Peter Kivy, who revisited this controversy in the 1980s.[17] Kivy maintains that bird songs are not music, but rather "natural sounds that are 'very like music.'" He concedes that bird sounds differ from the croaks or "inarticulate cries" of other wild creatures, but insists nevertheless that birds do not sing, and their songs are not music.[18] His proof is that you can't notate birdsong in the well-tempered scale of Western music. (That's funny. Actually birdsong was often notated this way in the nineteenth century, before the advent of sound-recording technology.) In this later reworking of aesthetic principles, composers could create music from the sounds of birds so long as they didn't just imitate them. As composer and ornithologist Emily Doolittle explains it, "The sounds of the animal songs were secondary to the human structure and narrative, and the intervention of the human composer was considered necessary to turn them into music."[19] This is a prescriptively anthropocentric formula, in which humans can appropriate anything from nature but must purify their language of animal referents even as they open the door to them. One can trace a fairly direct path from this aesthetic principle to the virtual menageries described in this book in that they make access to the digital the precondition for access to the experience of the animal. In the case of classical composition, musical instruments must not sound like animals, even (or especially) when they are made from animal parts. The voice must be purified of the nonhuman or racialized body, and the human soul purified of all traces of the animal. Similarly, animal bodies are referenced and marginalized in the choreography of fantasy works like Tchaikovsky's *Swan Lake* or Stravinsky's *Firebird Suite*, which barely resembles the movements of a bird.[20] These artists appropriate a gesture while diminishing its animality, visibly disciplining their own movement in the process so that it remains clearly human, i.e., defined and approved by appropriate aesthetic and social principles. Seeing this mimicry or extraction at work is a reminder that the human body is never fully or autonomously human; it is always supplemented, always necessarily but problematically appropriating the powers of the animal and the machine.

Other twentieth-century composers turned away from the ideal of self-generating musical evolution to investigate different kinds of listeners. Erik Satie enshrined this idea in music history, writing:

> We must bring about a music which is like furniture—a music, that is, which will be part of the noises of the environment, will take them into consideration. I think of it as melodious, softening the noises of the knives and forks, not dominating them, not imposing itself. It would fill up those heavy silences that sometimes fall between friends dining together. It would spare them the trouble of paying attention to their own banal remarks. And at the same time, it would neutralize the street noises which so indiscreetly enter into the play of conversation. To make such music would be to respond to a need.[21]

Satie's call for a music that harmonizes with listeners' everyday lives challenges the heroism and complexity of the Western canon and the way it demands rapt attention and silence from its listeners, but he is not challenging its anthropocentrism. Satie's manifesto-like statement nevertheless evokes an unavoidable analogy between furniture, indoor music, and the birdcages with songbirds inside that so often adorned these same interiors.

When Kivy published his stern guide to the human species' unique musicality, bird watchers and scientists had been researching birdsong for years. Since there was no interdisciplinary education for Anglo-American musicology, Kivy knew nothing of these developments, and he stepped inadvertently into a century of controversy. Having spent much of his life observing and making notes about birds, Charles Darwin concluded that "the taste for beautiful music was more consistent among birds than among human savages."[22] While venerated as the founder of evolutionary biology, Darwin firmly rejected the belief that birds sing only for instinctive or functional reasons and lack aesthetic inclinations. In his book *Why Birds Sing*, naturalist and composer David Rothenberg reminds his readers of Darwin's belief in the musicality of birds (while of course rejecting the racist comparison). For Rothenberg, the view that birds sing solely for mating and territorial purposes and thus are not making music is an overly reductive functionalist analysis. Birdsong is more than a simple routine, he insists, and nature is not a business.[23] (At least, not for the birds.)

I encountered another version of this controversy about instinct and expression in birds when I witnessed a murmuration, that miraculous cloud of starlings that forms and dissolves and reforms as it soars and twists over the fields. I was driving a rental car toward Lancaster, Pennsylvania, for a conference on affect theory. The sight was so stunning that I pulled off the road and together with my travel companions watched the birds in speechless awe. Ah yes, said conference attendees when I told them about it, the birds are getting ready to migrate. This magical performance evoked the commonsense view of the functional, more or less mechanical obligations of the birds, even among scholars dedicated to a posthumanist study of affect, sensation, and aesthetics. This quasi-scientific myopia about birds' capacities reappeared a few months later when I attended a film screening of Albert Hitchcock's movie *The Birds*. The guest commentator, a psychologist and animal behaviorist, proposed that Hitchcock's birds had nothing to do with real birds. Birds are clever, but not intelligent, he insisted; they possess no psychic or metaphysical capabilities, and they do not learn, create, or plan to act together, even in a murmuration. In this case, the incapacity to escape the reductivist view of animal instinct can be seen as a legacy of scientists' rejection of teleaesthesia at the turn of the last century. As Lisa Blackman writes:

> Teleaesthesia was defined as "perception at a distance or power of vision transcending time and space" (Bingham Newland, 1916: 189). In other words, instincts were not simply hard-wired biological drives, to be understood by physiology, but represented complex systems of communication or affective transfer, which were shared, transmitted and co-constituted between members of species. Thus, the idea of telepathic rapport, or action at a distance, was a common way to understand communication processes, whether the discussion was focused on machines, animals, insects, humans or technologies. The idea of telepathic transfer largely became discredited, overtaken by an increasing focus on what were billed as more rational communication processes. These were represented in the psychological sciences by concepts such as the attitude (see Rose, 1985). However, arguably the cultural fantasies conveyed by telepathic transfer have refused to go away.[24]

The Smithsonian Institution reports that research on telepathic transfer has returned, but this time experiments are being conducted with the intermediary aid of digital technology.[25] One hopes that the electrodes being implanted in a bird's brain will be an improvement over the way they were once inserted into a cat's skull to measure the transfer of sound in research preliminary to the invention of the telephone.[26] These stories illustrate how hard our institutions and discourses work to contain what we hear or see within established structures of truth. People working in different research disciplines have professional stakes in preferring their own explanations for what animals feel, sense, or do. The human sciences often defer to the evolutionary biologists when it comes to questions of species differentiation, intelligence, and feeling. Keeping a "rational" or anthropocentric grip on sense and meaning plays an important role in distinguishing between music and noise. By confounding the assumption that aesthetic sensibility is confined to humans, birdsong confuses the aesthetic distinction between music and noise. Just as W. J. T. Mitchell asks us "What do pictures want?," we can ask "What do these sonic objects want us to hear?"[27]

The Ears of Science

How sounds come to us and what we think they mean result from a complex set of agencies and relationships. A review of musicology's history will not tell us how birdsong became a sought-after part of music. Even when listeners could notate the songs, they weren't widely accepted as music. Automata or mechanical singing birds, exquisite devices that were made and collected as early as the Middle Ages, could imitate birdsong, composers could draw inspiration from birdsong, poets could write odes to songbirds, and people could keep caged songbirds in their homes, but birdsong was not thought of as meaningful communication or expression on its own terms.

Researchers in the nineteenth century used musical notation to transcribe them because it was the easiest and quickest way to describe and study what they heard. For these researchers, it was not a matter of adapting music to the vocalizations of the birds (the idea to which Hiller so strongly objected) so much as it was identifying the sonic details of birdsong by translating what they heard into the grammar of Western notation. Over time, researchers abandoned the musical score in favor of simpler graphic forms that were more conducive to their scientific goals.[28] With the arrival of sound-recording devices, ornithologists and civilians began to record the sounds of birds directly, first in laboratories where birds were kept in cages, and then, when recording technology made it possible, out in the field. They used this technology to learn to identify an individual bird or species through its sound, to discover "the limits of each vocalization," as Bernie Krause puts it in *The Great Animal Orchestra*. This research was mainly taxonomical rather than semiotic or aesthetic. The goal was to isolate and analyze each bird's sonic output and to identify it with a specific species, kind of like my parents' clock, rather than to understand it in reference to other entities or activities present in the bird's environment.

Figure 7.3
Tanner with Parabola, 1935. Courtesy of the Albert Rich Brand papers, #21-18-899, Division of Rare and Manuscript Collections, Cornell University Library.

When men went into the fields or forests in those dawn recording raids, they were in pursuit of sounds, not music. Few of them would have denied the magic of finding and hearing the birds; even fewer would have been able to ignore the competitive urgency of having ever more precise ways of locating, identifying, capturing, and comparing the songs they heard. For this purpose they needed recording technology that could eliminate the "noise" from the birds' environments. By the 1920s, such researchers had access to parabolic dish microphones left over from World War I that were able to find and isolate the sound of the bird separately from its sonic environment. They used these more focused recordings to explore how birds learn to sing, when they sing, and how their dialects differ from one place to another. Their recordings made it possible to ascertain which birds varied their tunes more than others, and in what situations.[29]

World War II bequeathed another technology that would be important for bird science: the sonogram. In 1940, early in the war, researchers at the

Bell Telephone Laboratories set out to develop methods for making sonic details *visible*. Their efforts were driven by "the need to monitor movements of ships and submarines, analyzing their far-traveling ocean-born sounds, each with its own particular signature."[30] This research made it possible to isolate and translate sound into visual information, so that personnel could "see" storms that were not visual objects. The goal to visualize data drove research practice in fields as diverse as meteorology, as I have documented in earlier research, medicine, satellite exploration, and ornithology.[31] As is often the case, technologies developed for military use shook off their associations with death once they found new purpose in the civilian world. Recording technologies designed to focus on the isolation and comparison of individual sounds became increasingly mobile and precise. As Krause recollects, "In a short time, the recording world became dominated by digital recording systems, moving from complex, heavy, and power dependent technologies to extremely light versatile and high-quality handheld models." He adds, "Each time I think I have a version of the ultimate system, I'm seduced by a new and better one."[32] Seduced by the results of these long-distance recording technologies, bird recordists made few whole-habitat recordings; they were virtually unheard of when Krause began field recordings in the late 1960s. "Rather," he writes, "sound fragmentation—acoustic snapshots of solo animals, like those in my nightmare—remained the dominant field recording model from the onset of the craft."[33] Such hauntings and nightmares appear frequently in this literature.[34]

Krause came to the forest as a music producer, not an ornithologist; this background inspired him to hear habitats holistically and to record them with stereo microphones in 3D sound.[35] Describing the forest soundscape as an "animal orchestra" was not a metaphor for Krause. But the recording practice of isolating single voices was already well established. Even today, the Sound Archive of the British Library catalogs and shelves its collection of birdsong recordings separately from those of their habitats. These archives invite us to listen to birds as though their songs bear no relation to who or what is near them, just as photographs of fish are photoshopped, as Stacy Alaimo has shown, to eliminate the organisms around them that fish must eat to survive.[36] This evaporation of habitat is the usual condition for the appearance of the animal in these virtual menageries. We hear birds as disembodied voices detached from their habitats, their food, their enemies, and one another, as though they are singing just for us—which is odd when you consider that the belief in the nonaesthetic functionalism of their warbling presupposes interactions among birds and with other species that are embedded in territory.

Using ever-improving technologies of translation, sound recordists have taught us a great deal about birds. They have demonstrated that many bird species are not born with their songs but learn them; that some species vary their songs more than others; and that there are regional dialects and inexplicable repetitions. Some birds sing not only to accomplish instinctual and evolutionary functions, like attracting mates or defending territories, but also because they love to sing, embellish, repeat, mimic, and vary, that is to say for something like aesthetic reasons, or for reasons we don't understand. A sedge warbler, for instance, "has as many as fifty recognizable elements in a song and draws on them almost at random to pour out long streams of songs which virtually never repeat themselves."[37] The knowledge that they "virtually never repeat themselves" could only come from a digital comparison of field recordings. Each bird has a slightly different voice, so that birds can learn to recognize the voices of neighboring birds, along with their mates and their chicks, and to distinguish them from other birds.[38]

The desire to capture sounds more accurately drove the development and commercial adaptation of new technologies and sound techniques, often from military research trajectories, which in turn have stimulated the creation of new audiences and markets. To make the "nature soundtracks" so popular today, birds are recorded separately or simulated digitally and remixed with other sounds to create the being-in-nature listening experience. The bird's natural habitat is simulated through sound mixing (adding ocean waves or piano noodling, always in major chords) in direct reversal of the way that its song was produced as a sound object, first by caging the bird, then by building beautiful automata with mechanical singing birds, then by recording its sound, and then by reproducing that sound with Raven software. Most listeners listen to birdsong singularly or collectively without recognizing or understanding the particular voices or their inflections. Indeed, some people may enjoy listening to these "nature CDs" for precisely that reason. Birds are "others" because we cannot interpret their meaning, because they make beautiful sound that does not speak to us in our language, and of course because we cannot fly. Like world music, from whose global popularity the market in nature music partially derives, their sounds seem to transcend our distance from birds and speak to our longing for harmony and hope in nature and in art. As scientists continue to enter their habitats and research their songs, we might be feeling other things. Habitats are shrinking and soon birds will have no hiding places. Will we hear this in their songs?

And No Birds Sing: The Poetry of Loss

O what can ail thee, knight-at-arms,
Alone and palely loitering?
The sedge has withered from the lake,
And no birds sing.
John Keats, "La Belle Dame Sans Merci," 1819

In John Keats's poem, a voluptuous evocation of love and death, the birds' silence is a metaphor for loss. This metaphor performs what literary critics call a natural fallacy; it symbolizes human feeling with images of nature. We all know this conceit, having heard so many songs about blue skies and love, raindrops and tears.[39] Rachel Carson's earth-shattering 1962 book *Silent Spring* takes Keats's romantic phrase as its epigraph. Spurred by the disturbing realization that birds had stopped singing around the waterways she was exploring, Carson revealed that dichlorodiphenyltrichloroethane (DDT) was being unloaded on consumers. DDT was the first modern insecticide, developed in the 1940s by military researchers seeking to combat malaria and typhus, and its use as a pesticide was poisoning the earth, the water, and many species of birds and other animals. Her readers were shocked to discover that when they poisoned the earth with chemicals, the chemicals could bite them back.

Carson was devastated not only by the silence of the birds but also by the readiness of her fellow scientists to break their objects of study into manageable bits, which allowed them to overlook the links between birds, habitats, and the poison entering the earth and water. Like Krause, she was haunted by a nightmare: her fellow scientists' refusal to know. "The shadow of sterility," she wrote, "lies over all the bird studies and indeed lengthens to include all living things within its potential range."[40] Her book ignited a storm of public controversy. She was described as "some kind of agricultural propagandist in the employ of the Soviet Union," accused of being a "communist sympathizer, and dismissed as a spinster with an affinity for cats."[41] The public relations war that followed the publication of her book was unleashed upon her as she was dying of cancer, almost certainly a consequence of her research activities.

Carson was the most controversial but not the first scientist to address birds in relation to environmental risk. In 1905, Walter Rothschild, a student of Charles Darwin, presented the first public systematic account of animal extinction. His lecture, "On Extinct and Vanishing Birds," was delivered at the 4th Ornithological Congress in 1905.[42] Like Carson, Rothschild saw these endangered birds as the so-called "canaries in the coal mine," meaning that the coal mine was already expanding to encompass the planet. By 1920, "the scientific foundations of extinction were firm enough that the issue could be recast as a political problem, subject not only to inexorable natural laws but to the interventions and choices made by societies."[43] Carson was nonetheless the first public science writer to associate science explicitly with poison and death. Seeing that the pesticides were creating more harm than good, Carson "quite self-consciously decided to write a book calling into question the paradigm of scientific progress that defined postwar American culture."[44] "Silent Spring," the title of the chapter on birds, became the title of her book, making the silence of the birds a metonym for the hubris of modern science, much as Keats had made it a metonym for the fragility of love. The book conveyed her findings with a rich, evocative prose that took poetry and nature writing rather than science as its inspiration. It spoke to public feelings as well as scientific practice, and opened the door to what Alex Lockwood describes as "new forms of writing [that] place affect at the very centre of contemporary narratives that call for pro-environmental beliefs and behaviours."[45]

The idea that humans had colonized and poisoned the natural world had arrived in full public view, and it was introduced by the motif of the silent bird. A later book by Mark Jaffe, *And No Birds Sing*, its title echoing both Keats and Carson, explores the mystery surrounding the extinction of birds on the island of Guam. Keats's phrase "and no birds sing" had ceased to be a metaphor.[46] The onset of species extinctions provided a new context for recording birds' songs, but the sonic grammar of recording practice largely remained the same. As a result, the recording of endangered and extinct birds can resemble frozen zoos rather than forests.

Our hearing of recorded natural sound is informed not only by ideas about poetry and music and by technological mediation, but also by ideas about what such technological mediation can do. It is also informed by the anxiety of living in a world in which species are becoming extinct faster than at any time in history, because of us. If we are "lulled" by the sound of them, it is in the dual sense outlined by English dictionaries: "i) to soothe (a person or animal) by soft sounds or motions (esp in the phrase *lull to sleep*); ii) to calm (someone or someone's fears, suspicions, etc), esp by deception."[47] The nature soundtrack offers us a lull in time passing, where if you are lucky, if you are in David Byrne's heaven, you have arrived in a place of deception "where nothing, nothing ever happens."[48]

Before there were CDs and Internet streams, people kept songbirds in cages. Owning a songbird brought the exotic beauty of the colonies into the living room to sing to the owner's sensibility and status.[49] The white myna bird or white starling of Bali, known worldwide for its beautiful singing, is now critically endangered because so many were captured for the caged-bird market. As numbers dropped, their value rose, and they became as valuable as the gilded singing automata now sold as antiques. But the extinction of a bird species is different from the obsolescence of a recording technology. There is nothing left to improve upon it. When all the birds of a species are gone, a sound recording, a drawing or photograph, a set of bones is all we have left of that species. Becoming aware of a life through loss and silence produces melancholy and apprehension in relation to which birdsong is not so much a symbol as an antidote.

Rothenberg writes, "Bird song makes its most attentive human listeners surge into poetry. … We want to stretch beyond its ability to explain, into its chance to evoke."[50] Since birds are more present and more absent to us than before, Rothenberg's "we" in "we want to stretch beyond our ability to explain" seems to be less about transcendence than about the shared experience of capture from which singer and listener long to escape. Scientists who used former military technologies to isolate birds from their sonic habitats in order to construct this sound object were part of the same technical universe that enabled sound recordists to construct purified tracks that could be recombined to emulate the feel of being wrapped in nature. Both practices participate in Latour's "never-been-modern" hybrid condition following modernity's separation and recombination of nature and culture. These networks or assemblages of human and nonhuman agency play a crucial role in the ongoing construction and management of subjectivities for the scientist, the sound producer, the therapist who purchases the CDs or internet services, the patient seeking to relax, as I was when I began this inquiry. Haraway calls upon us to produce what she calls "situated knowledge" when we investigate a phenomenon.[51] Using situated knowledge, we can hear differently the diverse human, animal, and technological agencies in these mixes and also acknowledge the sounds we don't hear. Let us now turn our attention to the patient.

From Bird Science to Human Science

While early twentieth-century bird researchers were creating new tools to study birdsong and sound producers were turning them into sound objects on tape, vinyl, or radio, other researchers were beginning to study people as embodied recipients of these media. There is no evidence that such researchers made explicit links between the precise technological inscription of birdsong and the quantification of physical sensations in listeners, but these processes were occurring at the same time. Scientists sought to "'get below' people's own experiences of electronic media by employing various technologies that measured a range of bodily processes presumably impacted by media use," Brenton Malin writes. "The new media technologies made emotions tangible, the argument went, allowing them to be captured and transmitted with a new kind of power. In the process, emotions themselves came to be seen as particular kinds of mechanical impulses—reflecting the apparatuses through which both media producers and academics attempted to take control of people's emotional lives."[52] These bodies are being examined as conductors or mediums whose "mechanical impulses" respond to or mimic the media experience to which they are exposed. The technologically enhanced confirmation that birds express more than mechanical impulses thus emerged in close proximity to the technologically enhanced realization that human bodies have physical and more or less mechanical responses that, whether they are instinctive or socially produced, can be measured and perhaps adjusted.

Malin describes the ideas guiding this research, an early version of what Horkheimer and Adorno called administrative (as opposed to critical) communication research, as "the new media physicalism." Concepts of musical "pathologies" or emotions were giving way to a more instrumental conceptualization of affect in which human feelings and behaviors could be located, measured, and studied with some of the same methods used in the study of animals. It has been shown that we share the evolution of our language, our anatomies, and our neurological systems with nonhuman species, but humanism continues to posit a difference between animal and human. As animals in this assemblage become less machine-like, humans become more so. This conjunction has the potential to turn humanist aesthetics on its head. Meanwhile it has actualized a huge industry in the dissemination of sales of the kind of soundtrack I heard in the spa in Jordan, Ontario.

Such soundtracks furnish a space in which our own ambivalent affect can be captured, treated, and released. According to one advertisement, "Listeners are set to find our new soundtrack a soothing experience. A recent psychological study found that natural sounds have restorative qualities. Apparently the calls of songbirds and other sounds of nature help people recover much quicker from stressful scenarios compared with the noise of urban living." "It makes sense that people should find birdsong calming," as University of Surrey environmental psychology PhD student Eleanor Ratcliffe, the study's author, explains in the same promotional text.

Elaborating her investigation of the psychological impact of birdsong, Ratcliffe explains: "Songbirds tend to sing when it's safe, and it makes evolutionary sense that we should feel calmer in a safe natural environment." Like the conceptualization of affect, the reference to evolution suggests a closer resemblance between human and bird than was previously permitted. Commenting on this proposed similarity or resonance between species, Eric Clarke writes that "an organism does not have to do complex processing to "decode" the information within the source: it needs to have a perceptual system that will *resonate* to the information."[53]

What ecological listening means to Clarke is quite different from what Ratcliffe (or Krause) is describing. Ratcliffe's research is functionalist, instrumental, and lab-based, making it as innocent of the social implications of interdisciplinary knowledge as Kivy's work on music and birds some thirty years earlier. What Ratcliffe's research on interspecies listening suggests is that humans don't feel safe, which is not surprising. Further, it proposes that humans are evolutionarily programmed to benefit from therapeutic treatment through prescribed, scrupulously edited listening shaped by evolutionary and biofeedback theory. Here birds are the chosen mediators between the science of evolutionary biology and the management of human experience in a culture that no longer makes time for human well-being. In this biopolitical feedback loop, people go to the birds to help deal with a stressful milieu that includes the impending silence of extinction and unexpressed fear and human self-loathing.

Nature recordings and apps have become hugely successful in recorded music sales and a favorite resource in affective self-management. By identifying and collaborating with creative expression in nonhuman species like birds, such recordings have the capacity to destabilize the categorical separation of human and animal, while at the same time enacting the technologies of personal self-governance that help us stay human and productive.

Encounters with birds on tape or with animals in film draw the listener's attention toward nonhuman bodies. Their expressions are captured by increasingly precise technologies that channel and contain our shared life with all its precarity.[54] Depending on the context, this presence can enhance or undermine our habitual sense of human superiority. Human and nonhuman circle one another searching for "an as yet unidentified coexistence," as Philip Warnell puts it; "These shamanic advents for the spirits of repressed animality are implicit in the production of animal form and performing figuration."[55] Coming to life, coming to technology, are reconciled through this experience now and for some unwritten future.

Figure 7.4
Dawn Chorus, 2017, screenshot. App designed by Carnegie Museum of Natural History and The Innovation Studio. Illustrations by Sam Ticnor.

The discovery of the aesthetic capacities of birds arose from some of the same technical capabilities that discovered that people feel something while listening to birds. The recognition that listening produces particular kinds of human affect (or "resonance") came about in part through the history of techniques for measuring and massaging human sensations. As a consequence, recorded birdsong has become an affective technology of risk culture. As Kember and Zylinska write, echoing Marx's analysis of the tension between means and relations of production, "It is precisely in the tension between the generative potentiality of mediation and the constraining aspects of the particular media setups and networks that biopolitics as a historically specific management and regulation of life presents itself in full force."[56]

Sound Objects and the Biopolitics of Listening

You can buy CDs of soothing nature soundscapes of birds mixed with music, or download birdsong specimens that last a few seconds or birdsong soundtracks that last up to ten hours. You can hear the syntax of affect management in these recordings. In metaphorical and lyrical contexts, the bird takes flight and carries our imagination with it into the skies. Whether evoking liberation or melancholy and loss, the lyrical bird is in motion. Temporality and ending seem immanent to both flight and sound, for both flight and the sound of music fill time and then disappear. Yet nature and bird recordings do not build on this impression. These recordings all render the bird's presence as geographically fixed. The bird calls and chirps above the sound of the water, pausing thoughtfully but predictably between intervals, and then it reappears to repeat its call precisely in the same distance. Time is fugitive but it does not have to lead to loss. The disparity between the poetic bird that flies away and the sonic bird that stays where it is offers a clue to understanding the recording of birdsong as biopolitical mediation.

Adorno's mediation theory teaches us that the social contradictions underlying a sound work are mediated through and voiced in its very sonic material and structure.[57] These hybrid sonic bird objects express and mediate the contradictions of our relationship with nonhuman musicality and the nonhuman world, which are in turn mediated by the history of appropriation of animal value and the strategy of mood management. These sound mixes in turn modulate our affective experience in work, domestic, and therapeutic environments. This is not the deterritorializing bird that Deleuze and Guattari describe on the move in forests and mountains. The social functions of these recordings seem to require curtailed possibilities for lines of flight.

Bird watchers learned that birds are musical subjects through technical means of sonic individualization that eliminated the background noises of nature. In *The Sixth Extinction*, Elizabeth Kolbert notes that acoustical engineers speak of "background noise" in the same way that biologists talk about "background extinction."[58] Birdsong recordings aimed at the self-healing marketplace actualize this metaphorical link by making habitat, and by extension sustainability, simultaneously exploitable and imperceptible. Today, with the technical and creative means at our disposal, we might hear a more truthful version of birdsong when it includes the frogs and ducks the musicologists abhorred, along with the people making the recordings and the other sounds nearby. The sounds of singing birds speak to us of the complexity of presence, interaction, noise, and loss. We can find a truer solidarity with them when we are ready to hear what is there as well as what is not, and what is not there as well as what is, differently.[59] It is a matter of learning (situatedly) to listen.

Encountering the voice of a bird that is gone forever produces an uncomfortable feeling that is both melancholy and apprehensive. These "nature" soundtracks evoke romantic associations with nature and yet devalue such associations with their bland sonic purity and careful engineering. Evoking and overturning the voice of the animal makes these recordings comparable to the menageries described in earlier chapters. They too are a form of risk management. They invite the listener to release her apprehension, to make an affective bargain to believe comparable to the "articles of faith" that let zoo visitors believe the animals are happy and their species' futures are ensured.[60]

This bargain is what these menageries and recordings ask of us. By conjoining technical precision with audible beauty, and by shaping the sound output to help us adapt to our everyday environments, these birdsong recordings help us to remain "comfortably unaware"[61] of the changing circumstances of bird habitats. To put this in a more negative light, they provide motivation for *not* thinking about how these technical capacities might also be ravaging the planet. That would not be relaxing or fun. The soothing sounds of birdsong in this context enable what Lauren Berlant describes as "cruel optimism"—"a relation of attachment to compromised conditions of possibility." "What is cruel about these attachments," Berlant explains, "and not merely inconvenient or tragic, is that the subjects who have *x* in their lives might not well endure the loss of their object or scene of desire, even though its presence threatens their well-being, because whatever the *content* of the attachment, the continuity of the form of it provides something of the continuity of the subject's sense of what it means to keep on living on and to look forward to being in the world."[62]

The nature evoked in these soundtracks is one "object or scene of desire" that is central to "what it means to keep on living." Holding on to this object as a "scene of desire" relies on access to commodities that are designed to enhance the listener's complicity with nature's commercial subsumption. Listeners have to split the object of desire, in this case the sound of singing birds, not only from nature and place, but also from personal knowledge of nature and place. In the context of contemporary biopolitics, this implicit contract is a continuation of the splitting, the "as-if" response noted by Sherry Turkle in her study of children and robot animal toys, where the children play with them "as if" they are animals while they know they are not.[63]

The childish yet pragmatic splitting of knowledge that Turkle describes is the condition of remaining attached to these "nature" commodities and logos in the new world ecology. We will away the background noise as though it doesn't matter, but we do this at our peril, and our attachment to this not quite music is not quite love.

There are other avenues into exploring birdsong. Early sound recordists said they heard a more truthful version of birdsong once they could take the technology into the field, rather than keeping the birds in their labs and cages. These bird watchers knew something that we have forgotten with our habit of extracting value from animals for consumption in zoos, images, and recordings. "Place defines a bird and what it is," states Simon Barnes, in *The Meaning of Birds*. "Place sums up the global mystery of species: and species is the way that life on earth works."[64] Witnessing the increasing severance of bird and place, Bernie Krause and Rachel Carson both describe their experience of powerful connections between birds, nightmares, and the fragmentation of knowledge. Florence of Florence and the Machine, whose "old familiar tweet tweet tweet" from "Bird Song" inspired the title of this chapter, also encounters the bird as a nightmare apparition.

"Bird Song" challenges us to wonder why dreams of birds must be happy ones when we are driven to reduce them to spirits or machines or to silence them altogether. The singer sees a bird outside her window who finds out "what she has become." She invites it into her room, but it won't stop singing. Finally she can stand it no longer, and she enacts the violence that is implicit in the imaginary disembodiment of the other that we have been tracing.

Well I didn't tell anyone, but a bird flew by.
Saw what I'd done. He set up a nest outside,
and he sang about what I'd become.
He sang so loud, sang so clear.
I was afraid all the neighbors would hear,
So I invited him in, just to reason with him.
I promised I wouldn't do it again.
[...]
I picked up the bird and above the din I said
"That's the last song you'll ever sing."
Held him down, broke his neck,
Taught him a lesson he wouldn't forget.[65]

Still, "the old familiar tweet tweet tweet" haunts her, and rather than falling silent, the song of the bird begins to come "from my mouth from my mouth from my mouth." This is profoundly a song about voices. The singer cannot break her attachment to the bird, even after she has killed it. She has become the bird. In psychoanalytic terms, she is experiencing the return of the repressed. Anthropologically, by killing the animal she has become one. In feminist terms, she is acknowledging that what you take into your body becomes you. In performative terms, she has exposed the violent politics of the subsumption of nature. Her body has become the medium for the bird, if we accept the mediological premise that she is not an object standing between preformed subjects or entities, but rather a subject caught in shifting relations that speak from and disturb a multiplicity of entities acting in relation to one another. Just as observers discovered that birdsong can elaborate as well as reiterate, and so express musical feeling as well as territorial difference, so our own creative mediations of birdsong can create diverse new modulations of the human-bird-digital-sound affective network in which we find ourselves.

Conclusion

Our response to hearing nature soundtracks with their ever-present birds relies on historically produced pleasures and sensations that blend objects taken from nature with increasingly complex undertakings of science and art. Techniques of digitization and visualization are absorbed by the commercial turn in the inscription of bird songs as sounds meant for human ears. The development of techniques for isolating and reconstituting bird voices emerged alongside the development of techniques for studying human responses to media stimulation. Each of these histories works to constitute its subjects as autonomously functioning entities comprised of and directed by assembled bits of information.

Our use of technology ushers the bird into the plane of human subjectivity by lifting it from its habitat. We gain greater proximity to the sound of the bird but find a continuing elusiveness of bird being, with all its complex pleasures, interactions, hazards, and potentials. The bird we hear is a hybrid object, to borrow a term made familiar by Latour, Haraway, and Debray. The person who listens to the birdsong that has been recorded, mixed, and streamed into her personal space is a hybrid object; the affective purpose of this listening experience is a hybrid object; when people play those recordings in the woods, the birds hear them and now they are hybrid objects. We listen to them in the setting of the Anthropocene, which haunts us with uncertainty about our powers and our complicity with loss. The bad feelings that plague us are soothed by hearing the songs of birds whose habitats are being destroyed by our own activities. One day we could be living

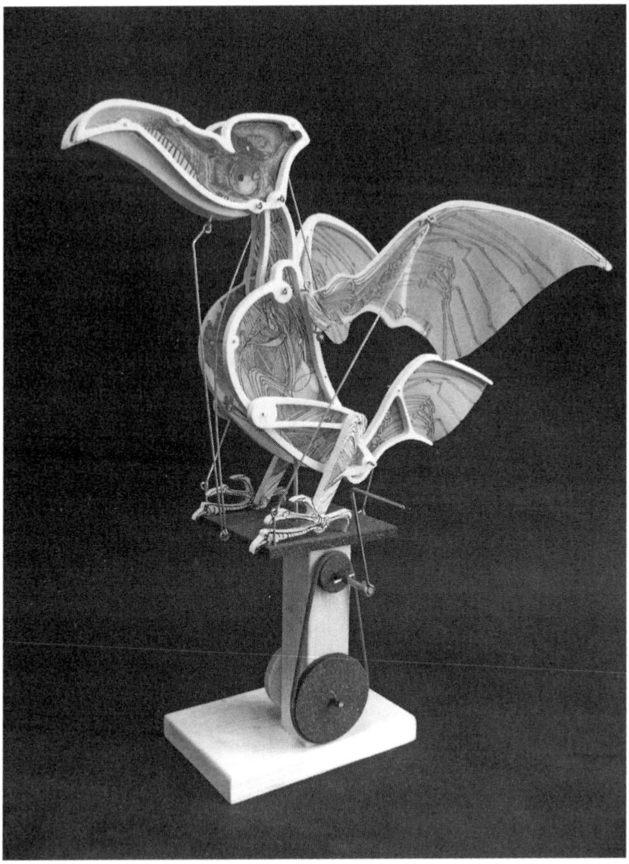

Figure 7.5
The Ghost of a Bird, 2011, Keith Newstead. Image courtesy of the artist.

among the robot dogs and electric sheep and owls found in Sherry Turkle's research and Philip K. Dick's transcendent nightmare. Being lulled to sleep will not ameliorate this glimpse of hell.

By exploring the experience of hearing a loon on a snowy day in Jordan, Ontario, I have untangled an instance of biopolitical mediation that involved the networked agency of singing birds, recording technologies, scientists, musicians, ornithologists, digital information processing, military technological innovations, massage therapists, neurological researchers, CD sales, the everyday disciplining of work and relaxation regimes, irreversible processes of extinction and loss, YouTube, grieving daughters, the ongoing capitalist subsumption of nature, and dreams of nature in springtime. As a result of these mediations, birds have been reconstituted as phantoms, humans have become the objects of neurological research and systematic affective regulation, and new bird-human grammars have begun to emerge. These developments may enable listeners to know themselves differently.

What happens if human listeners open their ears to all that background noise? What happens if the lookers and listeners determine to reconcile the animals they love with their natural habitats, and to save those habitats? Could they forgo the pleasure of seeing and hearing the submissive gazes and captured voices of animals so attractively imaged and recorded in this constant loop of mediations? What does it mean to create spaces for new modulations of animality, territory, loss, and love?

Conclusion: There Be Monsters

In 2013, four students publishing under the name "Pugachelli" posted a video they had produced for a communications theory course to illustrate the idea of commodity fetishism. They illustrated this idea by acting out their overwhelming urge to collect Pokémon cards.[1] The illustration is an apt one, for Pokémon games and cards were, during the childhood of these students, intensely desired commodities that riveted together play and collection with heightened levels of competition in children's culture. Pokémon is the most successful computer game series ever made, the top-selling trading card game of all time, and one of the most popular television programs ever produced.[2] Its time of market ascendancy, from the mid 1990s to the mid 2000s, kept children glued to their screens, convinced users and advocates that Pokémon play was educational, caused schoolyard fights, made the acquisition of cell phones obligatory, and fundamentally changed how children understood the practice of learning.[3]

Pokémon offers a quasi-animal or "monster" mediator that involves both object and practice. It brings together the animal spirits of the child at play, the taxonomical mentalities of the collector, the drive to compete, and the compulsory connectivity whose effects resonate throughout this book. The quest to understand the Pokémon phenomenon from a mediological perspective is thus an opportunity to revisit themes that organized this study and summarize the implications of my virtual menageries.

Pokémon gamers do not simply play; they collect and trade things. The games, cards, and toys associated with the brand are configured to comprise a collection that takes time, money, but above all effort and attention to build. The Pokémon challenge to trade and collect is not unprecedented, as it follows a tradition of collecting and trading cards for sports and superheroes, and even earlier cigarette cards illustrated with movie stars. But the drive to trade and collect is intensified by the development of cross-media platforms, including games and television, the invention of a menagerie of virtual monsters, and the targeting of younger children. The ascendance of goal-oriented play, the linking of fun, anxiety, and the desire to accumulate, and the highly digital, cross-media nature of this experience are actualized in the playfully simple forms of the unique Pokémon menagerie that dances before the eyes fixed determinedly upon their screens and other possessions.

Because it contains monsters, Pokémon could be viewed as a revival of the compulsion to collect heterogeneous objects that emerged with curiosity cabinets in the sixteenth and seventeenth century. These early collectors could display their collections and expertise and the most rare or obscure addition or the largest collection to their peers. Su Ballard writes of "the thrills of identification and classification that marked modernity's engagement with animals";[4] Pokémon provides a vestigial but more systematic elaboration of these thrills. In addition to the games, cards, and toys that are on the collecting agenda, there is always a new spinoff, a new software for recording and displaying their results, a new entity or app to chase, and collectors must resume their quests as new children join the pack. By playing with these toys and games, children strive to master a complex network of images, technologies, techniques, and drives.

In addition to enacting the thrill of the modern taxonomical drive that Ballard describes, and the thrill of possession described by the aforementioned communications students in their performative definition of commodity fetishism, Pokémon collecting can also be linked to the "archive fever" described by Derrida and addressed in chapter 3 of this book. Its relevance here is akin to its relevance to beaver images and exotic animal collections and birdsong variations, but now fueled by digital platforms and cross-media extensions and more intense rules for trading and collecting. In Derrida's description, the individual or collective subject is driven to locate every possible item to complete the archive, obsessively seeking to actualize evidence of her mastery by creating order from multiplicity. While there is a hypothetically finite number of objects in the Pokémon collection, as there would be with other playing cards, postage stamps, or LPs, the collection is never really complete. In addition to scope and variations, there is always going to be something new, so that the goal recedes indefinitely into the distance. This drive becomes more frantic as commodities fill the spaces once provided by humanist ways of framing and ensuring the self and its connection with others. To connect to one another through these irresistible commodities, Pokémon players compete with one another just as adults are increasingly obliged to compete with one another, whether for jobs, job security, assignments, advancements, dates, fashions, friends, online hits, certain possessions, recognition, power, all the supportive infrastructure and perks of the good or at least safe life.

In 2016, seeing its sales drop, Pokémon launched a program that invited a new mode of collecting. Pokémon Go is an app available on users' cell phones that is linked to global positioning systems (GPS); it sends players out into the streets, buses, and malls to chase down Pokémon monsters. Floating flirtatiously against the backdrop of the street or bus, these virtual beings are only visible through cell phones equipped with the Pokémon Go app. The idea is to follow the assigned routes, locate the monsters, and record their finds on the same cell phone. Users are now out in the "real world" with their mobile devices, instead of sitting in front of their computers. This real world has now become a backdrop for mobile devices carried on a briefly exciting safari to capture, not giraffes or birdsongs, but cute virtual monsters.

Just as the medieval menagerie reappeared in twentieth-century software and commercial imagery, so the specter of the medieval monster invoked by Pokémon reappears in the screens and laboratories of twenty-first-century labs and digital culture. The menagerie and the monster both arise through the fracturing of animal families and habitats, and through the creation of hybrids—in the first case, the creation of new hybrid or heterotopic spaces for exotic animals, and in the second, the creation of chimeric entities in the spaces of science and corporate culture. Just as menageries triangulated the empire, the animal, and the colony, so that human specimens were displayed in early zoos along with the animals, so hybrid monsters join the contemporary menagerie, strategically triangulated with the machine on one side and the hunter on the other. They are not animals, in other words, but how one views them can be considered in connection with how one views animals. Thinking about them together enriches our understanding of the threads intermittently connecting live and digital menageries, but also accidental and intentional monsters, and what they communicate about structures of power.

In Dick's novel *Do Androids Dream of Electric Sheep?*, cited earlier in this book, the very few remaining live animals are prestigious possessions for wealthy people and corporations; everyone else has to settle for electric animals that simulate the real thing. The central character's job is to distinguish real humans from fake humans by measuring their compassion. The artificial goat, owl, and toad assembled in Dick's novel extend the royal menagerie rhetorically and functionally into the domestic landscapes of postapocalyptic life. Pokémon creatures are not simulations of animals, however; they are not even eerie monsters or chimeras, the way the giraffe was once perceived to be, but intentionally created cartoon-like monsters that have no interest in the credibility or compassion that might be claimed by a giraffe or the horror evoked by a monster. These Pokémon monsters reach out to capture children and youth and keep them glued to their screens. They place a spell on them that is in some ways continuous with the magic conveyed by menageries as described in previous chapters, but modified by the "as-if" response Terkel identified in children playing with robot pets. They play with them "as if" they were what they simulate in order to join with others and follow the rules of the game.

Pokémon is unique in the world of games, but like other video games it performs an affective capture of players' sensations, working not only to grab their attention but also to harmonize their responses with the neoliberal logics of competition, adaptation, and pragmatism. It is not only toys or images or hours or days that are captured, in other words; it is the human brains that interact with them. In *Biopolitical Screens: Image, Power, and the Neoliberal Brain*, Pasi Väliaho theorizes the social and affective life of screen culture as an interaction of images and responses within a biopolitical apparatus.[5] Through toys, pictures, and games, subjects are shaped from childhood to be what Väliaho calls strategic and adaptive. There is an important correspondence between contemporary neurological research that approaches the human brain as an adaptive, self-organizing system and the "economic order of present-day societies and the neoliberal rationalities sustaining them."[6] This connection, he argues, is "critical to the biopolitical apparatus in charge of our lives today."[7] By biopolitics, Väliaho is referring to a complex of entertainment-military-scientific-financial institutions and practices that conducts and employs research on human neurology to enhance both screens and viewers' adaptation to screens. With the ability to capture subjects not just visually but also emotionally, and not just emotionally but also neurologically, this complex apparatus can shape our feelings and forms of knowledge to ensure that they adapt better to the needs of neoliberal capitalism. This complex certainly shapes our feelings and forms of knowledge in relation to nonhuman animals, as I have illustrated in previous chapters.

Neoliberalism may shape our relationships with screen interfaces, but it does not solely depend on these affective techniques for management of subjects' subjectivities: it has other weapons at its disposal, including the genetic, neurological, and medical modification of human and animal bodies. At the same time, if becoming strategic and adaptive is the desired consequence of these intensified screen interactions, being strategic and adaptive can take more than one shape, whether in relation to screens, tools, animals, or politics. Roughly nine in ten teens, for instance, now "view spending too much time online as a problem facing people their age, including 60% who say it is a *major* problem." Unfortunately, this anti-adaptive response produces its own tensions. The same survey that produced this finding also reviewed teens' emotions "when they do not have their cellphones, and 'anxious' (mentioned by 42% of teens) is the one cited by the largest share. Around one-quarter say they feel lonely (25%) or upset (24%) in these instances. In total, 56% associate the absence of their cellphone with at least one of these negative emotions."[8] Being with their devices produces negative responses; being without them produces negative responses as well. This quandary gives the content providers for these devices great responsibility for the provision of positive, fun, happy, and exciting experiences.

To best understand these emergent patterns, it is important to recognize the limits of representation as the central mode of analysis for understanding them. The Pokémon drive to collect extends the subsumption of what has been conventionally analyzed as either representation or narrative or both. This subsumption arises from the prominent serialization and abstraction of animal imagery in digital culture. This is an ambiguous achievement. The characters that make up these entities, like those in the Pokémon collection, are part animal, part robot, part virtual entity, part concept, part friend, part monster.

We are living in a time of monsters, Jeffrey Cohen claims, a time of widely created and commodified "ambient fear" that "saturates day-to-day living, prodding and silently antagonizing but never speaking its own name."[9] This ambient fear that cannot speak its name concerns the unacknowledged anxiety that we are being made less or other than human. This fear is exacerbated by the proliferation of hybrid creatures and genetically modified organisms; in other words, by monsters. This anxiety is significantly different from the well-documented fascination with monsters in the early modern period. Hybrid entities were once viewed as mistakes, sometimes as punishments, but always as monsters, whose hideous flaws were markers of their unnatural incapacity to live or reproduce themselves. As unnatural mixes of different species, body parts, or genders, they were interruptions of natural process and therefore of biological time. The Pokémon monster lightly augurs a virtual future that similarly ruptures the boundaries of the present, while providing enough entertainment to inoculate us against the "ambient fear" that Cohen describes.

Another bridge between the medieval monster and the contemporary virtual animal/hybrid is the idea that heroism arises from taking control of the challenges posed by the natural world. In the early modern world, taking control meant capturing or destroying the monster. This sense of imminent threat clearly distinguishes the monster from the parable or animated figure. In the contemporary world, taking control, according to postevolutionary thought, means making, playing with, or being the monster. This modern nature arises with live animals that one might capture one way or another for calculable profit and pleasure, and is transformed by late modernity, the "time of monsters," when corporate science creates the monsters it needs in the form of software icons, digital experiments, processed animal spirits, plastics, eyes, thumbs, nervous systems, and finally a totality of "artificial" or human-mediated life. These late modern monsters combine the trajectories of global science and culture, the fracturing of habitats and bodies, the prescient imagination of science fiction writers and artists, the genetic manipulation and commodification of smaller and smaller bits of life, and the dramatic implosion of narratives of evolution. Like the connection between live and digital menageries, the tenuous bond between accidental and intentional monsters communicates something important and complicated about contemporary human-animal relations and structures of power.

Monster Power

Etymologically, monsters are objects of display (*montrer*, to show) of the impossible. By combining contradictory organisms that do not belong together, these unnatural or supernatural monsters challenge the discourses that are used to make sense of organic life. Because they disrupt our understanding of the order of nature and time, they provoke what Freud called our repressed animistic impulses, which appear before us as though foreign to our being.[10] Freud proposes that people manage such impulses symptomatically in order to assert their humanity against specters of animality. In popular terminology and film criticism this is called the "return of the repressed." Psychoanalysis is often evoked in talking about monsters, just as about animal spirits, because it focuses less on defining the body as the instantiation of definite physical boundaries of the individual self, and more on recognizing the degree to which the mind succeeds or fails at projecting a single "body ego" or "skin ego" to mark its own boundaries.[11]

Monsters can create a tremor of fear. In his much-celebrated book *Imaginary Beings*, Borges describes some very frightening monsters that defy the boundary of any known entity. They include the Mantichora, ancient inhabitant of Ethiopia, which "has a triple row of teeth, which fit into each other like those of a comb, the face and ears of a man, and azure eyes, is of the color of blood, has the body of a lion, and a tail ending in a sting, like that of the scorpion." Can you imagine? According to Borges, Flaubert sought to improve upon Pliny's earlier description of this monster, describing "a gigantic red lion, with human face, and three rows of teeth."[12] Like the legendary fire-breathing monster comprised of lion, goat, and serpent formerly celebrated in Greek epic poetry, such monsters were comprised of various unnatural combinations of species. As Tom Tyler observes in tracing the history of monsters: "Not all these diverting, distracting creatures are monsters, but all the monsters are mixtures."[13] Such monsters might be matched against heroic men called upon to rescue their fellows and the rule of law, thus providing "an emblem—of culture over nature, of spirit over matter, and of right over might."[14]

Like records of the colonial conquest of distant lands that resulted in the capture of exotic animals, the epic stories and pictures of brave men fighting hideous monsters rely on the notion that heroic men who fight for culture, for spirit, and for right, against their opposites, are entitled to the treasures they collect. The enchantment of capture and possession and the thrill of fear feed each other in the collection of these foreign objects. As Rosi Braidotti remarks, "to be significant and to signify potentially contradictory meanings is precisely what the monster is supposed to do."[15] While the animal mediator is a connector, a magnetic figure that appears in and helps to animate a time of transition, the monster is a disrupter that historically destabilizes the human capacity and desire to be whole, and so challenges the understanding of what can and cannot be understood or lived.

Alison Griffiths traces a series of correspondences between medieval monsters and contemporary special effects.[16] With special effects, the form of the animal can be altered at will.[17] Rather than providing omens of the struggle between God and an unruly nature, however, these posthumanist monsters evoke an entirely human-centered universe in which the natural world signified by animals is detonated and all its animal body parts put to work. Griffiths's research extends our thematic pursuit of these extractions and renderings into the appropriation of modified monster imagery as homeopatheic intervention into ambient fear. The Pokémon monster intentionally evokes the idea of the monster—that is, it defies the identities or boundaries of biological life—and embodies postevolutionary creations while providing enough entertainment to inoculate players against the "ambient fear" that monsters evoke.

Contemporary monsters are part data, part organism, part human, the outcome of a cumulative machinic assemblage of organic and nonorganic parts. Pokémon is certainly not the only place they appear. Jussi Parikka describes digital networks as swarms or insects, probing the interactions and testing the boundaries between form and metaphor, language and life, animals and machines, whose collapse makes the appearance of the contemporary monster possible.[18] Similarly, designers are researching the biodynamics of octopus intelligence to model digital information management systems so that the building blocks of biology and information become increasingly interchangeable. In a more frightening context, robotic engineers are studying the physics of bird flight in order to build simulated hummingbirds as surveillance robots. The translation of tiny biological entities into tiny informatic entities, and vice versa, cedes the growing human responsibility to cohabit more compassionately with nonhuman life. If biological matter is being translated into networks, as Eugene Thacker suggests, our data networking instruments are being translated into post-rendered menageries and zoos.[19] These cyberzoos contribute to the administration and disruption of contemporary life by stimulating and altering the connectivities of organic life.[20] They are also teaching us more and more about human and animal brains and bodies.

For the most part, our culture has ceased to be frightened of monstrous assemblages. Floating Pokémon monsters, tomatoes with fish genes, artificial life forms, virtual and robotic pets, genetically modified seeds, insects and birds with digital information-gathering or photographic prostheses, and headless robot dogs opening doors are all hybrid entities that could be viewed as monsters. Whether appearing in the context of fantasy, play, science, art, or weaponry, the hybrid bio-object or quasi-life form actualizes the conjunction of distinct entities that ambiguously defy the so-called laws of nature. Unlike their predecessors, whose appearances were interpreted as unsought punishment for human sin and therefore frightening in more than one respect, the contemporary hybrid is not necessarily frightening or even visible outside the spectacular realm of science fiction. When monstrosity is visible outside that world, it is figured with varying degrees of frankness as the product of human intent. What makes *Okja* so remarkable as a science fiction movie is that it thoroughly empathizes with the monster created and then mercilessly hunted by money-hungry corporate science. *Okja* sides with the power of the monster's loving relationship with its human friend.[21]

Haraway's embrace of the cyborg, part of the conjuncture of cultural and technological developments described in chapter 4, challenged readers to recognize the degree to which every human subject is hybrid or part machine. Haraway's work extends Latour's theorization of the hybrid object as an entity created by the separation and reconjoining of nature and culture. Her purpose in emphasizing intersections between culture and nature was to describe human gendered bodies as more and other than their biology, and biology itself as authorized by narratives that may not understand its subject matter. Today's monsters display and sometimes advocate for the need to negotiate with multiple kinds of otherness, not just human others but also animals, not just animal others but also artificial animals, not just robots but monsters, bits, data, genes, and artificial intelligences, so much of them harshly instrumentalized (more than Haraway would acknowledge) in their conception and design. As knowing parts of these assemblages, we humans can no longer naturalize the animal, the machine, or the mediologies that engender our responses to them, as external to ourselves.

The point of a mediological approach is to broaden our understanding of what is being mediated and what is being set into motion by these entities. The practice of recombination precedes and surrounds us on every side. To describe something as a hybrid today, whether a menu or cuisine, plant, artwork, ethnicity, family, car, dog breed, robot, musical style, or performance event, is to enhance its cultural and economic value. This valorization of recombination and recommodification echoes the valorization of capture and possession that made colonial menageries and collections of curiosities possible and upheld their perceived value. While this thematic thread links new hybrids to old collections, contemporary monsters do not originate in such a straightforward lineage. Unlike classical monsters, these hybrids are easily reproduced, for they proliferate in serial form. Creators and users of these hybrid creatures need not fear them, because they were generated by human agents processing matter down to the smallest bit and reassembling it as a submissive and malleable monster (although not so malleable that they do not cause accidents and small catastrophes). These hybrids perform the semiotic antinomy of contradictory entities and meanings once performed by monsters, but from the neoliberal side of the scientific revolution, when anything can be accepted so long as it works and advances your interests. Under the aegis of corporate sponsorship, science has so successfully naturalized hybrid creations that it can seemingly manufacture monsters without limits.

The ever-expanding digitization and commodification of the world are joined in this process. In fact, you can be a monster, too. Instagram offers filters that turn your selfies or photos of friends into talking cats, birds, and other animals. You can be the animal and speak your text message. You are not a representation of that animal, or mimic, or simulacra, or heroic slayer. The loss of fear in the face of monsters, and the proliferation of monsters in films and games that represent little more than the playful skillfulness of comic digital reconfiguration, could be a promising outcome, or it could be another manifestation of cruel optimism. Will the extinctions, storms, fires, and droughts visible on the horizon restore fear to observers as though in a biblical shakedown? How far might the capture of children's bodies and minds be turned against itself? As Alexa Weik von Mossner suggests, "emotion and affect are the basic mechanisms that connect us to our environment, shape our knowledge, and motivate our actions."[22] Exploring emotion and affect in the context of human-animal-machine relations is essential for restoring kind and sustainable human-animal relations and possibly to preserving life on the planet.

People Power

It can be argued that the idea of using affect and emotion to save animal species from extinction is deeply anthropometric and problematically humanist, particularly in light of the importance of generating affect to the mode of biopolitical rule emphasizing growth in consumer capitalism.[23] In *Death of the PostHuman*, Claire Colebrook argues, echoing Lovelock's Gaia principle, that if we really cared about the environment we would just let our species become extinct.[24] As a critique of this instrumentalization of affect and emotion, it seems logical to dismiss growing concerns about climate change and extinction because they reiterate the patterns of human-centered thought that selfishly mourn the loss of species, especially beautiful and charismatic species like elephants, giraffes, parrots, orangutans, passenger pigeons, wallabies, western black rhinoceros, and any minute now, white rhinos, giraffes, and some species of penguins. Note that many of these species were featured in classical colonial menageries, reminding us that the spaces from which they originate are still colonial spaces whose sustainability is being threatened by the continued pursuit of pleasure and profit derived from animal extraction. Recent announcements that by 2030 there will be more plastic than fish in the ocean, or that humans will become extinct if climate change is not remedied by 2023, could be read as proof of Colebrook's idea. Wouldn't the giraffes and fish be better off without us? I see this idea expressed on social media all the time.

Others argue that the pain some of us feel when we hear this prognosis, or when we see dead sea animals or birds filled with plastic, giraffes murdered for high-priced fashion commodities, orangutans swinging from their last tree, still challenges what we think about being human and potentially forces us to be different and perhaps better humans. If birds and fish are dying from what they eat, surely it is the plastic, not the animal that died from it, that is the monster. It is the need to keep making plastic and palm oil that compels corporations to glue us to our seats and armies to build robot dogs and militarized birds to defend their masters' ruination of the earth's resources. So then it is the corporations that are the monsters, notwithstanding their lovely lion and polar bear emblems. Feeling rage and compassion for the birds and fish, the beavers and giraffes, engenders the demand that their habitats be protected. This position reiterates the idea with which I introduced this book, that responding to the magnetism or spirits or beauty or pain of animals is part of what makes us human. Compassion for and engagement with the strategically adaptive children and adults glued to their screens is another viable reaction, particularly when strategic and adaptive young people are taking to the streets, while strategic and adaptive governments are scrapping environmental regulations and endangered species protections in many parts of the world.

Genetic science has embarked on a new, more spectacular option to address the crisis of the unprecedented loss of species arising from these developments. Experiments in the genetic recreation of wooly mammoths, passenger pigeons, the great auk, and other extinct species have created flurries of excitement in the world of genetic "de-extinction" and beyond.[25] The genetic scientists undertaking these experiments believe that the restoration of these and other lost species might be an appropriate environmental solution because their return would cause the restoration of their habitats and even slow or reverse the permafrost thaw.[26] The creation of these "facsimiles"[27] or un-extinct animals would produce animals that are patentable, edible, and/or endangered, creating problems that compromise the showy brilliance of the science or the welcome return of a charismatic or beloved species. The environments in which these animals once lived no longer exist. As Wray argues in her careful review of this debate, the spectacular de-extinctions or cloned animal facsimiles or natural-looking monsters that might result from these experiments would not lessen the need to protect, engineer, moderate, and conserve—that is, render "hybrid"—the habitats that were once viable, even as we mourn the irreversible loss of hundreds of species that are disappearing.[28]

The many innovations afforded by the mediologies of the digital—the knowledge of animals, the aestheticization of animal bodies and voices, the instrumental research on human and nonhuman neurology and affect, the global satellite eyes and internet connections, the pragmatic adaptations, commodity compulsions, graphic abstractions, therapeutic resources, cat obsessions, endangered species webcams, animal rescue sites and secret horrifying videos, visible and invisible monsters, clonings and necrofauna, and virtual menageries galore are not the only solutions to the natural disasters or managerial biopolitics of the present. As Marx so powerfully observed, "Men [sic] make their own history, but they do not make it as they please; they do not make it under self-selected circumstances, but under circumstances existing already, given and transmitted from the past. The tradition of all dead generations weighs like a nightmare on the brains of the living."[29] It may be the animals that wake us up.

Notes

Introduction

1. John Berger, *About Looking* (New York: Vintage Books, 1980), 4.

2. I draw on Joost van Loon, *Risk and Technological Culture: Towards a Sociology of Virulence* (London: Routledge, 2002), which defines the relationship between the cultivation and management of risk as a fundamental clash of values in technocratic capitalist society. As opposed to the medieval and early modern cultural milieus with which this book begins, subjects in risk culture believe themselves responsible for the risks and management of risks they encounter.

3. Cited in Régis Debray, *Media Manifestos: On the Technological Transmission of Cultural Forms*, trans. Eric Rauth (London: Verso, 1996), 115.

4. Ibid., 13.

5. Ibid., 18; italics in original.

6. Ibid., 17; italics in original.

7. Ibid., 19.

8. Tom Tyler, introduction to *Animal Encounters*, ed. Tom Tyler and Manuela Rossini (The Hague: Brill Academic, 2009), 4.

9. Randy Malamud, *An Introduction to Animals and Visual Culture* (New York: Palgrave Macmillan, 2012); Nicole Shukin, *Animal Capital: Rendering Life in Biopolitical Times* (Minneapolis: University of Minnesota Press, 2009).

10. Anat Pick, *Creaturely Poetics: Animality and Vulnerability in Literature and Film* (New York: Columbia University Press, 2011). Elaborating the philosophy of Simone Weil to include nonhuman animals, Pick proposes a "creaturely" approach to animal representations in which the viewer's response is based on the felt recognition of the shared embodiedness of humans and animals.

11. Ibid., 4.

12. Mary Midgley, *Animals and Why They Matter* (Athens: University of Georgia Press, 1983).

13. Alexander Pschera, *Animal Internet: Nature and the Digital Revolution*, trans. Elisabeth Lauffer (New York: New Vessel Press, 2016).

14. Bertolt Brecht, "The Modern Theatre Is the Epic Theatre," in *Brecht on Theatre: The Development of an Aesthetic*, ed. and trans. John Willett (London: Methuen, 2001). Cf. Walter Benjamin, "The Artist as Producer," in *Reflections: Essays, Aphorisms, Autobiographical Writings*, ed. Peter Demetz, trans. Edmund Jephcott (New York: Schocken, 1986).

15. Félix Guattari, *The Three Ecologies* (London: Athlone Press, 2000). "Here we are talking about a reconstruction of social and individual practices which I shall classify under three complementary headings, all of which come under the ethico-aesthetic aegis of an ecosophy: social ecology, mental ecology and environmental ecology" (48). "Rather than speak of the 'subject', we should perhaps speak of components of subjectification, each working more or less on its own. This would lead us, necessarily, to re-examine the relation between concepts of the individual and subjectivity, and, above all, to make a clear distinction between the two. Vectors of subjectification do not necessarily pass through the individual, which in reality appears to be something like a 'terminal' for processes that involve human groups, socio-economic ensembles, data-processing machines, etc. Therefore, interiority establishes itself at the crossroads of multiple components, each relatively autonomous in relation to the other, and, if need be, in open conflict" (38).

16. Sarah Kember, *Cyberfeminism and Artificial Life* (London: Routledge, 2003), 216.

17. Michael Hardt and Antonio Negri, *Empire* (Cambridge, MA: Harvard University Press, 2000), 352, 356.

18. Eleanor Wilkinson, "On Love as an (Im)properly Political Concept," *Environment and Planning D: Society and Space* 35, no. 1 (2017): 64. She is referring to Sarah Ahmed, *The Cultural Politics of Emotion* (2004; London: Routledge, 2013).

19. Michel Foucault, "Of Other Spaces," trans. Jay Miskowiec, *Diacritics* 16 (1986): 22–27.

20. Richard Grusin, *Premediation: Affect and Mediality after 9/11* (London: Palgrave Macmillan, 2010).

21. John Maynard Keynes, *The General Theory of Employment, Interest and Money* (London: Macmillan, 1936).

22. Adam Smith, *The Theory of Moral Sentiments* (1759; Amherst, NY: Prometheus Books, 2000), 29.

23. Quoted in George Lowenstein and Ted O'Donohue, "Animal Spirits: Affective and Deliberative Processes in Economic Behavior," CAE Working Paper #04-14,

2004, Cornell University, https://cae.economics.cornell.edu/04-14.pdf, accessed August 9, 2018.

24. https://www.investopedia.com/terms/a/animal-spirits.asp.

25. John Maynard Keynes, *Essays in Persuasion*, cited in E. G. Winslow, "Keynes and Freud: Psychoanalysis and Keynes' Account of the 'Animal Spirits' of Capitalism," *Social Research* 53, no. 4 (1986): 563.

26. Winslow, "Keynes and Freud."

27. Quoted in ibid.

28. Akira Lippitt, *Electric Animal: Toward a Rhetoric of Wildlife* (Minneapolis: University of Minnesota Press, 2008), 116.

29. See Jody Berland, "Cultural Technologies and the 'Evolution' of Technological Cultures," in *North of Empire: Essays on the Cultural Technologies of Space* (Durham: Duke University Press, 2009).

30. Sherry Turkle, *Alone Together: Why We Expect More from Technology and Less from Ourselves* (New York: Basic Books, 2012). A good example of an interactive toy with "animal spirits" is Zoomer Chimp, a spirited robot monkey advertised as "your REAL best friend," released by Spinmaster in 2016. Interactivepuppy.com reviews this toy as "a multitalented, engaging, attention-grabbing (if not sometimes naughty) primate playmate." See http://interactivepuppy.com/spinmaster-zoomer-chimp-interactive-monkey-toy-review/

31. Ozgun Atasoy and Carey K. Morewedge, "Customers Won't Pay as Much for Digital Goods—and Research Explains Why," *Harvard Business Review*, December 22, 2017, https://hbr.org/2017/12/customers-wont-pay-as-much-for-digital-goods-and-research-explains-why. The story is illustrated by a neatly gridded wooden shelf populated by small statues of animals.

32. Fredric Jameson, "The Vanishing Mediator: Narrative Structure in Max Weber," *New German Critique*, no. 1 (Winter 1973): 52–58.

33. Yuk Hui, "What Is a Digital Object?" *Metaphilosophy* 43, no. 4 (2012): 387.

34. Pasi Väliaho, *Biopolitical Screens: Image, Power, and the Neoliberal Brain* (Cambridge, MA: MIT Press, 2014), 89.

35. "Using Cute Animals in Pop Culture Makes Public Think They're Not Endangered—Study," Agence France-Presse, April 13, 2018. The study by Franck Courchamp and William Ripple was published in *PLOS Biology*.

36. Alan Liu, *The Laws of Cool: Knowledge Work and the Culture of Information* (Chicago: University of Chicago Press, 2004).

37. Gayatri Chakravorty Spivak, *An Aesthetic Education in the Era of Globalization* (Cambridge, MA: Harvard University Press, 2012), 96–97.

Chapter 1

1. W. J. T. Mitchell, *What Do Pictures Want? The Lives and Loves of Images* (Chicago: University of Chicago Press, 2005), 13.

2. Tuan, cited in Randy Malamud, *An Introduction to Animals and Visual Culture* (New York: Palgrave Macmillan, 2012), 117. Eric Baratay and Elisabeth Hardouin-Fugier also comment on the inclusion of human specimens in colonial zoos in *Zoo: A History of Zoological Gardens in the West* (London: Reaktion Books, 2004).

3. Iris Braverman, *Zooland: The Institution of Captivity* (Stanford: Stanford University Press, 2013), 16.

4. Braverman, *Zooland.*

5. John Berger, *About Looking* (Toronto: Vintage, 1980), 19.

6. Ibid., 24.

7. Akira Mizuto Lippitt, *Electric Animal: Toward a Rhetoric of Wildlife* (Minneapolis: University of Minnesota Press, 2000), 196.

8. Walter Benjamin, "The Work of Art in the Age of Mechanical Reproduction," in *Illuminations: Essays and Reflections*, ed. Hannah Arendt, trans. Harry Zohn (New York: Schocken, 1969), 217–252; John Berger, *Ways of Seeing: Based on the BBC Series with John Berger* (London: Penguin Group, 1972).

9. Berger, *Ways of Seeing.*

10. Michel Foucault, "Of Other Spaces," *Diacritics* 16, no. 1 (Spring 1986): 15.

11. Raymond Williams, *Towards 2000*, 177.

12. Eric Ames, *Carl Hagenbeck's Empire of Entertainments* (Seattle: University of Washington Press, 2009), 6.

13. Ibid., 7. The concept of "antigeographic space" is attributed to Michael Sorkin, "See You in Disneyland," in *Variations on a Theme Park: The New American City and the End of Public Space*, ed. Michael Sorkin, 205–232 (New York: Hill and Wang, 1992), 208. In particular, Disney's Animal Kingdom has been cited as an example of Disney's participation in animal trade.

14. Heather Davis and Zoe Todd, "On the Importance of a Date, or, Decolonizing the Anthropocene," *ACME: An International Journal for Critical Geographies* 16, no. 4 (December 2017): 761–780, https://www.acme-journal.org/index.php/acme/article/view/1539, accessed February 10, 2018.

15. See Susan Buck-Morss, *Dreamworld and Catastrophe: The Passing of Mass Utopia in East and West* (Cambridge, MA: MIT Press, 2000).

16. Jody Berland, "Angels Suspended," *Assemblage: Critical Journal of Architecture and Design Culture* 20 (1993): 16–17.

17. Walter Benjamin, "N [Re the Theory of Knowledge, Theory of Progress]," in *Benjamin: Philosophy, Aesthetics, History*, ed. Gary Smith (Chicago: University of Chicago Press, 1989), 44.

18. Cf. Jussi Parikka, *Insect Media: An Archaeology of Animals and Technology* (Minneapolis: University of Minnesota Press, 2010).

19. Matt Applegate and Jamie Cohen, "Communicating Graphically: Mimesis, Visual Language, and Commodification as Culture," *Cultural Politics* 13, no. 1 (2017): 81–100. The reference is to Jussi Parikka, *What Is Media Archaeology?* (Cambridge: Polity Press, 2012).

20. Jonathan Burt, *Animals and Film* (London: Reaktion Books, 2002), 34.

21. Ibid., 35.

22. Ibid., 112.

23. The menagerie was located on Branson's privately owned "paradise," Necker Island, which was devastated by Hurricane Irma in 2017: https://www.thesun.co.uk/news/4447836/hurricane-irma-richard-branson-necker-island-damage-photos/, September 17, 2017, accessed August 2, 2018. Some of the animals, including 250 flamingos and 60 lemurs, survived.

24. Philip K. Dick, *Do Androids Dream of Electric Sheep*? (New York: Ballantine Books, 2008). It is no longer relevant or sufficient to refer to this book as the basis of the *Bladerunner* film. The book is built on the central character's obsession with animals, animal robots, menageries, and extinction.

25. Edison's film can be seen at https://www.youtube.com/watch?v=RoHeGhfWMzM.

26. Ames, *Carl Hagenbeck's Empire of Entertainments*, 201.

27. Donald Heraldson, *Creators of Life: A History of Animation* (New York: Drake, 1975), 56.

28. Pramod Nayer, "Touchscreens and Architexture," *MCC: Journal of Language and Social Sciences* 1, no. 1 (2016): 10.

29. Tracy Staedter, "Octopus Inspires AI Robots on a Mission," *Seeker*, https://www.seeker.com/octopus-inspires-ai-robots-on-a-mission-1771111049.html, accessed January 19, 2018.

30. "Each business is unique, but often the challenges are the same," the company explains on its home page, venturecapital.com.

31. Harold A. Innis, *The Bias of Communication* (Toronto: University of Toronto Press), 2008; Marshall McLuhan, *Understanding Media: The Extensions of Man* (Cambridge, MA: MIT Press, 1994); Jody Berland, *North of Empire: Essays on the Cultural Technologies of Space* (Durham: Duke University Press), 2009.

32. Applegate and Cohen, "Communicating Graphically," 83.

33. Terrence W. Gordon, *McLuhan: A Guide for the Perplexed* (New York: Continuum, 2010), 56; emphasis added.

34. Ibid., 86–87.

35. Cf. Derek Sayer, *The Violence of Abstraction: The Analytical Foundations of Historical Materialism* (London: Basil Blackwell, 1987).

36. W. J. T. Mitchell and Mark B. N. Hansen, eds., *Critical Terms for Media Studies* (Chicago: University of Chicago Press, 2010), xiii.

37. According to Martha Nussbaum, the seven basic features of treating things as objects include instrumentality, denial of autonomy, inertness, fungibility (the perception that one entity can be replaced with another similar one), violability, ownership, and denial of subjectivity. Nussbaum, "Objectification," *Philosophy and Public Affairs* 24, no. 4 (1995): 249–291. Objectification cannot occur to an object; it can only occur to something that is not an object, like a person or an animal. These features of objectification are taken up by Selena Nemorin in relation to the objectification of animals and of consumers who are animalized when they are targeted by neuromarketing. Selena Nemorin, "Augmenting Animality: Neuromarketing as a Pedagogy of Communicative Surveillance," PhD dissertation, Ontario Institute for Studies in Education, University of Toronto, 2015, 135–136.

38. Annie van den Oever and Geoffrey Winthrop-Young, "Rethinking the Materiality of Technical Media: Friedrich Kittler, Enfant Terrible with a Rejuvenating Effect on Parental Discipline—A Dialogue," in *Techné/Technology: Researching Cinema and Media Technologies, Their Development, Use and Impact*, ed. Annie van den Oever (Amsterdam: Amsterdam University Press, 2014), 235.

39. Ibid.

40. Lawrence Grossberg, *Cultural Studies in the Future Tense* (Durham: Duke University Press, 2010), 210.

41. Ibid., 189.

42. McLuhan compares our (mis)understanding of media with the error of Narcissus: "A youth stares, utterly captivated, at his image in the water. He does not realize that he has become a 'servomechanism' of his own image. In a similar vein, humans become the 'sex organs' that ensure the advancement and expansion of the machine world." McLuhan, *Understanding Media*, 41, 46. The myth of Narcissus is also "fundamentally a story about ecological retribution, as the Earth spirits offended by Narcis-

sus call down a divine and absolute retribution against him, ending in a death that Narcissus could have avoided simply by looking away. Nemisis's curse offers a terrible justice for creatures of nature injured by the self-absorption and vanity of human beings, a retribution that is played out to the point of an extinction." Joseph Masco, "The Six Extinctions: Visualizing Planetary Ecological Crisis Today," in *After Extinction*, ed. Richard Grusin (Minneapolis: University of Minnesota Press, 2018), 83–84. My thanks to Brian McCormack for drawing this circle.

43. Donna Haraway, *Companion Species Manifesto: Dogs, People, and Significant Otherness* (Chicago: Prickly Paradigm Press, 2003).

44. "Cats Against Capitalism," *Facebook*, https://www.facebook.com/CATSNOTCAP/, accessed December 10, 2017.

45. Derrida, *The Animal That Therefore I Am*, 7; Montaigne, "Apology for Raymond Sebond," 331.

46. Terry O'Sullivan, "Animal Magic," OpenLearn, Open University, June 6, 2006, http://www.open.edu/openlearn/money-management/management/business-studies/animal-magic, accessed April 15, 2018.

47. Nicole Shukin, *Animal Capital: Rendering Life in Biopolitical Times* (Minneapolis: University of Minnesota Press, 2009); Jonathan Sterne, "The Cat Telephone," *The Velvet Light Trap: A Critical Journal of Film and Television* 64 (Fall 2009): 83–84.

48. For discussion of the relationship between images, electronic reproduction, and animal rights activism, see Keri Cronin, "'A Mute Yet Eloquent Protest': Visual Culture and Anti-Vivisection Activism in the Age of Mechanical Reproduction," in *Critical Animal Studies: Thinking the Unthinkable*, ed. John Sorenson (Toronto: Canadian Scholars' Press, 2014), 284–297.

49. "A spider conducts operations that resemble those of a weaver, and a bee puts to shame many an Architect in the construction of her cells. But what distinguishes the worst architect from the best of bees is this, that the Architect raises his structure in imagination before he erects it in reality. At the end of every labour process, we get a result that already existed in the imagination of the labour at his commencement." Karl Marx, *Capital* (1867; London: Penguin Books, 1976), 284.

50. Hannah Arendt, *The Human Condition* (Chicago: University of Chicago Press, 1998), 353.

51. Carolyn Marvin, *When Old Technologies Were New: Thinking about Electric Communication in the Late Nineteenth Century* (New York: Oxford University Press, 1990), 141.

52. Jane Bennett, *The Enchantment of Modern Life: Attachments, Crossings, and Ethics* (Princeton: Princeton University Press, 2001), 94–95.

53. Cf. Max Haiven, *Cultures of Financialization: Fictitious Capital in Popular Culture and Everyday Life* (Basingstoke, UK: Palgrave Macmillan, 2014).

54. Richard Grusin, "Mediation Is the Message," *Journal of Visual Culture* 13, no. 1 (April 2014): 56.

55. Ibid.

56. Rachel Carson, *Silent Spring* (Boston: Houghton Mifflin, 1962).

57. Andrew Whitehouse, "Listening to Birds in the Anthropocene: The Anxious Semiotics of Sound in a Human-Dominated World," *Environmental Humanities* 6, no. 1 (2015): 53–71.

58. Ibid., 54.

59. Gilles Deleuze, "On Spinoza," August 10, 2017, http://deleuzelectures.blogspot.com/2007/02/on-spinoza.html, accessed December 6, 2017.

60. Tonya K. Davidson, Ondine Park, and Rob Shields, eds., *Ecologies of Affect: Placing Nostalgia, Desire, and Hope* (Waterloo: Wilfrid Laurier University Press, 2011), 4.

61. Ibid.

62. Matthew Tiessen, "(In)Human Desiring and Extended Agency," in Davidson, Park, and Shields, *Ecologies of Affect*, 129.

63. Lisa Blackman, *Immaterial Bodies* (Thousand Oaks, CA: Sage Publications, 2013), 89.

64. As Mary Midgley points out, this is not a very parsimonious theory, since the level of genetic programming needed to instruct a leaf-cutter ant would require more DNA than the creature possesses. Mary Midgely, "Beasts, Brutes and Monsters," in *What Is an Animal?*, ed. Tim Ingold (Boston: Routledge, 1994).

65. Ben Highmore, "Bitter After Taste: Affect, Food and Social Aesthetics," in *The Affect Theory Reader*, ed. Melissa Gregg and Gregory J. Seigworth (Durham: Duke University Press, 2010), 123; Anat Pick, *Creaturely Poetics: Animality and Vulnerability in Literature and Film* (New York: Columbia University Press, 2011).

66. Ben Anderson, "Affect and Biopower: Towards a Politics of Life," *Transactions of the Institute of British Geographers* 37, no. 1 (2012): 1–16.

67. Patricia Clough, "The Affective Turn: Political Economy, Biomedia and Bodies," *Theory, Culture and Society* 25, no. 1 (2008): 2.

68. Ben Anderson, "Affect and Biopower: Towards a Politics of Life," *Transactions of the Institute of British Geographers* 37, no. 1 (2012): 28–43. See also Nemorin, "Augmenting Animality."

69. Mark B. N. Hansen, *Feed-Forward: On the Future of Twenty-First-Century Media* (Chicago: University of Chicago Press, 2015), 58.

70. Ibid., 59.

71. Ibid., 63.

72. Hiroki Azuma, *Otaku: Japan's Database Animals* (Minneapolis: University of Minnesota Press, 2009), 87.

73. Grossberg, *Cultural Studies in the Future Tense*, 198.

74. Jeremy Gilbert, *Anticapitalism and Culture: Radical Theory and Popular Politics* (London: Bloomsbury Academic, 2008), 8.

75. Anderson, "Affect and Biopower," 8.

76. Paul Virilio, *Politics of the Very Worst: An Interview by Philippe Petit*, trans. Michael Cavaliere, ed. Sylvère Lotringer (New York: Semiotext(e), 1999).

77. Edward Tenner, *Why Technology Bites Back: Technology and the Revenge of Unintended Consequences* (New York: Vintage Books, 1997), 4; Foucaultian scholars of surveillance document the manner in which increasingly mandatory forms of participation mediate our enrolment in the disciplinary apparatus of the state and the consumer economy, spontaneously providing it with the data it needs to accomplish its work of categorization, ordering, and knowledge production; while those drawn to Foucault's later accounts of governmentality and biopower emphasize participation as the means by which we perform and reproduce ourselves as self-responsible, empowered, and exible subjects adapted to the demands of neoliberalism. Lacanians such as Slavoj Žižek locate the ideological function of participation in the injunction to enjoy—in this case, to enjoy the sensation of doing something without enduring the burden of actually doing anything: interactivity as a sublimated form of "interpassivity." And, finally, there is Jodi Dean's comprehensive account of the role that the "fantasy of participation" enacted and encouraged by emerging media technologies plays in bolstering the regime of contemporary communicative capitalism. Jodi Dean, *Democracy and Other Neoliberal Fantasies: Communicative Capitalism and Left Politics* (Durham: Duke University Press, 2009), 31.

78. Erica Fudge, *Animal* (London: Reaktion Books, 2002), 8.

79. Jacques Derrida, *The Animal That Therefore I Am*, ed. Marie-Louise Mallet, trans. David Wills (New York: Fordham University Press, 2008), 7; Michel de Montaigne, "Apology for Raymond Sebond," in *The Complete Works of Montaigne*, trans. Donald M. Frame (Stanford: Stanford University Press, 1958), bk. 2, chap. 12, 331.

80. Walt Kelly, "We have met the enemy and he is us," in *Pogo* comic strip, 1970.

81. Fudge, *Animal*, 89.

82. Michel Serres, *The Parasite*, trans. Lawrence R. Schehr (Baltimore: Johns Hopkins University Press, 1982), 36; cf. Matteo Pasquinelli, *Animal Spirits: A Bestiary of the Commons* (Rotterdam: NAi Publishers, Institute of Networked Cultures, 2008), 61.

83. Pasquinelli, *Animal Spirits*, 64–65.

Chapter 2

1. William Wordsworth, "She Was a Phantom of Delight," https://www.poetryfoundation.org/poems/45550/she-was-a-phantom-of-delight.

2. Paul Boulineau, 1934, cited in Eric Baratay and Elizabeth Hardouin-Fugier, *Zoo: A History of Zoological Gardens in the West* (London: Reaktion Books, 2004), 130.

3. Jason W. Moore, "The Rise of Cheap Nature," in *Anthropocene or Capitalocene? Nature, History and the Crisis of Capitalism*, ed. Jason W. Moore (Oakland, CA: PM Press, 2016), 85–86.

4. "Giraffa camelopardalis," The IUCN Redlist of Threatened Species.

5. The African Wildlife Leadership Foundation (AWLF) was founded in 1961 by Russell E. Train, a wealthy judge and hunter and member of the Washington Safari Club. Other founding members from the Safari Club were Nick Arundel, a former United States Marine Corps combat officer and journalist, Kermit Roosevelt, Jr. of the CIA, James S. Bugg, a businessman, and Maurice Stans, later to be Richard Nixon's campaign finance chairman. "African Wildlife Foundation," Wikipedia, accessed January 2018.

6. Ibid.

7. Dipesh Chakrabarty, "The Climate of History: Four Theses," *Critical Inquiry* 35, no. 2 (Winter 2009): 219–220.

8. Alan Liu, "Imagining the New Media Encounter," in *A Companion to Digital Literary Studies,* ed. Ray Siemens and Susan Schreibman (New York: Wiley-Blackwell, 2008), 3–26.

9. Ibid.

10. Jody Berland, "Animal and/as Medium: Symbolic Work in Communicative Regimes," *Global South* 3, no. 1 (2009): 42–65, 90.

11. Irving Goffman, *The Presentation of the Self in Everyday Life* (New York: Anchor, 1959).

12. In *Penguins, Pineapples and Pangolins: First Encounters with the Exotic* (London: British Library Publishing, 2016), Claire Cock-Starkey claims that giraffes were known in Europe since Julius Caesar brought a giraffe to Rome as part of his menagerie (11). Cf. Lisa J. Kiser, "Animals in Medieval Sports, Entertainments and

Menageries," in *A Cultural History of Animals in the Medieval Age*, ed. Brigitte Resl (Oxford: Berg, 2007), 103–126; Eric Ringmar, "Audience for a Giraffe," *Journal of World History* 17, no. 4 (2006): 375–397.

13. Ringmar, "Audience for a Giraffe," 376.

14. Baratay and Hardouin-Fugier, *Zoo*, 122.

15. Ringmar, "Audience for a Giraffe," 377–378.

16. Nicholas Thomas, "Objects of Knowledge: Oceanic Artifacts in European Engravings," in *Empires of Vision: A Reader*, ed. Martin Jay and Sumathi Ramaswamy (Durham: Duke University Press, 2014), 141–158.

17. Edgar Williams, *Giraffe* (London: Reaktion Books, 2011), 52.

18. Ringmar, "Audience for a Giraffe," 379.

19. Fredric Jameson, "The Vanishing Mediator: Narrative Structure in Max Weber," *New German Critique* 1 (Winter 1973): 52–58.

20. Ringmar, "Audience for a Giraffe," 388. There are other versions of this story in which the giraffe's loss is publicly mourned, however.

21. Thierry Buquet, "La belle captive. La girafe dans les menageries principes au Moyen Âge," in *La bête captive au Moyen Âge et à l'époque moderne*, ed. Corinne Beck and Fabrice Guizard (Amiens: Encrage, 2012), 65–90.

22. Comerio was "a pioneer of documentary film making who traveled widely and often recorded the interaction of people and animals; indeed, the abundant animal footage here is the contemporary film makers' most chilling material." Janet Maslin, "From the Pole to the Equator," *New York Times*, April 6, 1988.

23. Scott MacDonald, review of *From the Pole to the Equator* by Yevant Gianikian and Angela Ricci Lucchi, *Film Quarterly* 42, no. 3 (Spring 1989): 36.

24. "Using Cute Animals in Pop Culture Makes Public Think They're Not Endangered—Study," Agence France-Presse, April 13, 2018, reporting on a study by Franck Courchamp and William Ripple published in *PLOS Biology*.

25. John Durham Peters, *The Marvelous Clouds: Toward a Philosophy of Elemental Media* (Chicago: University of Chicago Press, 2015).

26. Ibid., 15.

27. Ibid., 29.

28. Cf. Joost van Loon, *Risk and Technological Culture: Towards a Sociology of Virulence* (London: Routledge, 2002).

29. Isabell Lorey, *State of Insecurity: Government of the Precarious* (London: Verso, 2015), 19; emphasis in original.

30. Charlie Gere, *Digital Culture*, rev. ed. (London: Reaktion Books, 2008).

31. Giraffe Conservation Foundation, "Africa's Giraffe Conservation Guide," 2017, accessed February 13, 2018.

32. Alister Doyle, "Giraffes Suffer 'Silent Extinction' in Africa," *Scientific American* (December 2015), accessed December 28, 2017.

33. Giraffe Conservation Foundation, "Africa's Giraffe Conservation Guide."

34. Cheryl Lousley, "Charismatic Life: Spectacular Biodiversity and Biophilic Life Writing," *Environmental Communication* 10, no. 6 (2016): 710.

35. See chapter 1.

36. Anat Pick, *Creaturely Poetics: Animality and Vulnerability in Literature and Film* (New York: Columbia University Press, 2011).

37. Peters, *The Marvelous Clouds*, 55.

38. W. J. T. Mitchell and Mark B. N. Hansen, eds., *Critical Terms for Media Studies* (Chicago: University of Chicago Press, 2010), xi.

39. W. J. T. Mitchell, *What Do Pictures Want? The Lives and Loves of Images* (Chicago: University of Chicago Press, 2004).

Chapter 3

1. Margaret Atwood, *Surfacing* (1972; Toronto: Emblem Editions, 2010), 39–40.

2. "Talk: Margaret Atwood," *Wikiquote*, https://en.wikiquote.org/wiki/Talk:Margaret_Atwood, accessed December 15, 2017.

3. Jennifer R. Wolch and Jody Emel, *Animal Geographies: Place, Politics, and Identity in the Nature-Culture Borderlands* (London: Verso, 1998), xvi–xvii.

4. Roland Barthes, *Mythologies* (New York: Farrar, Straus and Giroux, 1972). Notable exceptions to this dehistoricization include Keith Thomas, *Man and the Natural World* (Harmondsworth, UK: Penguin, 1992), and Clive Ponting, *A New Green History of the World: The Environment and the Collapse of Great Civilizations* (London: Penguin Books, 2007).

5. See Jacques Derrida, *Archive Fever: A Freudian Impression*, trans. Eric Prenowitz (Chicago: University of Chicago Press, 1998), 194; Bruno Latour, *Politics of Nature: How to Bring the Sciences into Democracy*, trans. Catherine Porter (Cambridge, MA: Harvard University Press, 2004); Bruno Latour, *We Have Never Been Modern* (Cambridge, MA: Harvard University Press, 1993); Cary Wolfe, *Before the Law: Humans and Other Animals in a Biopolitical Frame* (Chicago: University of Chicago Press, 2012), 9.

6. Jody Berland, *North of Empire: Essays on the Cultural Technologies of Space* (Durham: Duke University Press, 2009).

7. Cf. Mary Midgley, *Animals and Why They Matter* (Athens: University of Georgia Press, 1983); Mary Midgley, "Beasts, Brutes and Monsters," in *What Is an Animal?*, ed. Tim Ingold (London: Routledge, 1994), 35–46.

8. Von Uexküll notes, "We comfort ourselves all too easily with the illusion that the relations of another kind of subject to the things of its environment play out in the same space and time as the relations that link us to the things of our human environment. This illusion is fed by the belief in the existence of one and only one world, in which all living beings are encased. From this arises the widely held conviction that there must be one and only one space and time for all living beings." Jakob von Uexküll, *A Foray into the Worlds of Animals and Humans, with A Theory of Meaning* (Minneapolis: University of Minnesota Press, 2010), 54.

9. Ibid.

10. Margot Francis, *Creative Subversions: Whiteness, Indigeneity and the National Imaginary* (Vancouver: UBC Press, 2011), xx.

11. This theme is explored extensively in Berland, *North of Empire*, and previously in Stephen Slemon, "Unsettling the Empire: Resistance Theory for the Second World," *World Literature Written in English* 30 (1990): 30–41 (excerpted in *Contemporary Postcolonial Theory: A Reader*, ed. Padmini Mongia [New Delhi: Oxford University Press, 1997], and *New Contexts of Canadian Criticism*, ed. Ajay Hable, Donna Palmateer Penee, and J. P. [Tim] Struthers [Peterborough, ON: Broadview Press, 1997]).

12. Derrida, *Archive Fever*.

13. Steve Baker, *Picturing the Beast: Animals, Identity, and Representation* (Champaign-Urbana: University of Illinois Press, 2001).

14. Glynnis Hood, *The Beaver Manifesto* (Victoria, BC: RMB, 2011), 6.

15. In Argentina and Belgium, on the other hand, the animal is largely represented as a pest wreaking devastation onto the land. There is no historic or symbolic value attached to its presence.

16. Baker, *Picturing the Beast*, 47.

17. Cf. Linda Hutcheon, *The Canadian Postmodern: A Study of Contemporary English-Canadian Fiction* (New York: Oxford University Press, 1988).

18. For an important discussion of the concept of "rendering" of the animal's body in the production of culture, see Nicole Shukin, *Animal Capital: Rendering Life in Biopolitical Times* (Minnesota: University of Minnesota Press, 2009).

19. Harold Adams Innis, *The Fur Trade in Canada : An Introduction to Canadian Economic History* (New Haven: Yale University Press, 1962), 4.

20. Ibid., 5.

21. Ibid., 6.

22. Ponting, *A New Green History of the World*, 156.

23. Ibid., 157.

24. Alice B. Outwater, *Water: A Natural History* (New York: Basic Books, 1996).

25. Innis, *The Fur Trade in Canada*, "Conclusion."

26. Hood, *The Beaver Manifesto*, 39.

27. The idea of the topos offers a geopolitical extension of Derrida's notion of the archive, used to analyze the layering of texts, imprints, and spatial politics of the new world. Cf. Benjamin Keith Belton, *Orinoco Flow: Culture, Narrative, and the Political Economy of Information* (Lanham, MD: Scarecrow Press, 2003), and Berland, *North of Empire*, for a fuller discussion of this idea.

28. Michel Foucault, *Security, Territory, and Population: Lectures at the Collège de France, 1977–1978* (New York: Palgrave Macmillan, 2007).

29. Jody Berland, "Weathering the North," in *North of Empire*, 210–241.

30. Innis, *The Fur Trade in Canada*, 42.

31. Sam W. McKegney, "Second-Hand Shaman: Imag(in)ing Indigeneity from Le Jeune to Pratt, Moore and Beresford," *TOPIA: Canadian Journal of Cultural Studies*, no. 12 (Fall 2004): 25–40.

32. Such consideration for beavers appeared only in the twentieth century with the publication of books by trapper-turned-writer Grey Owl, who adopted beavers as pets, described them as "Little People," and endowed them with endearing qualities; see Grey Owl, *The Collected Works of Grey Owl : Three Complete and Unabridged Canadian Classics* (Toronto: Discovery Books, 1999). His writing was a deliberate intervention into the anthropocentrism and indifference of the entrepreneurs of the fur trade, for whom the animal was a serviceable tool for and index of their own imperial prowess over the territories they mapped and the bodies they encountered.

33. Steven Chase, "Beavers Can't Cut It as National Emblem, But Polar Bears Can, Senator Says," *Globe and Mai*, October 27, 2011.

34. My use of this concept is indebted to correspondence with Pauline Greenhill.

35. See Midgley, "Beasts, Brutes and Monsters"; Wolfe, *Before the Law*.

36. Innis cites Lahonton's work in his own research on the fur trade, with reference to the debate in fur trade literature whether Indians are closer to the beaver or the white man.

37. David M. Hayne, "Lom D'Arce De Lahonton, Louis-Armand de, Baron de Lahontan," in *Dictionary of Canadian Biography*, vol. 2 (1701–1740), University of Toronto/Université Laval, 1969/1982, http://www.biographi.ca/en/bio/lom_d_arce_de_lahontan_louis_armand_de_2E.html, accessed December 15, 2017.

38. Lewis O. Saum, *The Fur Trader and the Indian* (Seattle: University of Washington Press, 1965), 91.

39. A detailed examination of this process in seventeenth-century political philosophy can be found in Craig McFarlane, "Early Modern Speculative Anthropology," PhD dissertation, Department of Sociology, York University, 2014.

40. Saum, *The Fur Trader and the Indian*, 96.

41. Ibid.

42. Cf. Johannes Fabian, *Time and the Other: How Anthropology Makes Its Object* (New York: Columbia University Press, 1983); and Georges E. Sioui, *For an Amerindian Autohistory: An Essay on the Foundations of a Social Ethic*, trans. Sheila Fischman (Montreal: McGill-Queen's University Press, 1992), on othering through concepts of time. For further discussion of colonial discourse and its reliance on a Western view of the mastery of nature, see Berland, "Weathering the North."

43. Laura Peers, "Fur Trade History, Native History, Public History: Communication and Miscommunication," in *New Faces of the Fur Trade: Selected Papers of the Seventh North American Fur Trade Conference, Halifax, Nova Scotia, 1995*, ed. Jo-Anne Fiske, Susan Sleeper-Smith, and William Wicken (East Lansing: Michigan State University Press, 1998).

44. Ibid., 101.

45. Ibid., 105–106.

46. Derrida, *Archive Fever*.

47. Ibid., 89–90.

48. In his 1868 book *The American Beaver and His Works*, "[Lewis Henry] Morgan felt that the thinking principle was *not* unique to humanity. To the contrary, he believed that the Creator had endowed *all* animal species, and not mankind alone, with a mind as well as a body. If anything convinced him of this, it was his observations of the technical accomplishments of the Beaver." Tim Ingold, "The Animal in the Study of Humanity," in Ingold, *What Is an Animal?*, 87.

49. Rachel Price, "Archive Fever and Twentieth-Century Critical Theory," manuscript, Duke University, 2001, 5; cited in Bettina Funcke, *Pop or Populus: Art between High and Low* (Berlin: Sternberg Press, 2009), 47.

50. James M. Cameron, *The Canadian Beaver Book: Fact, Fiction and Fantasy* (Burnstown, ON: General Store Publishing House, 1991).

51. Chantal Nadeau, *Fur Nation: From the Beaver to Brigitte Bardot* (London: Routledge, 2001).

52. Julia Emberley, *The Cultural Politics of Fur* (Ithaca: Cornell University Press, 1997), 93.

53. Hood, *The Beaver Manifesto,* 2.

54. Francis, *Creative Subversions.*

55. Wolfe, *Before the Law.*

56. Ministry of Environment, Conservation Species Act, Beavers, http://www.pskf.ca/publications/beavers.htm.

57. Timothy Morton, *The Ecological Thought* (Cambridge, MA: Harvard University Press, 2012), 34.

58. Wolch and Emel, *Animal Geographies,* xvi–xvii.

59. Félix Guattari, *The Three Ecologies* (London: Athlone Press, 2000), 43.

60. Outwater, *Water: A Natural History.*

61. "The discourse about the thing, or evaluative discourses more generally, are fundamental to the spatio-temporal practices of valuing both the thing and the person. Without naming, memory, discourses, and the like, the whole process of constituting a mediated world of space-time relations would fall apart"; see David Harvey, *Justice, Nature and the Geography of Difference* (Cambridge, MA: Wiley-Blackwell, 1997), 221.

62. Jean Baudrillard, *For a Critique of the Political Economy of the Sign,* trans. C. Levin (St. Louis: Telos Press, 1981), 102.

63. Ibid.

64. See Jonathan Burt, *Animals in Film* (London: Reaktion Books, 2002).

65. Alan Liu, *The Laws of Cool: Knowledge Work and the Culture of Information* (Chicago: University of Chicago Press, 2004).

66. Ibid., 103.

67. Shukin, cited in Wolfe, *Before the Law,* 51–52.

68. John Ralston Saul, *A Fair Country: Telling Truths about Canada* (Toronto: Penguin Canada, 2009), 35.

Chapter 4

1. Régis Debray, *Media Manifestos: On the Technological Transmission of Cultural Forms,* trans. Eric Rauth (London: Verso, 1996), 18; italics in original.

2. Fred Turner, *From Counterculture to Cyberculture: Stewart Brand, the Whole Earth Network, and the Rise of Digital Utopianism* (Chicago: University of Chicago Press, 2006).

3. Howard Rheingold, *The Virtual Community: Homesteading on the Electronic Frontier* (Cambridge, MA: MIT Press, 2000).

4. See "The Corporate Animal" listed in menu at *Virtual Menageries*, www.virtualmenageries.com.

5. BBDO, "'Morrie's Menagerie' Is What They Call It at 'The Other Computer Company,'" *BBDO Newsletter*, March 1972, 4.

6. Ibid., 7.

7. O'Reilly Media, "About O'Reilly," http://www.oreilly.com/about/, accessed February 12, 2013.

8. Randy Malamud, *An Introduction to Animals and Visual Culture* (London: Palgrave Macmillan, 2012), 33.

9. Evelyn Fox Keller, "Marrying the Premodern to the Postmodern: Computers and Organisms after World War II," in *Prefiguring Cyberculture: An Intellectual History*, ed. Darren Tofts, Annemarie Jonson, and Alessio Cavallaro (Cambridge, MA: MIT Press, 2002), 64.

10. Kevin Kelly, "Futurist Stewart Brand Wants to Revive Extinct Species," *Wired*, August 17, 2012, https://www.wired.com/wiredenterprise/2012/08/ff_stewartbrand/. Cf. Turner, *From Counterculture to Cyberculture*.

11. Morris Wolfe, *Jolts: The TV Wasteland and the Canadian Oasis* (Toronto: J. Lorimer, 1985).

12. Roy Tennant, John Ober, and Anne G. Lipow, *Crossing the Internet Threshold: An Instructional Handbook* (Berkeley, CA: Library Solutions Press, 1994), 95.

13. Ibid.

14. Ragib Hasan, "History of Linux," 2002, http://ragibhasan.com/linux/.

15. Jody Berland, "The Work of the Beaver," in *Material Cultures in Canada*, ed. Tom Allen and Jennifer Blair (Waterloo: Wilfrid Laurier University Press, 2015), 25–50.

16. Cf. Paul Wells, *The Animated Bestiary: Animals, Cartoons, and Culture* (New Brunswick, NJ: Rutgers University Press, 2009).

17. Stuart Ewen, *All Consuming Images: The Politics of Style in Contemporary Culture* (New York: Basic Books, 1988), 183.

18. I discuss this technocratic concept of liberation in "Cultural Technologies and the 'Evolution' of Technological Cultures," in *North of Empire: Essays on the Cultural Technologies of Space* (Durham: Duke University Press, 2009).

19. Ibid.

20. As explained in the introduction, I am using the concept of "animal spirits" more or less as outlined by Keynes in his study of human economic behavior.

21. Hiroki Azuma, *Otaku: Japan's Database Animals* (Minneapolis: University of Minnesota Press, 2009).

22. Randy Malamud, *An Introduction to Animals and Visual Culture* (London: Palgrave Macmillan, 2012), 3

23. Jussi Parikka, *Insect Media: An Archaeology of Animals and Technology* (Minneapolis: University of Minnesota Press, 2010), 153.

24. Walter Benjamin, "The Work of Art in the Age of Mechanical Reproduction," in *Illuminations: Essays and Reflections*, ed. Hannah Arendt, trans. Harry Zohn (New York: Schocken, 1969), 217–252.

25. Debray, *Media Manifestos*, 17.

26. Gilles Deleuze, *The Fold* (New York: Continuum, 2006), 86.

27. Debray, *Media Manifestos*, 19.

28. Donna Jeanne Haraway, "A Cyborg Manifesto: Science, Technology, and Socialist-Feminism in the Late Twentieth Century," in Haraway, *Simians, Cyborgs and Women: The Reinvention of Nature* (London: Free Association Books, 1991), 149–181; Richard Stallmen, "The GNU Manifesto," 1985, http://www.gnu.org/gnu/manifesto.html, accessed February 2017.

29. Hasan, "History of Linux."

30. Michel Foucault, "The Confession of the Flesh," in *Power/Knowledge: Selected Interviews and Other Writings 1972–1977*, ed. Colin Gordon (New York: Pantheon Books, 1980), 194–228.

31. Keller, "Marrying the Premodern to the Postmodern," 60.

32. Ibid., 61.

33. Nicole Shukin, *Animal Capital: Rendering Life in Biopolitical Times* (Minneapolis: University of Minnesota Press, 2009).

34. Microsoft, "A History of Windows," https://windows.microsoft.com/en-us/windows/history, accessed February 12, 2013.

35. Chris Noonan, director, *Babe* (Universal Pictures, 1995).

36. Jodi Dean, ed., *Democracy and Other Neoliberal Fantasies: Communicative Capitalism and Left Politics* (Durham: Duke University Press, 2009).

37. Jakob von Uexküll, *A Foray into the World of Animals and Humans, with A Theory of Meaning* (Minneapolis: University of Minnesota Press, 2010). Cf. Brian McCormack, "Among *Umwelten*: Meaning-Making in Critical Posthumanism," PhD dissertation, York University, 2018.

38. Susan Buck-Morss, "Aesthetics and Anaesthetics: Walter Benjamin's Artwork Essay Reconsidered," *October* 62 (1992): 33.

39. Lorraine Daston, "Intelligences: Angelic, Animal, Human," in *Thinking with Animals: New Perspectives on Anthropomorphism*, ed. Lorraine Daston and Gregg Mitman (New York: Columbia University Press, 2005), 50.

40. Lev Manovich, *The Language of New Media* (Cambridge, MA: MIT Press, 2001), 217.

41. Ibid., 218. At the same time, Manovich argues that the practice of assemblage was formative to the development of film. Quoting Mikhail Kaufman, cinematographer of *Man with a Movie Camera* (1929): "An ordinary person finds himself in some sort of environment, gets lost amidst the zillions of phenomena, and observes these phenomena from a bad vantage point. ... But the man with a movie camera is infused with the particular thought that he is actually seeing the world for other people. Do you understand? He joins these phenomena with others, from elsewhere, which may not even have been filmed by him. Like a kind of scholar, he is able to gather empirical observations in one place and then in another. And that is actually the way in which the world has come to be understood."

42. Azuma, *Otaku: Japan's Database Animals*, 33.

43. Susan McHugh, "Clever Pigs, Failing Piggeries," *Antennae*, no. 12 (Spring 2010): 19.

44. Gilles Deleuze, *Francis Bacon: The Logic of Sensation* (New York: Continuum, 2003), 31–32.

45. W. J. T. Mitchell, *What Do Pictures Want? The Lives and Loves of Images* (Chicago: University of Chicago Press, 2005).

46. Nigel Thrift, *Knowing Capitalism* (London: Sage, 2005), 154.

47. Jonathan Crary, *Techniques of the Observer: On Vision and Modernity in the Nineteenth Century* (Cambridge, MA: MIT Press, 1992); Michael Dorland, "Foucault, *The Order of Things* and Data Visualization" (paper presented at the Association for Cultural Studies Crossroads Conference, Paris, 2012).

48. Jonathan Burt, *Animals in Film* (London: Reaktion Books, 2004), 10.

49. Wikipedia, "History of YouTube," accessed October 2016.

50. Deleuze, *The Fold*, 87–88.

51. Alan Liu, *The Laws of Cool: Knowledge Work and the Culture of Information* (Chicago: University of Chicago Press, 2004), 103.

52. Carol Adams, *The Sexual Politics of Meat: A Feminist-Vegetarian Critical Theory* (New York: Continuum, 2000), 40.

53. In "The Storyteller," published in 1936, Benjamin writes that "the art of storytelling is coming to an end. Less and less frequently do we encounter people with the ability to tell a tale properly. More and more often there is embarrassment all around when the wish to hear a story is expressed. It is as if something that seemed inalienable to us, the securest among our possessions, were taken from us: the ability to exchange experiences. ... We have no counsel either for ourselves or for others. ... To seek this counsel, one would first have to be able to tell the story. Walter Benjamin, "The Storyteller: Reflections on the Works of Nikolai Leskov," in *Illuminations*, 83–109.

54. Liu, *The Laws of Cool*, 103.

55. Sherry Turkle, *Alone Together: Why We Expect More from Technology and Less from Each Other* (New York: Basic Books 2012).

56. Dean, *Democracy and Other Neoliberal Fantasies*.

57. Randy Malamud, "Americans Do Weird Things with Animals, or, Why Did the Chicken Cross the Road?," in *Animal Encounters*, ed. Tom Tyler and Manuela Rossini (Leiden: Brill, 2009), 73–96.

58. Timothy Morton, *The Ecological Thought* (Cambridge, MA: Harvard University Press, 2012), 11.

Chapter 5

1. Elizabeth Kolbert, "The Climate of Man—III," *New Yorker*, May 9, 2005, 52; Elizabeth Kolbert, *The Sixth Extinction: An Unnatural History* (New York: Henry Holt, 2014).

2. See for instance Martin Heidegger, *The Question Concerning Technology and other Essays* (New York: Harper Perennial, 1982); Max Horkheimer and Theodor W. Adorno, *Dialectic of Enlightenment* (Stanford: Stanford University Press, 2002); Jacques Ellul, *The Technological Society* (New York: Vintage, 1967); Lewis Mumford, *Technics and Civilization* (Chicago: University of Chicago Press, 2010); and in a different register, Rachel Carson's *Silent Spring* (Boston: Houghton Mifflin, 1962), which I discuss in chapter 7.

3. Lisa Nakamura, "Where Do You Want to Go Today?," in *The Visual Culture Reader*, ed. Nicholas Mirzoeff (London: Routledge, 1998), 258.

4. Josh N. Wolfenbarger, "The Culture of Cell Phone Charms," by truefaith7, https://bellatory.com/fashion-accessories, July 18, 2016, downloaded July 31, 2018.

5. Ibid.

6. The notion of risk culture I am drawing on here is elaborated by Joost van Loon in his book *Risk and Technological Culture: Towards a Sociology of Virulence* (London: Routledge, 2002).

7. Andrew Wernick, *Promotional Culture: Advertising, Ideology and Symbolic Expression* (Thousand Oaks, CA: Sage, 1991), 216.

8. Sherry Turkle, *Alone Together: Why We Expect More from Technology and Less from Each Other* (New York: Basic Books, 2010). Cf. Derrick Jensen, *The Culture of Make Believe* (New York: Basic Books, 2002).

9. Jodi Dean, *Democracy and Other Neoliberal Fantasies: Communicative Capitalism and Left Politics* (Durham: Duke University Press, 2009).

10. Grossman proposes the iPhone as the best invention of 2007 in wider installment of *Time*'s "Best Inventions of 2007." Lev Grossman, "Invention of the Year: The iPhone," *Time*, November 1, 2007, http://time.com/time/specials/2007/article/0,28804,1677329_1678542_1677891,00.html, accessed May 2008.

11. Akira Mizuta Lippit, "... From Wild Technology to Electric Animal," in *Representing Animals*, ed. Nigel Rothfels (Bloomington: Indiana University Press, 2002), 120.

12. Ingrid Richardson, "Mobile Techsoma: Some Phenomenological Reflections on Itinerant Media Devices," *Fibercultures* 6 (2005): 1.

13. For more on the rhetoric of connectedness in relation to corporate capitalism, see Dan Schiller, *How to Think about Information* (Urbana: University of Illinois Press, 2007). Also relevant is Richard Maxwell and Toby Miller, "Ecological Ethics and Media Technology," *International Journal of Communication* 2 (2008): 331–353.

14. Is the author a critical scholar or the author of a report to Motorola? (This is not a frivolous question, since digital theorist Sadie Plant wrote a report for Motorola advancing similar conclusions, and Motorola has also cosponsored research on the creative use of cell phones in Canada.) The question is difficult to answer because universities and corporations cosponsor countless symposia and collaborate on projects and creative experiments on the progressive capacities of "new media." Given their mandate to demonstrate that such media render earlier models and approaches obsolete, both organizations are hesitant to acknowledge hazardous connections between embodied communication and the embodiment of the planet, between personal use and the political judgment required of the global citizen.

15. Arnold Pacey, *The Culture of Technology* (Cambridge, MA: MIT Press, 1985), 36.

16. Jonathan Sterne, "Out with the Trash," in *Residual Media*, ed. Charles Acland (Minneapolis: University of Minnesota Press, 2007), 28. Cf. Sean Cubitt, *Finite Media: Environmental Implications of Digital Technologies* (Durham: Duke University Press, 2017).

17. Elizabeth Grossman, *High Tech Trash: Digital Devices, Hidden Toxics, and Human Health* (Washington, DC: Island Press, 2007), 112, 114.

18. Sabine Lebel, "The Life Cycle of the Computer: Studies in the Materialities of Risk," PhD dissertation, York University, 2014.

19. Maxwell and Miller, "Ecological Ethics and Media Technology," 337. Cf. Sean Cubitt, *Finite Media*.

20. Susan Buck-Morss, *Dreamworld and Catastrophe: The Passing of Mass Utopia in East and West* (Cambridge, MA: MIT Press, 2000), 119. The quotation is from Alla Efimova, "A Prescription for Life: Sun, Air, and Water in Socialist Realism and Soviet Health Care," unpublished manuscript.

21. Van Loon, *Risk and Technological Culture*, 196.

22. Ann Laura Stoler, *Haunted by Empire: Geographies of Intimacy in North American History* (Durham: Duke University Press, 2006), 10.

23. Jody Berland, "Locating Listening," in *North of Empire: Essays on the Cultural Technologies of Space* (Durham: Duke University Press, 2009), 185–209.

24. "The idea that mechanization of instruments made music accessible to the unskilled efforts of toddlers and children became a central motif in their promotion, and quickly became the chosen strategy for advertising automatic pianos. Gulbransen used the image of a baby accompanied by the slogan 'easy to play: All the family will quickly become expert. ... Without long practice! All the joy without hard work!' Or as Kodak put it in an important postwar marketing campaign: 'Just push a button. We do the rest.'" Jody Berland, "The Musicking Machine," in *North of Empire*, 166.

25. Regarding Lévi-Strauss and Volosinov, David Morley writes that both emphasized the "versatility or multi-accentuality of signs through which a community distinguishes itself from others. ... Their shared vocabulary allows people to share conceptual forms without, at the same time, necessarily requiring them to share their meanings." David Morley, *Home Territories: Media, Mobility, and Identity* (London: Routledge, 2000), 243. These postmodern animals are particularly versatile.

26. Margaret Shildrick, *Leaky Bodies and Boundaries: Feminism, Postmodernism and (Bio)ethics* (London: Routledge, 1997), 180.

27. Shaun Moores, *Media/Theory* (New York: Routledge, 2005), 124–126.

28. André H. Caron and Letizia Caronia, *Moving Cultures: Mobile Communication in Everyday Life* (Montreal: McGill-Queen's University Press, 2007), 34–35.

29. Ibid., 13.

30. Ibid., 11.

31. Ibid., 75.

32. The notion of concealment in relation to risk is covered usefully by van Loon.

33. From a recent conference on Deleuze, media, and movement: "A Deleuzian theory of media asks, 'what kind of variation at the level of events is afforded by our material culture?' We must then determine what kind of event is a medium. In keeping with Deleuze's ontology of immanence we do not align media practice with representation or simulation, only with more or less adequate models of repetition ... that co-ordinate a space where an event can occur. Events ... not predicated on this cultivation of space but erupt continuously as a disarticulating force, the multiple or variable index of forces and relations. A medium is a place of inscription, a possibility of life. The event is not merely a possibility but the actualization of a virtual, which is real but un-mediated." See Gavin Wittje, "Deleuze Conference: On Media and Movement," Department of Anthropology, University of California, Berkeley, http://gavinwit.googlepages.com/Deleuzeconference, accessed December 4, 2017.

34. Christopher Coker, *The Future of War: The Re-Enchantment of War in the Twenty-First Century* (Malden, MA: Wiley-Blackwell, 2004), 33.

35. Ibid.

36. Ibid., 35.

37. George Grant, cited in Darrin Barney, *Prometheus Wired: The Hope for Democracy in the Age of Network Technology* (Chicago: University of Chicago Press, 2000), 51.

38. Darin Barney's conception of technology as a form of life exempt from political judgment is a central argument in his book *Prometheus Wired*. See also his 2008 Hart House Lecture, "One Nation under Google: Citizenship and the Technological Republic," delivered at the University of Toronto.

39. Van Loon, *Risk and Technological Culture*, 5.

40. Erica Fudge, "A Left-Handed Blow: Writing the History of Animals," in *Representing Animals*, ed. Nigel Rothfels (Bloomington: Indiana University Press, 2002), 7.

41. Roy Scranton, *Learning to Die in the Anthropocene: Reflections on the End of a Civilization* (San Francisco: City Lights Books, 2015), 4.

42. Ibid., 95.

43. The idea was apparently shelved until 2002 when the RAND Corporation published "Space Weapons, Earth Wars," which raised the idea. In 2003 a U.S. Defense Department report referenced the feasibility of launching just such a weapon system

in light of technological advances. Accusations that the United States was in fact working on such a system were flatly denied. Independent military observers believe that it is: http://endwar.wikia.com/wiki/Kinetic_Strike, accessed August 19, 2018.

44. Jared Keller, "The Pentagon's New Super Weapon Is Basically a Weaponized Meteor Strike," *Task & Purpose*, June 7, 2017, https://taskandpurpose.com/kinetic-bombardment-kep-weaponry/, accessed August 19, 2018.

45. Brian Murphy, "Revolution in Military Affairs: Digital Technology and Network Theories Applied to War," paper presented at the Canadian Communication Association, 2007, quoted with kind permission of the author.

46. Ibid. See also Tim Blackmore's *War X: Human Extensions in Battlespace* (Toronto: University of Toronto Press, 2005).

47. Jason Kirby, "How to Squander a $52-Billion Empire," *Maclean's*, July 23, 2007, 42.

48. Coker, *The Future of War*, 135.

49. In addition to cybernetic theory, Coker is drawing here on Elaine Scarry's explanation of the merging and "building-in" of human skill with weapons. See Elaine Scarry, *The Body in Pain: The Making and Unmaking of the World* (New York: Oxford University Press, 1985), 152.

50. "Robot Hummingbird Spy Drone Flies for Eight Minutes, Spies on Bad Guys," *Fox News*, February 18, 2011, http://www.foxnews.com/tech/2011/02/18/robot-hummingbird-spy-drone-flies-minutes-spies-bad-guys.html.

51. Barney, *Prometheus Wired*, 51.

52. From Jonathan Burt, "The Aesthetics of Livingness," a conference paper presented at "Representing Animals," York University, 2007. I thank the author for allowing me access to this manuscript.

53. Michel Serres, *Angels: A Modern Myth* (Paris: Flammarion, 1995), 68.

54. John Durham Peters, *Speaking into the Air: A History of the Idea of Communication* (Chicago: University of Chicago Press, 2001), 29.

55. Donald F. Theall, "Speaking into the Air: A History of the Idea of Communication," *Canadian Journal of Communication* 26, no. 3 (2001): 413.

56. For example, see Mary Midgley's *Animals and Why They Matter* (Athens: University of Georgia Press, 1983).

57. See the recent posthumous translation and publication of Derrida's "The Autobiographical Animal" entitled *The Animal That Therefore I Am*, ed. Marie-Louise Mallet, trans. David Wills (New York: Fordham University Press, 2008).

58. Susan Hall writes further: "One of the things that stayed with me was that something we use on a daily basis is killing gorillas and other animals in central Africa. Believe it or not, it is our cell phones. Cell phones contain an ore called coltan that is mined in Africa. Even though many of the animals are in wildlife reserves or 'protected' parks, illegal miners continue to invade the area because demand for the ore is so high. Although I know it is hard to stop something that is happening so far away, we can help. Did you know that it is estimated that more than 100 million cell phones are thrown away or tucked in a drawer every year? Many times it is all too easy to throw something in the trash and let somebody else worry about it. But cell phones and their accessories contain chemicals such as arsenic, cobalt, copper, lead and zinc. So animals are not only put in danger while we mine the necessary products to produce the phone, they are put in jeopardy when we throw them away too. The Zoological Society of San Diego and Eco-Cell, a cell phone recycling company, have set up a recycling program just outside the zoo and the Wild Animal Park to encourage all of us to dispose of phones properly." Hall goes on to explain that it is not at all clear where the actual recycling takes place. See Susan Hall, "Cell Phones Can Harm Animals," *Californian/North County Times*, September 13, 2006, accessed http://www.nctimes.com:80/articles/2006/09/13/news/columnists/susan_hall/21_46_339_12_06.txt.

59. See the short article by Khushboo Sandhu, "Cell Phone Tower Radiation May Be Killing Plants and Animals," *Ludihana Newsline*, March 13, 2007, http://cities.expressindia.com/fullstory.php?newsid=226423.

60. Cubitt, *Finite Media*.

61. Maxwell and Miller, "Ecological Ethics and Media Technology," 346.

62. Jon Mooallem, "The Afterlife of Cellphones—Cellular Telephone—Waste Materials—Recycling," *New York Times*, January 13, 2008, 41. For an account of cell phone waste, see Grossman's *High Tech Trash*.

63. For example, the website for the Providence Animal Rescue League (PARL): "We Recycle Cell Phones & Empty Printer Cartridges! If you're wondering what to do with your old cell phones or empty printer cartridges, then give them to PARL! We recycle these items in exchange for funds to help us provide care and find new homes for the many pets at PARL. We can take the following items: Cell phones (all makes and models)." (See http://www.parl.org/.) Prior to recycling or disposal, personal data and information can be wiped or erased from a cell phone with an open-source Cell Phone Data Eraser tool. As instructed by Wireless Recycling—"the industry source for used wireless solutions"—to erase information and data from a phone, "Just search for the make and model of your phone and download the instructions." (See http://www.recellular.com/recycling/.)

64. See The Animal Rescue Site, https://shop.theanimalrescuesite.com/store/item.do?itemId=25644&siteId=310.

65. Carolyn Ellis, "Katrina and the Cat: Responding to Society's Expendables," *Cultural Studies ↔ Critical Methodologies* 7, no. 2 (2007): 188–201.

66. Jennifer Harding and E. Deidre Pribram, "The Power of Feeling: Locating Emotions in Culture," *European Journal of Cultural Studies* 5, no. 4 (May 2002): 407.

67. Neil Evernden, "Nature in Industrial Society," in *Cultural Politics in Contemporary America*, ed. Ian H. Angus and Sut Jhally (New York: Routledge, 1989), 164.

Chapter 6

1. Kevin Kelly, *What Technology Wants* (New York: Viking, 2010), 323.

2. Edith Podhovnik, The Meow Factor—An Investigation of Cat Content in Today's Media," in *Arts & Humanities Venice 2016*, conference proceedings, April 27, 2016, 130.

3. Cynthia Chris, *Watching Wildlife* (Minneapolis: University of Minnesota Press, 2006), 36.

4. Popular cat websites include: https://icanhas.cheezburger.com, www.lolcats.com, https://www.lovemeow.com, www.catsinsinks.com, www.kittenwar.com, dailykitten.com, simon's cat (youtube), www.cattime.com; all accessed August 21, 2018.

5. Erica Fudge, *Animal* (London: Reaktion Books, 2002), 28.

6. The origin of this proverb is unknown. It first appeared in print in a famous early collection of English proverbs, *The Proverbs and Epigrams of John Heywood* (1562):

Some hear and see him whom he heareth nor seeth not
But fields have eyes and woods have ears, ye wot
And also on my maids he is ever tooting.
Can ye judge a man, (quoth I), by his looking?
What, a cat may look on a king, ye know!
My cat's leering look, (quoth she), at first show,
Showeth me that my cat goeth a caterwauling;
And specially by his manner of drawing
To Madge, my fair maid.

See *The Phrase Finder*, https://www.phrases.org.uk/meanings/a-cat-may-look-at-a-king.htm, accessed December 2017.

7. Katherine Rogers writes, "Making much of any pet laid one open to suspicion under the 1604 statute against witchcraft in England, which declared it a felony 'to consult, covenant with, entertain, employ, feed, or reward any evil or wicked spirit.'" Katherine Rogers, "Agents of the Devil," in *The Cat and the Human Imagination: Feline Images from Bast to Garfield* (Ann Arbor: University of Michigan Press, 1988), 51. Needless to say, these familiars were usually cats.

8. Hugh Trevor-Roper, *The European Witch-Craze of the Sixteenth and Seventeenth Centuries* (London: Pelican Books, 1969), 93.

9. *The Tragedie of Gorbeduc* (also known as *Ferrex and Porrex*), by Thomas Norton and Thomas Sackville, the first tragedy and first drama written in blank verse, was performed before Queen Elizabeth in 1562. It was republished numerous times. See for example Thomas Norton and Thomas Sackville, "The Tragedie of Gorbeduc," in *Verse Libel in Renaissance England and Scotland*, ed. Steven W. May and Alan Bryson (Oxford: Oxford University Press, 2016), 198.

10. Inga Clendinnen, *Ambivalent Conquests: Maya and Spaniard in Yucatan, 1517–1570*, 2nd ed. (Cambridge: Cambridge University Press, 2003), 67.

11. J. Eric S. Thompson, *Maya Hieroglyphic Writing: An Introduction* (Norman: University Press of Oklahoma, 1966).

12. Carolyn Merchant, *The Death of Nature: Women, Ecology, and the Scientific Revolution* (New York: HarperCollins, 1990), 137.

13. A well-known study of such an event is Robert Darnton, "Workers Revolt: The Great Cat Massacre of the Rue Saint Séverin," in *The Great Cat Massacre and Other Episodes in French Cultural History* (New York: Basic Books, 1999).

14. Cf. Danny Lewis, "If You Want to Adopt a Black Cat, You May Need to Wait until Halloween Is Over," *Smithsonian SmartNews*, October 24, 2016, https://www.smithsonianmag.com/smart-news/if-you-want-adopt-black-cat-you-may-have-wait-until-halloween-is-over-180960868/, accessed February 13, 2018.

15. Steve Baker, *The Postmodern Animal* (London: Reaktion Books, 2000), 86.

16. https://www.independent.co.uk/life-style/cats-pretend-indifferent-humans-pet-study-oregon-state-university-a7653941.html.

17. "Endangered or Extinct Animals Won't Be Saved By Cloning," https://www.smithsonianmag.com/smart-news/endangered-or-extinct-animals-wont-be-saved-by-cloning-121647168/#uKciZ7j3VX8Xyq2b.99. The photograph shows a cat dressed in a panda suit reclining against a lineup of smiling oshaberi toys that appear to be dinosaurs.

18. For a directory of black cat superstitions and legends, see https://www.historicmysteries.com/black-cat-superstition/, accessed August 20 2018.

19. If you hear echoes of Hamlet's soliloquies, you are not mistaken; Shakespeare's play, which appeared twenty-three years later, was clearly influenced by Montaigne's essay.

20. Michel de Montaigne, "Apology for Raymond Sebond," in *The Complete Works of Montaigne*, trans. Donald M. Frame (Palo Alto, CA: Stanford University Press, 1958), 331. In another translation of this sentence, the cat is making a "pastime"

rather than a "toy" of its master: see Montaigne, *Apology for Raymond Sebond*, trans. Roger Ariew and Marjorie Grene (Indianapolis: Hackett, 2003), 15.

21. Jacques Derrida, "The Animal That Therefore I Am," trans. David Willis, *Critical Inquiry* 28, no. 2 (2002): 375.

22. Gilles Deleuze and Félix Guattari, *A Thousand Plateaus: Capitalism and Schizophrenia* (Minneapolis: University of Minnesota Press, 1987), 240. Derrida writes: "I must make it clear from the start, the cat I am talking about is a real cat, truly, believe me, a *little* cat. It isn't the *figure* of a cat. It doesn't silently enter the room as an allegory for all the cats on earth, the felines that traverse myths and religions, literature and fables. There are so many of them. The cat I am talking about does not belong to Kafka's vast zoopoetics, something that nevertheless solicits attention, endlessly and from a novel perspective" (Derrida, "The Animal That Therefore I Am," 374; italics in original).

23. Gerald L. Bruns, "Derrida's Cat (Who Am I?)," *Research in Phenomenology* 38, no. 3 (2008): 410.

24. Similarly, premodern Roman Catholic churchmen frowned upon pet owning and on the practice of giving "Christian" names to pets. Marc Shell, "The Family Pet," *Representations* 15 (1986): 135.

25. Deleuze and Guattari, *A Thousand Plateaus*, 305.

26. Quoted in Baker, *The Postmodern Animal*, 137.

27. Steve Baker, *Picturing the Beast: Animals, Identity, and Representation* (Champaign-Urbana: University of Illinois Press, 2001), 95.

28. Chris, *Watching Wildlife*, 71.

29. Alexander Wilson, *The Culture of Nature: North American Landscape from Disney to the Exxon Valdez* (Toronto: Between the Lines Press, 1991); Bill McKibben, *The Age of Missing Information* (New York: Random House, 1992).

30. Baker, *The Postmodern Animal*, 44.

31. James Serpell, *In the Company of Animals: A Study of Human-Animal Relationships* (Cambridge: Cambridge University Press, 1996).

32. Fudge, *Animal.*

33. Donna Haraway, *The Companion Species Manifesto: Dogs, People, and Significant Otherness* (Chicago: Prickly Paradigm Press, 2003), 12.

34. Michel de Certeau, *The Practice of Everyday Life*, trans. Steven F. Rendall, 3rd ed. (Berkeley: University of California Press, 2011), 169.

35. Ibid., 38.

36. Cited in Zygmunt Baumann, *Globalization: The Human Consequences* (New York: Columbia University Press, 1998), 28.

37. This obviously does not apply to male writers and philosophers (see note 1). Lévi-Strauss, Wood, Lyotard, and Derrida all evoke the cat's special value to (and in) their writing. Cats stop, Lyotard suggests, "at thresholds that we do not see, where they sniff some 'present beyond'" (cited in Baker, *The Postmodern Animal*, 184).

38. Haraway, *The Companion Species Manifesto*, 37.

39. Thanks to Zoe Lepiansky for this insight; that was a great discussion.

40. Research has shown that cats kill millions of birds each year in North America. Cats are not the only challenge; other constraints on bird sustainability include deforestation, tall buildings, avian botulism, and other environmental factors.

41. Keith Tester, *Animals and Society: The Humanity of Animal Rights* (New York: Routledge, 1991).

42. Katharine Rogers, *The Cat and the Human Imagination : Feline Images from Bast to Garfield* (Ann Arbor: University of Michigan Press, 1998), 163.

43. Penny Sparke, *As Long as It's Pink: The Sexual Politics of Taste* (Kitchener, ON: Pandora Press, 1995), 108.

44. Desmond Morris, *Catwatching: The Essential Guide to Cat Behavior* (London: Ebury, 2002).

45. Henri Lefebvre, *The Production of Space*, trans. Donald Nicholson-Smith (Oxford; Blackwell, 1992), 87.

46. Sarah Kember, *Virtual Anxiety: Photography, New Technologies and Subjectivity* (Manchester: Manchester University Press, 1998), 31.

47. Roland Barthes, *Camera Lucida: Reflections on Photography*, trans. Richard Howard (New York: Hill and Wang, 2010), 4.

48. Kember, *Virtual Anxiety*, 6.

49. Kevin Robins, *Into the Image: Culture and Politics in the Field of Vision* (East Sussex: Psychology Press, 1996), 12.

50. Edward Said, *Culture and Imperialism* (New York: Vintage Books, 1993).

51. Katherine Kete, *The Beast in the Boudoir: Petkeeping in Nineteenth-Century Paris* (Berkeley: University of California Press, 1995).

52. Lyotard, quoted in Baker, *The Postmodern Animal*, 18.

Chapter 7

1. Jonathan Sterne, *The Audible Past* (Durham: Duke University Press, 2003), 25.

2. Steven Feld, *Sound and Sentiment: Birds, Weeping, Poetics, and Song in Kaluli Expression* (Durham: Duke University Press, 2012), 79.

3. John Shepherd and Peter Wicke, *Music and Cultural Theory* (Malden, MA: Polity Press, 1997), 34.

4. Cf. Alexander Pschera, *Animal Internet: Nature and the Digital Revolution*, trans. Elisabeth Lauffer (New York: New Vessel Press, 2016).

5. "As the Government begins to shape the EU (Withdrawal) Bill, it has taken a vote to scrap EU legislation that sees non-human animals as sentient beings. Once we leave the EU in 2019, it's not only badgers and foxes that will be threatened by this change in law, but all animals that aren't pets. So basically all animals that it will be profitable to exploit." *The Independent*, November 20, 2017, https://www.independent.co.uk/voices/brexit-government-vote-animal-sentience-cant-feel-pain-eu-withdrawal-bill-anti-science-tory-mps-a8065161.html.

6. Emily Doolittle, "Animal Sounds or Animal Songs?," *Journal of Music*, August 11, 2017, 11, http://journalofmusic.com/focus/animal-sounds-or-animal-songs.

7. Nadia Whitehead, "Did Human Speech Evolve from Bird Song?," review of a *Nature World News* article, *Science*, June 12, 2014, http://www.sciencemag.org/news/2014/06/did-human-speech-evolve-bird-song, accessed April 5, 2018.

8. Brian Stallard, "Singing Primate Expose the Mystery of the Human Language," *Nature World News*, June 11, 2014, https://www.natureworldnews.com/articles/7529/20140611/singing-primate-expose-mystery-human-language.htm.

9. Shigeru Miyagawa, Shiro Ojima, Robert C. Berwick, and Kazuo Okanoya, "The Integration Hypothesis of Human Language Evolution and the Nature of Contemporary Languages," *Frontiers in Psychology*, June 2014, https://www.frontiersin.org/articles/10.3389/fpsyg.2014.00564/full, accessed August 5, 2018.

10. Michel Serres, *Thumbelina: The Culture and Technology of Millennials*, trans. Daniel W. Smith (New York: Rowman and Littlefield International, 2014).

11. John Luther Adams, *The Place Where You Go to Listen: In Search of an Ecology of Music* (Middletown: Wesleyan University Press, 2009), xi.

12. Peter Kivy, *Sound and Semblance: Reflections on Musical Representation* (Princeton: Princeton University Press, 1984), 20.

13. Edward A. Lippmann, *A History of Western Musical Aesthetics* (Lincoln: University of Nebraska Press, 1994), 91.

14. Ibid., 97.

15. John Shepherd et al., *Whose Music? A Sociology of Musical Languages* (London: Lattimer New Dimensions, 1977), 44.

16. These aesthetic pundits can be compared to the philosophers Montaigne lambasted in the late sixteenth century for their presumptive superiority as a species. This presumption was demonstrated, he argued, by the philosophers' culpable lack of curiosity about the world of animals. In the twentieth century, the practice was rather to learn as much as possible about animals but from a narrowly instrumental vantage point. Modernist social and electronic constructions validated the ideal of institutional and technical autonomy by pointing to an analogy between information structures and biological organisms. These analogous structures were based on understandings of evolution that had been severed from evidence of cross-organism and cross-species cooperation, as feminist biologists like Keller have argued.

17. Kivy, *Sound and Semblance*, 25.

18. Ibid., 243.

19. Doolittle, "Animal Sounds or Animal Songs?"

20. I am indebted to Jonathan Osborne for this insight.

21. Alan M. Gillmor, *Erik Satie* (Woodbridge, CT: Twayne Publishers, 1988), 232.

22. David Rothenberg, *Why Birds Sing: A Journey into the Mystery of Bird Song* (New York: Basic Books, 2006), 236.

23. Ibid., 236–237.

24. Lisa Blackman, *Immaterial Bodies Affect, Embodiment, Mediation* (London: Sage, 2014), viii.

25. Corinne Iozio, "Scientists Prove That Telepathic Communication Is Within Reach," Smithstonian.com, October 2, 2014, https://www.smithsonianmag.com/innovation/scientists-prove-that-telepathic-communication-is-within-reach-180952868/#lkagjRVOVsrUgMRK.99, accessed July 28, 2018.

26. Jonathan Sterne, "The Cat Telephone," *The Velvet Light Trap: A Critical Journal of Film and Television* (Fall 2009): 83–84.

27. W. J. T. Mitchell, *What Do Pictures Want? The Lives and Loves of Images* (Chicago: University of Chicago Press, 2005).

28. Alexandra Hui, *The Psychophysical Ear: Musical Experiments, Experimental Sounds, 1840–1910* (Cambridge, MA: MIT Press, 2012).

29. Don Stap, *Birdsong* (New York: Scribner, 2010).

30. Peter R. Marler and Hans Slabbekoorn, *Nature's Music: The Science of Birdsong* (Cambridge, MA: Academic Press, 2004), 1.

31. Jody Berland, "Mapping Space: Imaging Technologies and the Planetary Body," in *Technoscience and Cyberculture*, ed. Stanley Aronowitz, Barbara Martinson, Michael Menser, and Jennifer Rich (London: Routledge, 1996); Jody Berland, *North of Empire: Essays on the Cultural Technologies of Space* (Durham: Duke University Press, 2009).

32. Bernie Krause, *The Great Animal Orchestra: Finding the Origins of Music in the World's Wild Places* (Boston: Back Bay Books, 2013), 33–34. Paul Theberge, *Any Sound You Can Imagine: Making Music/Consuming Technology* (Hanover, NH: Wesleyan University Press, 1997) makes the same point about popular musicians, who must consume up-to-date technologies in order to be able to participate in pop music performance culture.

33. Krause, *The Great Animal Orchestra*, 33.

34. Feminist sociologist Avery Gordon argues against the Foucauldian idea of historical rupture for precisely this reason. As Blackman summarizes: "what is missed in such methodological framings are those aspects of historical continuity that are passed and transmitted through silences, gaps, omissions, echoes and murmurs." Blackman, *Immaterial Bodies*, xix, citing Gordon, *Ghostly Matters: Haunting and the Sociological Imagination* (2008).

35. As Krause notes, "in a short time, the recording world became dominated by digital recording systems, moving from complex, heavy, and Power dependent technologies to extremely light versatile and high-quality handheld models. ... Each time I think I have a version of the ultimate system, I'm seduced by a new and better one" (ibid., 33–34).

36. Stacy Alaimo, "Violet Black," in *Prismatic Ecology: Ecotheory beyond Green*, ed. Jeffrey Jerome Cohen (Minneapolis: University of Minnesota Press, 2013); with thanks to Brian McCormack for reminding me of this connection.

37. Christopher Perrins, *New Generation Guide to the Birds of Britain and Europe* (Austin: University of Texas Press, 1987), 23.

38. Ibid., 24.

39. See Jody Berland, "Blue Skies from Now On: Weather Motifs in Popular Songs," *Public* 10: Love (1994): 21–39.

40. Rachel Carson, *Silent Spring* (Boston: Houghton Mifflin, 1962), 108.

41. Eliza Griswold, "How 'Silent Spring' Ignited the Environmental Movement," *New York Times Magazine*, September 21, 2012, https://www.nytimes.com/2012/09/23/magazine/how-silent-spring-ignited-the-environmental-movement.html.

42. Richard J. Ladle and Paul Jepson, "Origins, Uses, and Transformation of Extinction Rhetoric," *Environment and Society* 1, no. 1 (2010): 96–115.

43. Amy Lynn Fletcher, *Mendel's Ark: Biotechnology and the Future of Extinction* (New York: Springer, 2014), 19–20.

44. Mark Hamilton Lytle, *The Gentle Subversive: Rachel Carson, Silent Spring, and the Rise of the Environmental Movement* (Oxford: Oxford University Press, 2007), 166.

45. Alex Lockwood, "The Affective Legacy of Silent Spring," Environmental Humanities 1, no. 1 (2012): 123–140, https://read.dukeupress.edu/environmental-humanities/article/1/1/123/8076/The-Affective-Legacy-of-Silent-Spring, accessed April 16, 2018.

46. Mark Jaffe, *And No Birds Sing: The Story of an Ecological Disaster in a Tropical Paradise* (New York: Simon & Schuster, 1994).

47. "Definition of 'Lull,'" *Collins Dictionary*, 4ttps://www.collinsdictionary.com/dictionary/english/lull, accessed February 9, 2018.

48. "Heaven," sang David Byrne, lead vocalist of the Talking Heads, "heaven is a place, a place where nothing, nothing ever happens." The deep ambivalence of our relationship to nature is so different from the affective ties of the past. (The Talking Heads, "Heaven," by David Byrne and Jerry Harrison, released August 3, 1979, track 8 on *Fear of Music*, Sire Records, 1979.)

49. In that respect owning a lyrical songbird was like owning a piano; it was a measure not only of the bird's beautiful singing but also of the owner's status and (his wife's) exquisite taste. Cf. Jody Berland, "The Musicking Machine," in *Residual Media: Residual Technologies and Culture*, ed. Charles R. Acland (Minneapolis: University of Minnesota Press, 2007), 303–328.

50. Rothenberg, *Why Birds Sing*, 54.

51. Donna Haraway, "Situated Knowledges: The Science Question in Feminism and the Privilege of Partial Perspective," *Feminist Studies* 14, no. 3 (Autumn 1988): 575–599.

52. Brenton J. Malin, *Feeling Mediated: A History of Media Technology and Emotion in America* (New York: NYU Press, 2014), 198.

53. Eric F. Clarke, *Ways of Listening: An Ecological Approach to the Perception of Musical Meaning* (Oxford: Oxford University Press 2005), 19. The preceding quotations are also from this source.

54. Anat Pick, *Creaturely Poetics: Animality and Vulnerability in Literature and Film* (New York: Columbia University Press, 2011).

55. Philip Warnell, "Writing in the Place of the Animal," in *Nancy and Visual Culture*, ed. Carrie Giunta and Adrienne Janus (Edinburgh: Edinburgh University Press, 2016), 148–149.

56. Sarah Kember and Joanna Zylinska, *Life after New Media: Mediation as a Vital Process* (Cambridge, MA: MIT Press, 2014), 160.

57. Max Paddison, *Adorno's Aesthetics of Music* (Cambridge: Cambridge University Press, 1997).

58. Elizabeth Kolbert, *The Sixth Extinction: An Unnatural History* (New York: Henry Holt, 2014), 15.

59. A number of sound artists are pursuing these ideas. I heard a work at Minding Animals 4 (Mexico City) by Catherine Clover, a sound artist from Melbourne, Australia, whose recording was comprised of the simultaneous sounds of birds and excited Chinese bird watchers. The sound was chaotic and infectious, and utterly different from everything I am describing.

60. Rob Laidlaw, dir., *Zoocheck* (Canada); lecture in my animal studies class, York University, January 2018.

61. Richard A. Oppenlander, *Comfortably Unaware—Global Depletion and Food Responsibility ... What You Choose to Eat* (Minneapolis: Langdon Street Press, 2011).

62. Lauren Berlant, "Cruel Optimism," in *The Affect Theory Reader*, ed. Melissa Gregg and Gregory J. Seigworth (Durham: Duke University Press, 2010), 94.

63. Sherry Turkle, *Alone Together: Why We Expect More from Technology and Less from Each Other* (New York: Basic Books, 2010).

64. Simon Barnes, *The Meaning of Birds* (New York: Pegasus Books, 2018), 82.

65. Well I didn't tell anyone, but a bird flew by.
Saw what I'd done. He set up a nest outside,
and he sang about what I'd become.
He sang so loud, sang so clear.
I was afraid all the neighbours would hear,
So I invited him in, just to reason with him.
I promised I wouldn't do it again.

But he sang louder and louder inside the house,
And no I couldn't get him out.
So I trapped him under a cardboard box.
stood on it to make him stop.
I picked up the bird and above the din I said
"That's the last song you'll ever sing."
Held him down, broke his neck,
Taught him a lesson he wouldn't forget.

But in my dreams began to creep
that old familiar tweet tweet tweet.

I opened my mouth to scream and shout,
I waved my arms and flapped about.
But I couldn't scream and I couldn't shout,
couldn't scream and I couldn't shout.

I opened my mouth to scream and shout
waved my arms and flapped about
But I couldn't scream I couldn't shout,
The song was coming from my mouth.
From my mouth,
From my mouth,
From my mouth.

From my mouth,
From my mouth,
From my mouth,
From my mouth.

From my mouth.
From my mouth.
From my mouth.
From my mouth.

From my mouth,
From my mouth,
From my mouth,
From my mouth.

Songwriters: Devonte Hynes / Florence Leontine Mary Welch. "Bird Song" lyrics © Universal Music Publishing Group, Spirit Music Group. Courtesy Florence and the Machine website.

Conclusion

1. Pugachelli, *Commodity Fetishism: Gotta Catch 'Em All*, YouTube, 3:37, November 23, 2013, https://www.youtube.com/watch?v=mynNwjyzly4, accessed February 26, 2018.

2. Joseph Tobin, introduction to *Pikachu's Global Adventure: The Rise and Fall of Pokémon*, ed. Joseph Tobin (Durham: Duke University Press, 2004), 9.

3. Julian Sefton-Green, "Initiation Rites: A Small Boy in a Poke-World," in Tobin, *Pikachu's Global Adventure*, 141; see also Nigel Thrift, *Knowing Capitalism* (London: Sage, 2005).

4. Su Ballard, "Stretching Out: Species Extinction and Planetary Aesthetics in Contemporary Art," *Australian and New Zealand Journal of Art* 17, no. 1 (2017): 2–16.

5. Pasi Väliaho, *Biopolitical Screens: Image, Power, and the Neoliberal Brain* (Cambridge, MA: MIT Press, 2014).

6. Ibid., 83.

7. Ibid., 16.

8. Jingjing Jiang, "How Teens and Parents Navigate Screen Time and Device Distractions," *Pew Research Center: Internet and Technology*, http://www.pewinternet.org/2018/08/22/how-teens-and-parents-navigate-screen-time-and-device-distractions/, accessed August 22, 2018.

9. Jeffrey Jerome Cohen, ed., *Monster Theory: Reading Culture* (Minneapolis: University of Minnesota Press, 1996), viii.

10. Cf. Michael Dylan Foster, *Pandemonium and Parade: Japanese Monsters and the Culture of Yokai* (Berkeley: University of California Press, 2008), 108.

11. Sharalyn Orbaugh, "Emotional Infectivity: Cyborg Affect and the Limits of the Human," *Mechademia* 3 (2008): 169.

12. Jorge Luis Borges, *The Book of Imaginary Beings*, trans. Andrew Hurley (1967; New York: Viking Penguin, 2005), 131.

13. Tom Tyler, "Deviants, Donestre, and Debauchees: Here Be Monsters," *Culture, Theory and Critique* 49, no. 2 (2008): xx.

14. Mario Iozzo, ed., *The Chimaera of Arrezo* (Florence: Edizioni Polistampa, 2009), 13.

15. Rosi Braidotti, "Signs of Wonder and Traces of Doubt: On Teratology and Embodied Differences," in *Monsters, Goddesses and Cyborgs: Feminist Confrontations with Science, Medicine and Cyberspace*, ed. Nina Lykke and Rosi Braidotti (Chicago: Zed Books, 1996), 135.

16. Alison Griffiths, "Wonder, Magic and the Fantastical Margins: Medieval Visual Culture and Cinematic Special Effects," *Journal of Visual Culture* 9, no. 2 (2010): 163–188.

17. Cf. Paul Wells, *The Animated Bestiary: Animals, Cartoons, and Culture* (New Brunswick, NJ: Rutgers University Press, 2009).

18. Jussi Parikka, *Insect Media: An Archaeology of Animals and Technology* (Minneapolis: University of Minnesota Press, 2010).

19. Eugene Thacker, *The Global Genome* (Cambridge, MA: MIT Press, 2005), 9.

20. Lev Manovich, *Language of New Media* (Cambridge, MA: MIT Press, 2001); Hiroki Azuma, *Otaku: Japan's Database Animals* (Minneapolis: University of Minnesota Press, 2009).

21. *Okja*, dir. Bong Joon-ho (South Korea / United States, 2017).

22. Alexa Weik von Mossner, ed., *Moving Environments: Affect, Emotion, Ecology, and Film* (Waterloo: Wilfrid Laurier University Press, 2014), cover.

23. Ben Anderson addresses this point when he writes: "I pose the question of the relation between affect and biopower from a particular context—advanced liberal democracies—in relation to the connections between a specific economic ordering—the 'real subsumption of life' (Hardt and Negri 2009)—and a specific logic of governing—neoliberalism (Foucault 2008). What links this ordering of capital / life relations with a logic of governing is a problematisation of life as contingent, as tensed between chaos and determination (as expressed through terms such as uncertainty, indeterminacy, discontinuity and turbulence). Summarising rather crudely, we could say that through neoliberal logics of governing the contingency of life has become a source of threat and opportunity, danger and profit (see Cooper 2008; Dillon 2007; Marazzi 2010; Massumi 2009, 40–63). If productive forces are to be 'generated', made to 'grow' and be 'ordered', then the contingencies of life must be known, assayed, sorted and intervened on. But contingency must never be fully eliminated, even if it could be." Ben Anderson, "Affect and Biopower: Towards a Politics of Life," *Transactions of the Institute of British Geographers* (2011): 2.

24. Claire Colebrook, *Death of the PostHuman: Essays on Extinction*, vol. 1 (London: Open Humanities Press, 2015).

25. See Britt Wray, *Rise of the Necrofauna: The Science, Ethics, and Risks of De-Extinction* (Vancouver: Greystone Books and David Suzuki Institute, 2017).

26. Ibid., 146.

27. Ibid., 188.

28. Ibid., 247.

29. Karl Marx, "The Eighteenth Brumaire of Louis Bonaparte."

Bibliography

Acampora, Ralph R. Nietzsche's Feral Philosophy: Thinking through an Animal Imaginary. In *A Nietzschean Bestiary: Becoming Animal beyond Docile and Brutal*, ed. Christa Davis Acampora and Ralph R. Acampora, 1–16. Lanham, MD: Rowman and Littlefield, 2004.

Adams, Carol J. *The Sexual Politics of Meat: A Feminist-Vegetarian Critical Theory*. New York: Continuum, 2000.

Adams, John Luther. The Place Where You Go to Listen. In *Search of an Ecology of Music*. Middletown, CT: Wesleyan University Press, 2009.

Adams, Vincanne, Michelle Murphy, and Adele E. Clarke. "Anticipation: Technoscience, Life, Affect, Temporality." *Subjectivity* 28, no. 1 (2009): 246–265.

France-Presse, Agence. "Using Cute Animals in Pop Culture Makes Public Think They're Not Endangered—Study." *Guardian*, April 13, 2018, https://www.theguardian.com/environment/2018/apr/13/using-cute-animals-in-pop-culture-makes-public-think-theyre-not-endangered-study (accessed August 21, 2018).

Ahmed, Sara. *The Cultural Politics of Emotion*. New York: Routledge, 2004.

Ahmed, Sara. *Living a Feminist Life*. Durham: Duke University Press, 2017.

Ahuja, Neel. "Postcolonial Critique in a Multispecies World." *PMLA* 124, no. 2 (2009): 556–563.

Alaimo, Stacy. Violet Black. In *Prismatic Ecology: Ecotheory beyond Green*, ed. Jeffrey Jerome Cohen, 233–251. Minneapolis: University of Minnesota Press, 2013.

Alaimo, S., and S. Hekman, eds. *Material Feminisms*. Bloomington: Indiana University Press, 2008.

Allen, A. S., and K. Dawe, eds. *Current Directions in Ecomusicology: Music, Culture, Nature*. New York: Routledge, 2015.

Allen, T., and J. Blair, eds. *Material Cultures in Canada*. Waterloo: Wilfrid Laurier University Press, 2015.

Aloi, Giovanni, ed. "Deconstructing the Animal in Search of the Real." *Anthrozoös* 25, suppl. 1 (2012): s73–s90.

Aloi, Giovanni, ed. *Virtual Animals*. Special issue, *Antennae: The Journal of Nature in Visual Culture* 30 (2014).

Ames, Eric. *Carl Hagenbeck's Empire of Entertainments*. Seattle: University of Washington Press, 2009.

Anderson, Ben. "Affect and Biopower: Towards a Politics of Life." *Transactions of the Institute of British Geographers* 37, no. 1 (2012): 28–43.

Anderson, Ben, and Paul Harrison. *Taking-Place: Non-Representational Theories and Geography*. Burlington, VT: Ashgate, 2010.

Angus, I. H., and S. Jhally, eds. *Cultural Politics in Contemporary America*. New York: Routledge, 1989.

Site, Animal Rescue. The. https://theanimalrescuesite.greatergood.com/clicktogive/ars/home (accessed August 21, 2018).

Applegate, Matt, and Jamie Cohen. "Communicating Graphically: Mimesis, Visual Language, and Commodification as Culture." *Cultural Politics* 13, no. 1 (2017): 81–100.

Arendt, Hannah. *The Human Condition*. Chicago: University of Chicago Press, 1998.

Armstrong, Philip. "The Postcolonial Animal." *Society & Animals* 10, no. 4 (2002): 413–419.

Atwood, Margaret. *Surfacing*. Toronto: Emblem Editions, 2010.

Atwood, Margaret. *Survival: A Thematic Guide to Canadian Literature*. Toronto: Anansi, 1972.

Azuma, Hiroki. *Otaku: Japan's Database Animals*. Minneapolis: University of Minnesota Press, 2009.

Bajec, Iztok Lebar, and Frank H. Heppner. "Organized Flight in Birds." *Animal Behaviour* 78, no. 4 (2009): 777–789.

Baker, Steve. *Picturing the Beast: Animals, Identity, and Representation*. Champaign-Urbana: University of Illinois Press, 2001.

Baker, Steve. *The Postmodern Animal*. London: Reaktion Books, 2000.

Balcombe, Jonathan, and J. M. Coetzee. *Second Nature: The Inner Lives of Animals*. New York: St. Martin's Griffin, 2011.

Ballard, Su. "Stretching Out: Species Extinction and Planetary Aesthetics in Contemporary Art." *Australian and New Zealand Journal of Art* 17, no. 1 (2017): 2–16.

Baratay, Eric, and Elisabeth Hardouin-Fugier. *Zoo: A History of Zoological Gardens in the West*. London: Reaktion Books, 2004.

Barnes, Simon. *The Meaning of Birds*. New York: Pegasus Books, 2018.

Barney, Darin. "One Nation under Google: Citizenship and the Technological Republic." 2008 Hart House Lecture, University of Toronto.

Barney, Darin. *Prometheus Wired: The Hope for Democracy in the Age of Network Technology*. Chicago: University of Chicago Press, 2000.

Barthes, Roland. *Camera Lucida: Reflections on Photography*. Trans. R. Howard. New York: Hill and Wang, 2010.

Barthes, Roland. *Mythologies*. New York: Farrar, Straus and Giroux, 1972.

Bartkowski, Frances. *Kissing Cousins: A New Kinship Bestiary*. New York: Columbia University Press, 2008.

Baudrillard, Jean. *For a Critique of the Political Economy of the Sign*. Trans. C. Levin. St. Louis: Telos Press, 1981.

Bauman, Zygmunt. *Globalization: The Human Consequences*. New York: Columbia University Press, 1998.

BBDO. "'Morrie's Menagerie' Is What They Call It at 'The Other Computer Company.'" *BBDO Newsletter*, March 1972, 4–7.

Beattie, Judith Hudson. "Indian Maps in the Hudson's Bay Company Archives: A Comparison of Five Area Maps Recorded by Peter Fidler, 1801–1802." *Archivaria* 21 (1985): 166–175.

Beck, Ulrich. *Ecological Politics in the Age of Risk*. Cambridge: Polity Press, 1995.

Bekoff, M., ed. *Ignoring Nature No More: The Case for Compassionate Conservation*. Chicago: University of Chicago Press, 2013.

Bekoff, Marc, and Jessica Pierce. *Wild Justice: The Moral Lives of Animals*. Chicago: University of Chicago Press, 2010.

Belton, Benjamin Keith. *Orinoco Flow: Culture, Narrative, and the Political Economy of Information*. Lanham, MD: Scarecrow Press, 2003.

Benjamin, Walter. "The Author as Producer." *Selected Writings*, vol. 2, part 2, *1931–1934*, ed. Michael W. Jennings, Howard Eiland, and Gary Smith, 768–782. Cambridge, MA: Harvard University Press, 2005.

Benjamin, Walter. N. [Re the Theory of Knowledge, Theory of Progress] In *Benjamin: Philosophy, Aesthetics, History*, ed. Gary Smith, 43–83. Chicago: University of Chicago Press, 1989.

Benjamin, Walter. "The Storyteller: Reflections on the Works of Nikolai Leskov." In *Illuminations: Essays and Reflections*, ed. Hannah Arendt, trans. Harry Zohn, 83–109. New York: Schocken, 1969.

Benjamin, Walter. "Theses on the Philosophy of History." In *Illuminations: Essays and Reflections*, ed. Hannah Arendt, trans. Harry Zohn, 253–264. New York: Schocken, 1969.

Benjamin, Walter. "The Work of Art in the Age of Mechanical Reproduction." In *Illuminations: Essays and Reflections*, ed. Hannah Arendt, trans. Harry Zohn, 217–252. New York: Schocken, 1969.

Bennetch, Paul. "Parrots Learn Their 'Names' from Their Parents, Study Shows." *Cornell Chronicle*, July 26, 2011, http://news.cornell.edu/stories/2011/07/parrots-learn-their-names-their-parents (accessed August 11, 2017).

Bennett, Jane. *The Enchantment of Modern Life: Attachments, Crossings, and Ethics*. Princeton, NJ: Princeton University Press, 2001.

Berardi, Franco. *Bifo—Franco Berardi: Transverse. Bilingual edition*. Ostfildern: Hatje Cantz, 2012.

Berger, John. *About Looking*. New York: Vintage Books, 1980.

Berger, John. *Ways of Seeing: Based on the BBC Series with John Berger*. London: Penguin Group, 1972.

Berkhead, Tim. *A Brand-New Bird: How Two Amateur Scientists Created the First Genetically Engineered Animal*. New York: Basic Books, 2003.

Berland, Jody. "Angels Suspended." *Assemblage: Critical Journal of Architecture and Design Culture* 20 (1993): 16–17.

Berland, Jody. "Animal and/as Medium: Symbolic Work in Communicative Regimes." *Global Society* 3, no. 1 (2009): 42–65.

Berland, Jody. "Blue Skies from Now On: Weather Motifs in Popular Songs." *Public* 10: Love (1994): 21–39.

Berland, Jody. "The Corporate Animal." *Virtual Menageries*, http://www.virtualmenageries.com/advertisements/ (accessed August 20, 2018).

Berland, Jody. Cultural Technologies and the 'Evolution' of Technological Cultures. In *North of Empire: Essays on the Cultural Technologies of Space*, 273–299. Durham: Duke University Press, 2009.

Berland, Jody. Locating Listening. In *North of Empire: Essays on the Cultural Technologies of Space*, 185–209. Durham: Duke University Press, 2009.

Berland, Jody. Mapping Space: Imaging Technologies and the Planetary Body. In *Technoscience and Cyberculture*, ed. Stanley Aronowitz, Barbara Martinson, Michael Menser and Jennifer Rich, 123–138. London: Routledge, 1996.

Berland, Jody. The Musicking Machine. In *Residual Media: Residual Technologies and Culture*, ed. Charles R. Acland, 303–328. Minneapolis: University of Minnesota Press, 2007.

Berland, Jody. *North of Empire: Essays on the Cultural Technologies of Space*. Durham: Duke University Press, 2009.

Berland, Jody. Weathering the North. In *North of Empire: Essays on the Cultural Technologies of Space*, 210–241. Durham: Duke University Press, 2009.

Berlant, Lauren. *Cruel Optimism*. Durham: Duke University Press, 2011.

Berlant, Lauren. Cruel Optimism. In *The Affect Theory Reader*, ed. Melissa Gregg and Gregory J. Seigworth, 93–117. Durham: Duke University Press, 2010.

Best, Steven, and Douglas Kellner. *The Postmodern Adventure: Science, Technology, and Cultural Studies at the Third Millennium*. New York: Guilford Press, 2001.

Blackman, Lisa. *The Body: The Key Concepts*. New York: Bloomsbury Academic, 2008.

Blackman, Lisa. "Embodying Affect: Voice-Hearing, Telepathy, Suggestion and Modelling the Non-Conscious." *Body & Society* 16, no. 1 (2010): 163–192.

Blackman, Lisa. *Immaterial Bodies: Affect, Embodiment, Mediation*. Thousand Oaks, CA: Sage, 2012.

Blackmore, Tim. *War X: Human Extensions in Battlespace*. Toronto: University of Toronto Press, 2005.

Blasdel, Alex. "'A Reckoning for Our Species': The Philosopher Prophet of the Anthropocene." *Guardian*, June 15, 2017, [REMOVED HYPERLINK FIELD]https://www.theguardian.com/world/2017/jun/15/timothy-morton-anthropocene-philosopher (accessed August 10, 2017).

Bolter, Jay David, and Richard Grusin. *Remediation: Understanding New Media*. Cambridge, MA: MIT Press, 2000.

Borges, Jorge Luis. *The Book of Imaginary Beings. Illus. Peter Sis*. Trans. A. Hurley. New York: Viking Penguin, 2005.

Braidotti, Rosi. Signs of Wonder and Traces of Doubt: On Teratology and Embodied Differences. In *Monsters, Goddesses and Cyborgs: Feminist Confrontations with Science, Medicine and Cyberspace*, ed. Nina Lykke and Rosi Braidotti, 135–152. Chicago: Zed Books, 1996.

Brecht, Bertolt. The Modern Theatre Is the Epic Theatre. In *Brecht on Theatre: The Development of an Aesthetic*, ed. John Willett, 33–42. New York: Hill and Wang, 1964.

de Brunhoff, John. *Animals in Music. CD.* Naxos Records, 2014.

Bruns, Gerald L. "Derrida's Cat (Who Am I?)." *Research in Phenomenology* 38, no. 3 (2008): 404–423.

Buck-Morss, Susan. "Aesthetics and Anaesthetics: Walter Benjamin's Artwork Essay Reconsidered." *October* 62 (1992): 3–41.

Buck-Morss, Susan. *Dreamworld and Catastrophe: The Passing of Mass Utopia in East and West.* Cambridge, MA: MIT Press, 2000.

Buquet, Thierry. La belle captive. La girafe dans les menageries principes au Moyen Âge. In *La bête captive au Moyen Âge et à l'époque moderne*, ed. Corinne Beck and Fabrice Guizard, 65–90. Amiens: Encrage, 2012.

Burns, Bill. *Safety Gear for Small Animals.* Installation and book. Museum of Contemporary Art, Toronto, 2005.

Burt, Jonathan. The Aesthetics of Livingness. Conference presentation. Toronto: York University, 2007.

Burt, Jonathan. *Animals in Film.* London: Reaktion Books, 2002.

Burt, Jonathan. "John Berger's 'Why Look at Animals?': A Closer Reading." *Worldviews* 9, no. 2 (2005): 203–218.

Byrne, David, and Jerry Harrison, songwriters. "Heaven" by The Talking Heads. Track 8 on *Fear of Music*, Sire Records, vinyl LP, August 3, 1979.

Calarco, Matthew. "Animals in Continental Philosophy." *H-Net,* April 23, 2007, [REMOVED HYPERLINK FIELD]https://networks.h-net.org/node/16560/pages/32233/animals-continental-philosophy-matthew-calarco (accessed October 29, 2007).

Cameron, James M. *The Canadian Beaver Book: Fact, Fiction and Fantasy.* Burnstown, ON: General Store Pub. House, 1991.

Caron, André H., and Letizia Caronia. *Moving Cultures: Mobile Communication in Everyday Life.* Montreal: McGill-Queen's University Press, 2007.

Carson, Rachel. *Silent Spring.* Boston: Houghton Mifflin, 1962.

"Cats Against Capitalism." Facebook.com, https://www.facebook.com/CATSNOTCAP/ (accessed December 10, 2017).

de Certeau, Michel. *The Practice of Everyday Life* (3rd ed.). Trans. S. F. Rendall. Berkeley: University of California Press, 2011.

Chakrabarty, Dipesh. "The Climate of History: Four Theses." *Critical Inquiry* 35, no. 2 (2009): 197–222.

Chase, Steven. "Beavers Can't Cut It as National Emblem, but Polar Bears Can, Senator Says." *Globe and Mail*, October 27, 2011.

Chris, Cynthia. *Watching Wildlife*. Minneapolis: University of Minnesota Press, 2006.

Church, Sally K. "The Giraffe of Bengal: A Medieval Encounter in Ming China." *Medieval History Journal* 7, no. 1 (2004): 1–37.

Cixous, Hélène. "The Cat's Arrival." *Parallax* 38 (January-March 2006): 21–42.

Clarke, Eric F. Music, Space and Subjectivity. In *Music, Sound and Space: Transformations of Public and Private Experience*, ed. Georgina Born, 90–110. Cambridge: Cambridge University Press, 2013.

Clarke, Eric F. *Ways of Listening: An Ecological Approach to the Perception of Musical Meaning*. Oxford: Oxford University Press, 2005.

Clendinnen, Inga. *Ambivalent Consequences: Maya and Spaniard in Yucatan, 1517–1570*. 2nd ed. Cambridge: Cambridge University Press, 2003.

Cliff, Stafford. *The Best in Retail Corporate Identities*. London: Pavilion Books, 1996.

Clough, Patricia T. "The Affective Turn: Political Economy, Biomedia and Bodies." *Theory, Culture & Society* 25, no. 1 (2008): 1–22.

Cock-Starkey, Claire. *Penguins, Pineapples and Pangolins: First Encounters with the Exotic*. London: British Library Publishing, 2016.

Code, Lorraine. *Ecological Thinking: The Politics of Epistemic Location*. Oxford: Oxford University Press, 2006.

Coetzee, J. M., and Amy Gutmann. *The Lives of Animals*. Princeton: Princeton University Press, 1999.

Cohen, J. J., ed. *Monster Theory: Reading Culture*. Minneapolis: University of Minnesota Press, 1996.

Coker, Christopher. *The Future of War: The Re-Enchantment of War in the Twenty-First Century*. Malden, MA: Wiley-Blackwell, 2004.

Colebrook, Claire. *Death of the PostHuman: Essays on Extinction*. vol. 1. London: Open Humanities Press, 2015.

Cooper, Simon. *Technoculture and Critical Theory: In the Service of the Machine?* London: Routledge, 2002.

Corbett, Julia. *Communicating Nature: How We Create and Understand Environmental Messages*. Washington, DC: Island Press, 2006.

Couldry, Nick, and Anna McCarthy. *MediaSpace: Place, Scale and Culture in a Media Age*. New York: Routledge, 2004.

Crary, Jonathan. *Techniques of the Observer: On Vision and Modernity in the Nineteenth Century*. Cambridge, MA: MIT Press, 1992.

Crew, Bec. "Cats Sailed with Vikings to Conquer the World, Genetic Study Reveals." *ScienceAlert*, October 1, 2016, https://thebestcatpage.com/2016/10/01/cats-sailed-vikings-conquer-world-genetic-study-reveals/ (accessed August 11, 2017).

Crist, Eileen. Ecocide and the Extinction of Animal Minds. In *Ignoring Nature No More: The Case for Compassionate Conservation*, ed. Marc Bekoff, 45–61. Chicago: University of Chicago Press, 2013.

Crist, Eileen. Ptolemaic Environmentalism. In *Keeping the Wild: Against the Domestication of Earth*, ed. George Wuerthner, Eileen Crist and Tom Butler, 16–30. Washington, DC: Island Press, 2014.

Cronin, Keri. 'A Mute yet Eloquent Protest': Visual Culture and Anti-Vivisection Activism in the Age of Mechanical Reproduction. In *Critical Animal Studies: Thinking the Unthinkable*, ed. John Sorenson, 284–297. Toronto: Canadian Scholars' Press, 2014.

Cronin, K., and K. Robertson, eds. *Imagining Resistance: Visual Culture and Activism in Canada*. Waterloo: Wilfrid Laurier University Press, 2011.

Cruikshank, Julie. *The Social Life of Stories: Narrative and Knowledge in the Yukon Territory*. Lincoln: University of Nebraska Press, 2000.

Cubitt, Sean. *Digital Aesthetics*. London: Sage, 1998.

Cubitt, Sean. *Finite Media: Environmental Implications of Digital Technologies*. Durham: Duke University Press, 2017.

Cubitt, Sean. *Simulation and Social Theory*. London: Sage, 2001.

Cubitt, S., and P. Thomas, eds. *Relive: Media Art Histories*. Cambridge, MA: MIT Press, 2013.

Cutler, Chris. Plunderphonia. In *Audio Culture: Readings in Modern Music*, ed. Christopher Cox and Daniel Warner, 138–156. New York: Continuum, 2004.

Darnton, Robert. Workers Revolt: The Great Cat Massacre of the Rue Saint Séverin. In *The Great Cat Massacre and Other Episodes in French Cultural History*. New York: Basic Books, 1999.

Daston, Lorraine. Intelligences: Angelic, Animal, Human. In *Thinking with Animals: New Perspectives on Anthropomorphism*, ed. Lorraine Daston and Gregg Mitman, 37–58. New York: Columbia University Press, 2005.

Davidson, T. K., O. Park, and R. Shields, eds. *Ecologies of Affect: Placing Nostalgia, Desire, and Hope*. Waterloo: Wilfrid Laurier University Press, 2011.

Davis, Heather, and Zoe Todd. "On the Importance of a Date, or, Decolonizing the Anthropocene." *ACME: An International Journal for Critical Geographies* 16, no. 4 (December 2017): 761–780, https://www.acme-journal.org/index.php/acme/article/view/1539 (accessed February 10, 2018).

Dean, Jodi. *Democracy and Other Neoliberal Fantasies: Communicative Capitalism and Left Politics*. Durham: Duke University Press, 2009.

Dean, Jodi. *Publicity's Secret: How Technoculture Capitalizes on Democracy*. Ithaca: Cornell University Press, 2002.

Debray, Régis. *Media Manifestos: On the Technological Transmission of Cultural Forms*. Trans. E. Rauth. London: Verso, 1996.

Deckha, Maneesha. "Toward a Postcolonial, Posthumanist Feminist Theory: Centralizing Race and Culture in Feminist Work on Nonhuman Animals." *Hypatia* 27, no. 3 (2012): 527–545.

"Definition of 'Lull.'" *Collins Dictionary*, https://www.collinsdictionary.com/dictionary/english/lull (accessed February 9, 2018).

Deleuze, Gilles. *The Fold*. New York: Continuum, 2006.

Deleuze, Gilles. *Francis Bacon: The Logic of Sensation*. New York: Continuum, 2003.

Deleuze, Gilles. *Kafka: Toward a Minor Literature*. Minneapolis: University of Minnesota Press, 1986.

Deleuze, Gilles. "On Spinoza." N.d., [REMOVED HYPERLINK FIELD]http://deleuzelectures[REMOVED HYPERLINK FIELD].blogspot.com/2007/02/on-spinoza.html (accessed August 10, 2017).

Deleuze, Gilles, and Félix Guattari. *A Thousand Plateaus: Capitalism and Schizophrenia*. Minneapolis: University of Minnesota Press, 1987.

Derrida, Jacques. *The Animal That Therefore I Am*, ed. Marie-Louise Mallet, trans. David Wills. New York: Fordham University Press, 2008.

Derrida, Jacques. *Archive Fever: A Freudian Impression*. Trans. E. Prenowitz. Chicago: University of Chicago Press, 1998.

Derrida, Jacques. Before the Law. In *Acts of Literature*, ed. Derek Attridge, 181–220. New York: Routledge, 1991.

Derrida, Jacques, and Derek Attridge. *Acts of Literature*. New York: Routledge, 1991.

Dick, Philip K. *Do Androids Dream of Electric Sheep?* New York: Ballantine Books, 2008.

Dixon, Dougal. *After Man: A Zoology of the Future*. New York: St. Martin's Griffin, 1998.

Dixon, Steve. Metal Performance: Humanizing Robots, Returning to Nature, and Camping About. In *Critical Digital Studies: A Reader*. 2nd ed., ed. Arthur Kroker and Marilouise Kroker, 485–541. Toronto: University of Toronto Press, 2013.

Donath, Judith. "Artificial Pets: Simple Behaviors Elicit Complex Attachments." N.d., http://www.vivatropolis.com/judith/ArtificialPets.pdf (accessed August 20, 2018).

Donath, Judith. Interfaces Make Meaning. In *The Social Machine: Designs for Living Online*, 41–76. Cambridge, MA: MIT Press, 2014.

Doniger, Wendy. Reflection. In *The Lives of Animals*, ed. J. M. Coetzee, 93–106. Princeton: Princeton University Press, 1999.

Donovan, J., and C. J. Adams, eds. *The Feminist Care Tradition in Animal Ethics: A Reader*. New York: Columbia University Press, 2007.

Doolittle, Emily. "Animal Sounds or Animal Songs?" *Journal of Music*, July 9, 2012, http://journalofmusic.com/focus/animal-sounds-or-animal-songs (accessed August 11, 2017).

Dorland, Michael. "Foucault, *The Order of Things* and Data Visualization." Unpublished paper presented at Crossroads in Cultural Studies, Paris, 2012.

Doyle, Alister. Giraffes Suffer 'Silent Extinction' in Africa. *Scientific American*, December 8, 2016. https://www.scientificamerican.com/article/giraffes-suffer-silent-extinction-in-africa/ accessed December 28, 2017.

Drain, Jim. *Catholic No. 1: Cats*. 2nd ed. D.A.P./Evil Twin Publications, 2005, http://www.eviltwinpublications.com/eviltwin.html.

Dugmore, A. Radclyffe. *Nature and the Camera: How to Photograph Live Birds and Their Nests; Animals, Wild and Tame; Reptiles; Insects; Fish and Other Aquatic Forms; Flowers, Trees, and Fungi*. New York: Doubleday, 1902.

Dugmore, A. Radclyffe. *The Romance of the Beaver: Being the History of the Beaver in the Western Hemisphere*. London: Heinemann, 1914.

Edison Manufacturing Co. "The Boxing Cats." Youtube.com, https://www.youtube.com/watch?v=RoHeGhfWMzM (accessed August 18, 2018).

Efimova, Alla. "A Prescription for Life: Sun, Air, and Water in Socialist Realism and Soviet Health Care." Unpublished manuscript.

Ellis, Carolyn. "Katrina and the Cat: Responding to Society's Expendables." *Cultural Studies ↔ Critical Methodologies* 7, no. 2 (2007): 188–201.

Ellul, Jacques. *The Technological Society*. New York: Vintage, 1967.

Emberley, Julia. *The Cultural Politics of Fur*. Ithaca: Cornell University Press, 1997.

Emberley, Julia. *Defamiliarizing the Aboriginal : Cultural Practices and Decolonization in Canada*. Toronto: University of Toronto Press, 2007.

EndWar Wiki. "Kinetic Strike." Wikia.com, http://endwar.wikia.com/wiki/Kinetic_Strike (accessed August 19, 2018).

Eveleth, Rose. Endangered or Extinct Animals Won't Be Saved by Cloning. *Smithsonian*, November 13, 2012. https://www.smithsonianmag.com/smart-news/endangered-or-extinct-and-animals-wont-be-saved-by-cloning-121647168/#uKciZ7j3VX8Xyq2b.99 (accessed August 21, 2018).

Evernden, Neil. Nature in Industrial Society. In *Cultural Politics in Contemporary America*, ed. Ian H. Angus and Sut Jhally, 151–166. New York: Routledge, 1989.

Ewen, Stuart. *All Consuming Images: The Politics of Style in Contemporary Culture*. New York: Basic Books, 1988.

Ewen, Stuart. *Captains of Consciousness: Advertising and the Social Roots of the Consumer Culture*. New York: Basic Books, 2001.

Ewen, Stuart, and Elizabeth Ewen. *Channels of Desire: Mass Images and the Shaping of American Consciousness*. Minneapolis: University of Minnesota Press, 1992.

Fabian, Johannes. *Time and the Other: How Anthropology Makes Its Object*. New York: Columbia University Press, 1983.

Fagan, Brian. *The Intimate Bond: How Animals Shaped Human History*. New York: Bloomsbury Press, 2015.

Feld, Steven. *Sound and Sentiment: Birds, Weeping, Poetics, and Song in Kaluli Expression*. Durham: Duke University Press, 2012.

Fiamengo, Janice. "Postcolonial Guilt in Margaret Atwood's Surfacing." *American Review of Canadian Studies* 29, no. 1 (2009): 141–163.

Findlen, P., ed. *Early Modern Things: Objects and Their Histories, 1500–1800*. New York: Routledge, 2013.

Fiske, Jo-Anne, Susan Sleeper Smith, and William Wicken eds. *New Faces of the Fur Trade: Selected Papers of the Seventh North American Fur Trade Conference, Halifax, Nova Scotia, 1995*. East Lansing: Michigan State University Press, 1998.

Fleming, Marnie. *Beaver Tales*. Catalogue of an exhibition, held May 16–July 20, 2000. Oakville, ON: Oakville Galleries, 2000.

Fletcher, Amy Lynn. *Mendel's Ark: Biotechnology and the Future of Extinction*. New York: Springer, 2014.

Florence and the Machine. *Birdsong. CD*. Universal Island Records Ltd, 2011.

Fornari, José. A Computational Environment for the Evolutionary Sound Synthesis of Birdsongs. In *Evolutionary and Biologically Inspired Music, Sound, Art and Design*, ed. Penousal Machado, Juan Romero and Adrian Carballal, 96–107. Berlin: Springer, 2012.

Foster, Michael Dylan. *Pandemonium and Parade: Japanese Monsters and the Culture of Yokai*. Berkeley: University of California Press, 2008.

Foucault, Michel. *Introduction to The History of Sexuality*. vol. 1. Trans. R. Hurley. New York: Vintage, 1990.

Foucault, Michel. ""Of Other Spaces: Utopias and Heterotopias. Des Espaces Autres." Trans. Jay Miskowiec." *Diacritics* 16 (1986): 22–27.

Foucault, Michel. *The Order of Things: An Archaeology of Human Sciences*. New York: Random House, 2012.

Foucault, Michel. *Security, Territory, and Population: Lectures at the Collège de France, 1977–1978*. New York: Palgrave Macmillan, 2007.

Fox News Tech. "Robot Hummingbird Spy Drone Flies for Eight Minutes, Spies on Bad Guys." *Fox News*, February 18, 2011, http://www.foxnews.com/tech/2011/02/18/robot-hummingbird-spy-drone-flies-minutes-spies-bad-guys.html (accessed August 21, 2018).

Francis, Margot. *Creative Subversions: Whiteness, Indigeneity and the National Imaginary*. Vancouver: UBC Press, 2011.

Franklin, Sarah. *Dolly Mixtures: The Remaking of Genealogy*. Durham: Duke University Press, 2007.

Franklin, Seb. "Cloud Control, or The Network as Medium." *Cultural Politics* 8, no. 3 (2012): 443–464.

Freud, Sigmund. *Totem and Taboo*. New York: Norton, 2010.

Fudge, Erica. *Animal*. London: Reaktion Books, 2002.

Fudge, Erica. *At the Borders of the Human: Beasts, Bodies, and Natural Philosophy in the Early Modern Period*. New York: St. Martin's Press, 1999.

Fudge, Erica. *Brutal Reasoning: Animals, Rationality, and Humanity in Early Modern England*. Ithaca: Cornell University Press, 2006.

Fudge, Erica. A Left-Handed Blow: Writing the History of Animals. In *Representing Animals*, ed. Nigel Rothfels, 3–18. Bloomington: Indiana University Press, 2002.

Fudge, Erica. *Pets*. Stocksfield, UK: Routledge, 2014.

Fuller, Matthew. *Media Ecologies: Materialist Energies in Art and Technoculture*. Cambridge, MA: MIT Press, 2007.

Gagnon, Francois-Marc. *Images du Castor Canadien | Septentrion. La Référence*. Quebec: Septentrion, 1994.

Genosko, G., ed. *Marshall McLuhan: Critical Evaluations in Cultural Theory*. London: Routledge, 2005.

Gere, Charlie. *Digital Culture*. Rev. ed. London: Reaktion Books, 2008.

Gianikian, Yervant, and Angela Ricci Lucchi. *From the Pole to the Equator*. Film, Museum of Modern Art, 1988.

Gilbert, Jeremy. *Anticapitalism and Culture: Radical Theory and Popular Politics*. London: Bloomsbury Academic, 2008.

Gillmor, Alan M. *Erik Satie*. Woodbridge, CT: Twayne Publishers, 1988.

Gilson, Dave. "In 1918, California Drafted Children into a War on Squirrels." *Atlas Obscura*, November 29, 2016, https://www.atlasobscura.com/articles/in-1918-california-drafted-children-into-a-war-on-squirrels (accessed August 20, 2018).

Giraffe Conservation Foundation. "Africa's Giraffe Conservation Guide." https://giraffeconservation.org/wp-content/uploads/2016/02/Conservation-Guide-poster-LR-c-GCF.pdf (accessed February 13, 2018).

Gitelman, Lisa. *Always Already New: Media, History, and the Data of Culture*. Cambridge, MA: MIT Press, 2008.

Goffman, Erving. *The Presentation of Self in Everyday Life*. New York: Anchor, 1959.

Gómez-Peña, Guillermo. "The New Global Culture, Somewhere between Corporate Multiculturalism and the Mainstream Bizarre (a Border Perspective)." *Drama Review* 45, no. 1 (2001): 7–30.

Goodall, Jane. *Giraffe Family: Animal Series*. Toronto: Madison Marketing, 1991.

Goodall, Jane. *Lion Family: Animal Series*. Toronto: Madison Marketing, 1991.

Goodall, Jane. "Tool Using." *Jane Goodall—Studies of the Chimpanzee*. Video recording, 1976.

Gordon, Avery F. *Ghostly Matters: Haunting and the Sociological Imagination*. Minneapolis: Minnesota University Press, 2008.

Gordon, W. *Terrence. McLuhan: A Guide for the Perplexed*. New York: Continuum, 2010.

Gould, James L. *Ethology: The Mechanisms and Evolution of Behavior*. New York: Norton, 1982.

Gould, Trevor. *Posing for the Public: The World as Exhibition*. Hamilton, ON: Art Gallery of Hamilton, 2003.

Government of Canada. *Government of Canada Response to Report of Standing Committee on Aboriginal Affairs and Northern Development: The Fur Issue: Cultural Continuity, Economic Opportunity*. Ottawa, ON: Indian and Northern Affairs Canada, 1987.

Greenberg, Clement. Avant-Garde and Kitsch. *Art and Culture*. Boston: Beacon Press, 1961. First published in *Partisan Review* 6, no. 5 (1939): 34–49.

Gregg, M., and G. J. Seigworth, eds. *The Affect Theory Reader*. Durham: Duke University Press, 2010.

Gregory, D., and A. Pred, eds. *Violent Geographies: Fear, Terror, and Political Violence*. New York: Routledge, 2006.

Owl, Grey. *The Collected Works of Grey Owl: Three Complete and Unabridged Canadian Classics*. Toronto: Discovery Books, 1999.

Griffiths, Alison. "Wonder, Magic and the Fantastical Margins: Medieval Visual Culture and Cinematic Special Effects." *Journal of Visual Culture* 9, no. 2 (2010): 163–188.

Griswold, Eliza. "How 'Silent Spring' Ignited the Environmental Movement." *New York Times Magazine*, September 21, 2012, https://www.nytimes.com/2012/09/23/magazine/how-silent-spring-ignited-the-environmental-movement.html[REMOVED HYPERLINK FIELD] (accessed. August 14, 2017).

Grossberg, Lawrence. *Cultural Studies in the Future Tense*. Durham: Duke University Press, 2010.

Grossman, Elizabeth, and Elisa Carlson. *High Tech Trash: Digital Devices, Hidden Toxics, and Human Health*. Washington, DC: Island Press, 2007.

Grossman, Lev. Invention of the Year: The iPhone—Best Inventions of 2007. *Time*, November 1, 2007. http://content.time.com/time/specials/2007/article/0,28804,1677329_1678542_1677891,00.html accessed August 20, 2018.

Grusin, Richard. "Mediation Is the Message." *Journal of Visual Culture* 13, no. 1 (2014): 55–57.

Grusin, Richard. *Premediation: Affect and Mediality after 9/11*. New York: Palgrave Macmillan, 2010.

Guattari, Félix. Remaking Social Practices. In *The Guattari Reader*, ed. Gary Genosko, 262–272. Oxford: Wiley-Blackwell, 1996.

Guattari, Félix. *The Three Ecologies*. London: Athlone Press, 2000.

Hackett, E. J., et al., eds. *The Handbook of Science and Technology Studies*. 3rd ed. Cambridge, MA: MIT Press, 2007.

Haiven, Max. *Cultures of Financialization: Fictitious Capital in Popular Culture and Everyday Life*. Basingstoke, UK: Palgrave Macmillan, 2014.

Haiven, Max. "Monsters of the Financialized Imagination: From Pokemon to Trump." In *State of Power*, ed. Nick Buxton and Deborah Eade, n.p. Washington: Transnational Institute, 2017, http://longreads.tni.org/state-of-power/age-of-monsters/ (accessed August 21, 2018).

Halberstam, Judith. *The Queer Art of Failure*. Durham: Duke University Press, 2011.

Hall, Susan. "Cell Phones Can Harm Animals." *Californian/North County Times*, September 12, 2006, http://www.sandiegouniontribune.com/sdut-cell-phones-can-harm-animals-2006sep13-story.html (accessed August 20, 2018).

Ham, Jennifer, and Matthew Senior. *Animal Acts: Configuring the Human in Western History*. London: Routledge, 1997.

Hammer, R., and D. Kellner, eds. *Media/Cultural Studies: Critical Approaches*. New York: Peter Lang, 2009.

Hansen, Elizabeth. *Animal Attractions*. Princeton: Princeton University Press, 2004.

Hansen, Mark B. N. *Feed-Forward: On the Future of Twenty-First-Century Media*. Chicago: University of Chicago Press, 2015.

Hanssen, Beatrice. *Walter Benjamin's Other History: Of Stones, Animals, Human Beings, and Angels*. Berkeley: University of California Press, 1998.

Haraway, Donna. *The Companion Species Manifesto: Dogs, People, and Significant Otherness*. Chicago: Prickly Paradigm Press, 2003.

Haraway, Donna. A Cyborg Manifesto: Science, Technology, and Socialist-Feminism in the Late Twentieth Century. In *Simians, Cyborgs and Women: The Reinvention of Nature*, 149–181. London: Free Association Books, 1991.

Haraway, Donna. "Situated Knowledges: The Science Question in Feminism and the Privilege of Partial Perspective." *Feminist Studies* 14, no. 3 (Autumn 1988): 575–599.

Haraway, Donna. *When Species Meet*. Minneapolis: University of Minnesota Press, 2007.

Harding, Jennifer E., and E. Deidre Pribram. "The Power of Feeling: Locating Emotions in Culture." *European Journal of Cultural Studies* 5, no. 4 (2002): 407–426.

Hardt, Michael, and Antonio Negri. *Empire*. Cambridge, MA: Harvard University Press, 2001.

Harley, Maria Anna. "Birds in Concert: North American Birdsong in Bartók's Piano Concerto No. 3." *Tempo* 189 (1994): 8–16.

Hartshorne, Charles. "The Aesthetics of Birdsong." *Journal of Aesthetics and Art Criticism* 26, no. 3 (1968): 311–315.

Harvey, David. *Justice, Nature and the Geography of Difference*. Cambridge, MA: Wiley-Blackwell, 1997.

Hasan, Ragib. "History of Linux." 2002, http://ragibhasan.com/linux/ (accessed February 12, 2013).

Hayne, David M. "Lom d'Arce de Lahontan, Louis-Armand de, Baron de Lahontan." *Dictionary of Canadian Biography*, vol. 2 (1701–1740). University of Toronto/Université Laval, 1969/1982, http://www.biographi.ca/en/bio/lom_d_arce_de_lahontan_louis_armand_de_2E.html (accessed December 15, 2017).

Hearne, Vicki. *Adam's Task: Calling Animals by Name*. New York: Alfred A. Knopf, 1986.

Heidegger, Martin. *The Question Concerning Technology and Other Essays*. New York: Harper Perennial, 1982.

Heidenreich, Conrad E. "Seventeenth-Century Maps of the Great Lakes: An Overview and Procedures for Analysis." *Archivaria* 6 (1978): 83–112.

Heimann, Jim. *All American Ads*. Cologne: Taschen, 2003.

Heise, Ursula. *Imagining Extinction*. Chicago: University of Chicago Press, 2016.

Heise, Ursula K., and Allison Carruth. "Introduction to Focus: Environmental Humanities." *American Book Review* 32, no. 1 (2011): 3.

Heraldson, Donald. *Creators of Life: A History of Animation*. New York: Drake, 1975.

Herzog, Hal. *Some We Love, Some We Hate, Some We Eat: Why It's So Hard to Think Straight about Animals*. New York: Harper Perennial, 2011.

Heywood, John. *The Proverbs and Epigrams of John Heywood (1562)*. The Spenser Society, 1867.

Highmore, Ben. "Bitter After Taste: Affect, Food and Social Aesthetics." In *The Affect Theory Reader*, ed. Melissa Gregg and Gregory J. Seigworth. Durham: Duke University Press, 2010.

Hofman, Ana. "The Affective Turn in Ethnomusicology." *Muzikologija* 18 (2015): 35–55.

Hong, Seung-Baeck. *21C Hit Design Hit Brand and Logo*. vol. 1. Seoul: DN Books, 2008.

Hood, Glynnis. *The Beaver Manifesto*. Victoria, BC: RMB, 2011.

Horkheimer, Max, and Theodor W. Adorno. *Dialectic of Enlightenment*, ed. Gunzelin Noeri. Trans. Edmund Jephcott. Stanford: Stanford University Press, 2002.

Hornung, P. Clarence. *Handbook of Early Advertising Art*. New York: Dover, 1956.

Hosie, Rachel. "Cats Are Only Pretending to Be Indifferent to Humans, Claims Study." Indy/Life, March 28, 2017, https://www.independent.co.uk/life-style/cats-pretend-indifferent-humans-pet-study-oregon-state-university-a7653941.html (accessed August 21, 2018).

Howell, James. "Thērologia, The Parly of Beasts, Or, Morphandra, Queen of the Inchanted Iland wherein Men Were Found, Who Being Transmuted to Beasts, Though Proffer'd to Be Dis-Inchanted, and to Becom Men Again, Yet, in Regard of the Crying Sins and Rebellious Humors of the Times, They Prefer the Life of a Brute Animal before that of a Rational Creture ... : With Reflexes upon the Present State of Most Countries in Christendom: Divided into a XI Sections." 1660. *Early English Books Online*. York University, https://www.library.yorku.ca/find/Record/1810207 (accessed August 20, 2018).

Huet, Marie-Hélène. *Monstrous Imagination*. Cambridge, MA: Harvard University Press, 1993.

Hui, Alexandra. *The Psychophysical Ear: Musical Experiments, Experimental Sounds, 1840–1910*. Cambridge, MA: MIT Press, 2012.

Hui, Yuk. "What Is a Digital Object?" *Metaphilosophy* 43, no. 4 (2012): 380–395.

Hutcheon, Linda. *The Canadian Postmodern: A Study of Contemporary English-Canadian Fiction*. Oxford: Oxford University Press, 1988.

Hynes, Devonte, and Florence Leontine Mary Welch, songwriters. "Bird Song" by Florence and the Machine. Universal Music Publishing Group, Spirit Music Group, disc 2, track 2 on *Lungs: Deluxe Edition*, 2009, compact disc.

I-Love-Cats. "Upload and Share Your Cute Cat & Kitten Images." http://i-love-cats.com/ (accessed August 21, 2018).

Ingold, T., ed. *What Is an Animal?* London: Unwin Hyman, 1988.

Innis, Harold A. *The Bias of Communication*. Toronto: University of Toronto Press, 2008.

Innis, Harold Adams. *The Fur Trade in Canada: An Introduction to Canadian Economic History*. New Haven: Yale University Press, 1962.

Iozio, Corinne. "Scientists Prove That Telepathic Communication Is Within Reach." *Smithsonian*, October 2, 2014, https://www.smithsonianmag.com/innovation/scientists-prove-that-telepathic-communication-is-within-reach-180952868/#lkagjRVOVsrUgMRK.99 (accessed July 28, 2018).

Iozzo, M., ed. *The Chimaera of Arrezo*. Florence: Edizioni Polistampa, 2009.

IUCN Redlist of Threatened Species. "Giraffa camelopardalis," Iucnredlist.org http://www.iucnredlist.org/details/9194/0 (accessed August 18, 2018).

Jaffe, Mark. *And No Birds Sing: The Story of an Ecological Disaster in a Tropical Paradise*. New York: Simon and Schuster, 1994.

Jameson, Fredric. "The Vanishing Mediator: Narrative Structure in Max Weber." *New German Critique, NGC* 1 (Winter 1973): 52–89.

Jay, M., and S. Ramaswamy, eds. *Empires of Vision: A Reader*. Durham: Duke University Press, 2014.

Jay, Roni. *The Kingdom of the Cat*. London: Apple Press, 2000.

Jensen, Derrick. *The Culture of Make Believe*. New York: Basic Books, 2002.

Jiang, Jingjing. "How Teens and Parents Navigate Screen Time and Device Distractions." *Pew Research Centre: Internet and Technology*, August 22, 2018, http://www.pewinternet.org/2018/08/22/how-teens-and-parents-navigate-screen-time-and-device-distractions/ (accessed August 22, 2018).

Kafka, Franz. A Report to an Academy. In *The Complete Stories*, ed. Nahum Norbert Glatzer, trans. Willa Muir and Edwin Muir, 257–258. New York: Schocken Books, 1983.

Katz, Cyndi. Banal Terrorism. In *Violent Geographies: Fear, Terror, and Political Violence*, ed. Derek Gregory and Allan Pred, 349–362. New York: Routledge, 2006.

Keats, John. *John Keats: Selected Poems*, rev. ed., ed. John Barnard. London: Penguin Classics, 2007.

Keller, Evelyn Fox. Marrying the Premodern to the Postmodern: Computers and Organisms after World War II. In *Prefiguring Cyberculture: An Intellectual History*, ed. Darren Tofts, Annemarie Jonson, and Alessio Cavallaro, 52–65. Cambridge, MA: MIT Press, 2002.

Keller, Jared. "The Pentagon's New Super Weapon Is Basically a Weaponized Meteor Strike." *Task & Purpose*, June 7, 2017, https://taskandpurpose.com/kinetic-bombardment-kep-weaponry/ (accessed August 19, 2018).

Kellogg, Louise P. "The Hudson Bay Company Tokens." *Wisconsin Magazine of History* 2, no. 2 (1918): 214–216.

Kelly, Kevin. "Futurist Stewart Brand Wants to Revive Extinct Species." *Wired*, August 17, 2012, https://www.wired.com/2012/08/ff_stewartbrand/.

Kelly, Walt. "We Have Met the Enemy and He Is Us." *Pogo*, comic strip, 1971.

Kember, Sarah. *Cyberfeminism and Artificial Life*. London: Routledge, 2003.

Kember, Sarah. *Virtual Anxiety: Photography, New Technologies and Subjectivity*. Manchester: Manchester University Press, 1998.

Kember, Sarah, and Joanna Zylinska. *Life after New Media: Mediation as a Vital Process*. Cambridge, MA: MIT Press, 2014.

Kete, Kathleen. *The Beast in the Boudoir: Petkeeping in Nineteenth-Century Paris*. Berkeley: University of California Press, 1995.

Keynes, John Maynard. *Essays in Persuasion*. New York: Lightning Source Inc, 2009.

Keynes, John Maynard. *The General Theory of Employment, Interest and Money*. New York: Createspace Independent, 2009.

Kirby, Jason. "How to Squander a $52-Billion Empire." *Maclean's* (July 23, 2007): 40–43.

Kiser, Lisa J. Animals in Medieval Sports, Entertainments and Menageries. In *A Cultural History of Animals in the Medieval Age*, ed. Brigitte Resl, 103–126. Oxford: Berg, 2007.

Kivy, Peter. *Sound and Semblance: Reflections on Musical Representation*. Princeton: Princeton University Press, 1984.

Klein, Bethany. *As Heard on TV: Popular Music in Advertising*. Farnham, UK: Routledge, 2010.

Kolbert, Elizabeth. "The Climate of Man—III." *New Yorker (New York, N.Y.)* (May 9, 2005): 52.

Kolbert, Elizabeth. *The Sixth Extinction: An Unnatural History*. New York: Henry Holt, 2014.

Krause, Bernie. *The Great Animal Orchestra: Finding the Origins of Music in the World's Wild Places*. Boston: Back Bay Books, 2013.

Krech, Shepard. *Indians, Animals, and the Fur Trade: A Critique of Keepers of the Game*. Athens: University of Georgia Press, 1981.

Krech, Shepard. *The Subarctic Fur Trade: Native Social and Economic Adaptations*. Vancouver: University of British Columbia Press, 1984.

Kroeber, A. L. *The Nature of Culture*. Chicago: University of Chicago Press, 1952.

Kroker, A., and M. Kroker, eds. *Critical Digital Studies: A Reader*. 2nd ed. Toronto: University of Toronto Press, 2013.

Ladle, Richard J., and Paul Jepson. "Origins, Uses, and Transformation of Extinction Rhetoric." *Environment and Society* 1, no. 1 (2010): 96–115.

Lagueux, Olivier. "Geoffroy's Giraffe: The Hagiography of a Charismatic Mammal." *Journal of the History of Biology* 36, no. 2 (2003): 225–247.

Lahonton, Louis-Armand Lom d'Arce, Baron de. *Different Ways of Hunting the Beaver*. London, 1703.

Lahonton, Louis-Armand Lom d'Arce, Baron de. In *New Voyages to North-America*, ed. Reuben Gold Thwaites and Victor Hugo Paltsits. Chicago: A. C. McClurg, 1905.

Lamarre, Thomas. "New Media Worlds; Final Fantasy: Computer Graphic Animation and the Dis[illusion] of Life; An Unrecognized Treasure Chest: The Internet as Animation Archive." In *Animated Worlds*, ed. Suzanne Buchan, 131–150. Bloomington, IN: John Libbey, 2006.

Latour, Bruno. "On Actor-Network Theory: A Few Clarifications." *Soziale Welt* 47, no. 4 (1996): 369–381.

Latour, Bruno. *Politics of Nature: How to Bring the Sciences into Democracy*. Trans. C. Porter. Cambridge, MA: Harvard University Press, 2004.

Latour, Bruno. *Reassembling the Social: An Introduction to Actor-Network-Theory*. Oxford: Oxford University Press, 2007.

Latour, Bruno. *We Have Never Been Modern*. Cambridge, MA: Harvard University Press, 1993.

Lawrence, M., and L. McMahon, eds. *Animal Life and the Moving Image*. London: British Film Institute, 2015.

Leach, William R. *Land of Desire: Merchants, Power, and the Rise of a New American Culture*. New York: Vintage, 1994.

Leakey, Richard E., and Roger Lewin. *The Sixth Extinction: Patterns of Life and the Future of Humankind*. New York: Anchor Books, 1996.

LeBel, Sabine. "The Life Cycle of the Computer: Studies in the Materialities of Risk." PhD dissertation, York University, 2014.

LeBel, Sabine. "Notes on Cool: The Temporal Politics of Friendly Monsters and the E-Waste Aesthetic by Sabine Lebel Nanocrit.com." *NANO: New American Notes Online* 7 (2015) https://www.nanocrit.com/issues/issue7/notes-cool-temporal-politics-friendly-monsters-and-e-waste-aesthetic (accessed August 20, 2018).

Lefebvre, Henri. *The Production of Space*. Trans. D. Nicholson-Smith. Oxford: Wiley-Blackwell, 1992.

Lévi-Strauss, Claude. *Totemism*. Boston: Beacon Press, 1971.

Lewis, Danny. "If You Want to Adopt a Black Cat, You May Need to Wait until Halloween Is Over." *Smithsonian SmartNews*, October 24, 2016, https://www.smithsonianmag.com/smart-news/if-you-want-adopt-black-cat-you-may-have-wait-until-halloween-is-over-180960868/ (accessed February 13, 2018).

Lewis-Kraus, Gideon. "Crazy for Kittehs: The Quest to Find the Purring Heart of Cat Videos." *Wired UK*, October 2012.

Lilley, Sasha, et al. *Catastrophism: The Apocalyptic Politics of Collapse and Rebirth*. Oakland: Between the Lines, 2012.

Lippit, Akira Mizuta. *Electric Animal: Toward a Rhetoric of Wildlife*. Minneapolis: University of Minnesota Press, 2000.

Lippit, Akira Mizuta. '... From Wild Technology to Electric Animal. In *Representing Animals*, ed. Nigel Rothfels, 119–136. Bloomington: Indiana University Press, 2002.

Lippmann, Edward A. *A History of Western Musical Aesthetics*. Lincoln: University of Nebraska Press, 1994.

Liu, Alan. "From Reading to Social Computing." [REMOVED HYPERLINK FIELD][REMOVED HYPERLINK FIELD][REMOVED HYPERLINK FIELD][REMOVED HYPERLINK FIELD]2013, https://dlsanthology.mla.hcommons.org/from-reading-to-social-computing/ (accessed August 20, 2018).

Liu, Alan. Imagining the New Media Encounter. In *A Companion to Digital Literary Studies*, ed. Ray Siemens and Susan Schreibman, 3–26. New York: Wiley-Blackwell, 2008.

Liu, Alan. *The Laws of Cool: Knowledge Work and the Culture of Information*. Chicago: University of Chicago Press, 2004.

Liu, Alan. "Where Is Cultural Criticism in the Digital Humanities?" January 7, 2011, http://liu.english.ucsb.edu/where-is-cultural-criticism-in-the-digital-humanities/ (accessed August 20, 2018).

Lockwood, Alex. "The Affective Legacy of Silent Spring." *Environmental Humanities* 1, no. 1 (2012): 123–140, https://read.dukeupress.edu/environmental-humanities/article/1/1/123/8076/The-Affective-Legacy-of-Silent-Spring (accessed April 16, 2018).

van Loon, Joost. *Risk and Technological Culture: Towards a Sociology of Virulence*. London: Routledge, 2002.

Lorey, Isabel. *State of Insecurity: Government of the Precarious*. London: Verso, 2015.

Lousley, Cheryl. "Charismatic Life: Spectacular Biodiversity and Biophilic Life Writing." *Environmental Communication* 10, no. 6 (2016): 704–718.

Loveridge-Green, Olivia, Holly Christodoulou, and Guy Birchall. "Irma's Wrath." *Sun*, September 17, 2017, https://www.thesun.co.uk/news/4447836/hurricane-irma-richard-branson-necker-island-damage-photos/ (accessed August 2, 2018).

Lovink, Geert. "Interview with Alan Liu." February 28, 2006, http://networkcultures.org/geert/interview-with-alan-liu/ (accessed August 20, 2018).

Lowenstein, George, and Ted O'Donohue. "Animal Spirits: Affective and Deliberative Processes in Economic Behavior." CAE Working Paper #04-14, 2004, Cornell University, https://cae.economics.cornell.edu/04-14.pdf. (accessed August 9, 2018).

Lu, Jican, and Fuguo Yu. *Big Brand*. Toronto: Designer Books, 2008.

Luther, David, and Luis Baptista. "Urban Noise and the Cultural Evolution of Bird Songs." *Proceedings of the Royal Society of London B: Biological Sciences* 277 (1680) (2010): 469–473.

Lytle, Mark Hamilton. *The Gentle Subversive: Rachel Carson, Silent Spring, and the Rise of the Environmental Movement*. Oxford: Oxford University Press, 2007.

MacDonald, Scott. "Review: From the Pole to the Equator by Yevant Gianikian, Angela Ricci Lucchi." *Film Quarterly* 42, no. 3 (Spring 1989): 33–38.

MacKay, Douglas. *The Honorable Company: A History of the Hudson's Bay Company*. Oxford: Tudor Press, 1938.

Mackey, Eva. *Unsettled Expectations: Uncertainty, Land and Settler Decolonization*. Halifax: Fernwood Publishing, 2016.

Malamud, Randy. Americans Do Weird Things with Animals, or, Why Did the Chicken Cross the Road? In *Animal Encounters*, ed. Tom Tyler and Manuela Rossini, 73–96. Leiden: Brill, 2009.

Malamud, Randy. *An Introduction to Animals and Visual Culture*. London: Palgrave Macmillan, 2012.

Malamud, Randy. *Reading Zoos: Representations of Animals and Captivity*. New York: New York University Press, 1998.

Malin, Brenton J. *Feeling Mediated: A History of Media Technology and Emotion in America*. New York: NYU Press, 2014.

Manovich, Lev. *The Language of New Media*. Cambridge, MA: MIT Press, 2001.

Marler, Peter R., and Hans Slabbekoorn. *Nature's Music: The Science of Birdsong*. Cambridge, MA: Academic Press, 2004.

Martin, Calvin, and Nancy Lurie. *Keepers of the Game: Indian-Animal Relationships and the Fur Trade*. Berkeley: University of California Press, 1982.

Marvin, Carolyn. *When Old Technologies Were New: Thinking about Electric Communication in the Late Nineteenth Century*. New York: Oxford University Press, 1990.

Marx, Karl. *Capital: A Critique of Political Economy*. vol. 1. Trans. Ben Fowkes. London: Penguin Books, 1976.

Masco, Joseph. The Six Extinctions: Visualizing Planetary Ecological Crisis Today. In *After Extinction*, ed. Richard Grusin, 71–105. Minneapolis: University of Minnesota Press, 2018.

Maslin, Janet. "From the Pole to the Equator." *New York Times*, April 6, 1988.

Masson, Jeffrey Moussaieff, and Susan McCarthy. *When Elephants Weep: The Emotional Lives of Animals*. New York: Delta, 1996.

Massumi, Brian. *Parables for the Virtual: Movement, Affect, Sensation*. Durham: Duke University Press, 2002.

Massumi, Brian. *Politics of Everyday Fear*. Minneapolis: University of Minnesota Press, 1993.

Maxwell, Richard, and Toby Miller. "Ecological Ethics and Media Technology." *International Journal of Communication* 2 (2008): 331–353.

May, John, and Michael Marten. *The Book of Beasts*. New York: Viking Press, 1983.

Mazlish, Bruce. *The Fourth Discontinuity: The Co-Evolution of Humans and Machines*. New Haven: Yale University Press, 1993.

Mbembe, Achille. *On the Postcolony*. Berkeley: University of California Press, 2001.

Mbembe, Achille. "On the Postcolony: A Brief Response to Critics." *Qui Parle* 15, no. 2 (2005): 1–49.

McCormack, Brian. "Among *Umwelten*: Meaning-Making in Critical Posthumanism." PhD dissertation, York University, 2018.

McGuigan, Jim. *Neoliberal Culture*. New York: Palgrave Macmillan, 2016.

McHugh, Susan. "Clever Pigs, Failing Piggeries." *Antennae* 12 (Spring 2010): 19–25.

McKegney, Sam W. "Second-Hand Shaman: Imag(in)ing Indigeneity from Le Jeune to Pratt, Moore and Beresford." *Topia* 12 (Fall 2004): 25–40.

McKibben, Bill. *The Age of Missing Information*. New York: Random House, 1992.

McLuhan, Marshall. *The Mechanical Bride: Folklore of Industrial Man*. Berkeley, CA: Gingko Press, 2008.

McLuhan, Marshall. "New Media as Political Forms." *Explorations* 3 (1955): 115–121.

McLuhan, Marshall. *Understanding Media: The Extensions of Man*. Cambridge, MA: MIT Press, 1994.

McLuhan, Marshall, and Quentin Fiore. *The Medium Is the Massage: An Inventory of Effects*. Berkeley, CA: Gingko Press, 2001.

McLuhan, Marshall, and Eric McLuhan. *Laws of Media: The New Science*. Toronto: University of Toronto Press, 1992.

McMurray, Andrew. "Critical Ecologies: Ten Years Later." *Electronic Book Review*, December 2006, http://electronicbookreview.com/essay/critical-ecologies-ten-years-later/ (accessed August 20, 2018).

Merchant, Carolyn. *The Death of Nature: Women, Ecology, and the Scientific Revolution.* New York: HarperCollins, 1990.

Meredith, Martin. *Elephant Destiny: Biography of an Endangered Species in Africa.* New York: Public Affairs, 2001.

Microsoft. "A History of Windows." https://windows.microsoft.com/en-us/windows/history (accessed February 12, 2013).

Midgley, Mary. *Animals and Why They Matter.* Athens: University of Georgia Press, 1983.

Midgley, Mary. *Beast and Man: The Roots of Human Nature.* London: Routledge, 1978.

Midgley, Mary. Beasts, Brutes and Monsters. In *What Is an Animal?* ed. Tim Ingold, 35–46. Boston: Routledge, 1994.

Midgley, Mary. Speech and Other Excellences. In *Beast and the Man: The Roots of Human Nature*, 203–251. London: Routledge, 1978.

Mills, Stephanie. "Everyday Life in the Modern World." *Journal of Wild Culture*, June 18, 2017, http://www.wildculture.com/article/everyday-life-modern-world/1495 (accessed August 20, 2018).

Miltner, Katharine. "Srsly Phenomenal: An Investigation into the Appeal of Lolcats." PhD dissertation, University of Queensland, 2013.

Mirzoeff, N., ed. *The Visual Culture Reader.* London: Routledge, 2012.

Misa, Thomas, Phillip Brey, and Andrew Feenberg. *Modernity and Technology.* Cambridge, MA: MIT Press, 2003.

Mitchell, W. J. T. *Image Science: Iconology, Visual Culture, and Media Aesthetics.* Chicago: University of Chicago Press, 2015.

Mitchell, W. J. T. *What Do Pictures Want? The Lives and Loves of Images.* Chicago: University of Chicago Press, 2005.

Mitchell, W. J. T., and Mark B. N. Hansen, eds. *Critical Terms for Media Studies.* Chicago: University of Chicago Press, 2010.

Miyagawa, Shigiru, Shiro Ojima, Robert C. Berwick, and Kazuyo Okanoya. "The Integration Hypothesis of Human Language Evolution and the Nature of Contemporary Languages." *Frontiers in Psychology*, June 2014, https://www.frontiersin.org/articles/10.3389/fpsyg.2014.00564/full (accessed August 5, 2018).

Mol, Arthur P. J. The Environmental Transformation of the Modern Order. In *Modernity and Technology*, ed. Thomas S. Misa, Philip Brey and Andrew Feenberg, 303–326. Cambridge, MA: MIT Press, 2003.

Montaigne, Michel de. Apology for Raymond Sebond. In *The Complete Works of Montaigne*, trans. D. M. Frame. Stanford: Stanford University Press, 1958.

Mooallem, John. "The Afterlife of Cellphones—Cellular Telephone—Waste Materials—Recycling." *New York Times*, January 13, 2008, 38–43.

Moore, Jason W. The Rise of Cheap Nature. In *Anthropocene or Capitalocene? Nature, History, and the Crisis of Capitalism*, ed. Jason W. Moore, 78–115. Oakland, CA: PM Press, 2016.

Moore, Jennifer, writer and producer. "Flux" by Jennifer Moore. Track 1 on *Twig*, Mp3, September 26, 2013.

Moores, Shaun. The Doubling of Place: Electronic Media, Time-Space Arrangements and Social Relationships. In *MediaSpace: Place, Scale and Culture in a Media Age*, ed. Nick Couldry and Anna McCarthy, 21–36. London: Routledge, 2004.

Moores, Shaun. *Media/Theory*. New York: Routledge, 2005.

Morgan, Lewis H. *The American Beaver and His Works*. London: Forgotten Books, 2015.

Morley, David. *Home Territories: Media, Mobility, and Identity*. London: Routledge, 2000.

Morris, Desmond. *Catwatching: The Essential Guide to Cat Behaviour*. London: Ebury, 2002.

Morton, Timothy. *The Ecological Thought*. Cambridge, MA: Harvard University Press, 2012.

Morton, Timothy. "Of Matter and Meter: Environmental Form in Coleridge's 'Effusion 35' and 'The Eolian Harp.'." *Literature Compass* 5 (2008): 1–26.

Mumford, Lewis. *Technics and Civilization*. Chicago: University of Chicago Press, 2010.

Murphie, Andrew, Larissa Hjorth, Gillian Fuller, and Sandra Buckley. "Editorial: Mobility, New Social Intensities, and the Coordinates of Digital Networks." *Fibreculture* 6 (2005): n.p.

Murphy, Brian. "Revolution in Military Affairs: Digital Technology and Network Theories Applied to War." Paper presented at the Canadian Communication Association, University of Saskatchewan, 2007.

Myerson, George. *Heidegger, Habermas and the Mobile Phone*. London: Icon, 2001.

Nadeau, Chantal. *Fur Nation: From the Beaver to Brigitte Bardot*. London: Routledge, 2001.

Nakamura, Lisa. Where Do You Want to Go Today? In *The Visual Culture Reader*, ed. Nicholas Mirzoeff, 255–263. London: Routledge, 1998.

Nayar, Pramrad K. "Touchscreens and Architexture: Tactile Technologies, the World and the Digital Uncanny." *MCC Journal for Language and Social Sciences* 1, no. 1 (2016): 7–13.

Necati, Yas. "The Tories Have Voted that Animals Can't Feel Pain." *Independent*, November 20, 2017, https://www.independent.co.uk/voices/brexit-government-vote-animal-sentience-cant-feel-pain-eu-withdrawal-bill-anti-science-tory-mps-a8065161.html (accessed June 18, 2018).

Nelson, Peter. "Cohabiting in Time: Towards an Ecology of Rhythm." *Organised Sound* 16, no. 2 (2011): 109–114.

Nemorin, Selena. "Augmenting Animality: Neuromarketing as a Pedagogy of Communicative Surveillance." PhD dissertation, Ontario Institute for Studies in Education, University of Toronto, 2015.

Niall. Ultimate Natural Sounds—Tranquil Birdsong. CD. Paradise Music, 2008.

Noble, Ian. *Picture Perfect: Fusions of Illustrations and Design*. Switzerland: RotoVision, 2003.

Nollman, Jim. *Playing Music with Animals: Interspecies Communication of Jim Nollman with 300 Turkeys, 12 Wolves and 20 Orcas. CD*. Smithsonian Folkways, 1982.

Noonan, Chris, dir. *Babe*. Film. Universal Pictures, 1995.

Norton, Thomas, and Thomas Sackville. The Tragedie of Gorbeduc. In *Verse Libel in Renaissance England and Scotland*, ed. Steven W. May and Alan Bryson. Oxford: Oxford University Press, 2016.

Noske, Barbara. *Beyond Boundaries*. Montreal: Black Rose Books, 1997.

Nott, George. "Talking with the Birds: It's a Hoot with Sound Artist Catherine Clover." *Independent*, June 28, 2011.

Nussbaum, Martha. "Objectification." *Philosophy & Public Affairs* 24, no. 4 (1995): 249–291.

van den Oever, Annie, and Geoffrey Winthrop-Young. Rethinking the Materiality of Technical Media: Friedrich Kittler, Enfant Terrible with a Rejuvenating Effect on Parental Discipline—A Dialogue. In *Techné/Technology: Researching Cinema and Media Technologies, Their Development, Use and Impact*, ed. Annie van den Oever, 219–239. Amsterdam: Amsterdam University Press, 2014.

Oppenlander, Richard A. *Comfortably Unaware—Global Depletion and Food Responsibility … What You Choose to Eat*. Minneapolis: Langdon Street Press, 2011.

Orbaugh, Sharalyn. "Emotional Infectivity: Cyborg Affect and the Limits of the Human." *Mechademia* 3 (2008): 150–172.

O'Reilly, Media. "About O'Reilly." http://www.oreilly.com/about/ (accessed February 12, 2013).

O'Sullivan, Terry. "Animal Magic." OpenLearn, Open University, June 6, 2006, http://www.open.edu/openlearn/moneymanagement/management/business-studies/animal-magic (accessed April 15, 2018).

Outwater, Alice B. *Water: A Natural History*. New York: Basic Books, 1996.

Pacey, Arnold. *The Culture of Technology*. Cambridge, MA: MIT Press, 1985.

Paddison, Max. *Adorno's Aesthetics of Music*. Cambridge: Cambridge University Press, 1997.

Parikka, Jussi. "Hidden in Plain Sight: The Steganographic Image." February 2017, https://unthinking.photography/themes/fauxtography/hidden-in-plain-sight-the-steganographic-image (accessed August 21, 2018).

Parikka, Jussi. *Insect Media: An Archaeology of Animals and Technology*. Minneapolis: University of Minnesota Press, 2010.

Parikka, Jussi. *What Is Media Archaeology?* Cambridge: Polity Press, 2012.

Pasquinelli, Matteo. *Animal Spirits: A Bestiary of the Commons*. Rotterdam: NAi Publishers, Institute of Networked Cultures, 2008.

Peers, Laura. "Fur Trade History, Native History, Public History: Communication and Miscommunication." In *New Faces of the Fur Trade: Selected Papers of the Seventh North American Fur Trade Conference, Halifax, Nova Scotia, 1995*, ed. Jo-Anne Fiske, Susan Sleeper-Smith, and William Wicken. East Lansing: Michigan State University Press, 1998.

Perrins, Christopher. *New Generation Guide to the Birds of Britain and Europe*. Austin: University of Texas Press, 1987.

Peters, John Durham. *The Marvelous Clouds: Toward a Philosophy of Elemental Media*. Chicago: University of Chicago Press, 2015.

Peters, John Durham. *Speaking into the Air: A History of the Idea of Communication*. Chicago: University of Chicago Press, 2001.

Pettman, Dominic. *Human Error: Species-Being and Media Machines*. Minneapolis: University of Minnesota Press, 2011.

Finder, Phrase. The. "The Meaning and Origin of the Expression: A Cat May Look at a King." https://www.phrases.org.uk/meanings/a-cat-may-look-at-a-king.htm (accessed August 21, 2018).

Pick, Anat. *Creaturely Poetics: Animality and Vulnerability in Literature and Film.* New York: Columbia University Press, 2011.

Pick, A., and G. Narraway, eds. *Screening Nature: Cinema beyond the Human.* New York: Berghahn Books, 2013.

Plumb, Christopher. "Reading Menageries: Using Eighteenth-Century Print Sources to Historicise the Sensorium of Menagerie Spectators and Their Encounters with Exotic Animals." *European Review of History: Revue européenne d'histoire* 17, no. 2 (2010): 265–286.

Podhovnik, Edith. "The Meow Factor—An Investigation of Cat Content in Today's Media." In *Arts & Humanities Venice 2016*, conference proceedings, April 27, 2016, 127–139.

Ponting, Clive. *A New Green History of the World: The Environment and the Collapse of Great Civilizations.* London: Penguin Books, 2007.

Powell, Douglas, and William Leiss. *Mad Cow and Mother's Milk: The Perils of Poor Risk Communication.* Montreal: McGill-Queen's University Press, 2004.

Powell, Mike. "Cover Story: Natural Selection." *Pitchfork*, November 2, 2016, http://pitchfork.com/features/cover-story/reader/natural-selection/ (accessed August 20, 2018).

Providence, Animal Rescue League. http://www.parl.org/ (accessed August 21, 2018).

Pschera, Alexander. *Animal Internet: Nature and the Digital Revolution.* Trans. E. Lauffer. New York: New Vessel Press, 2016.

Pugachelli. "Commodity Fetishism: Gotta Catch 'Em All." YouTube, 3:37, November 23, 2013, https://www.youtube.com/watch?v=mynNwjyzly4 (accessed February 26, 2018).

Ratcliffe, Eleanor, Birgitta Gatersleben, and Paul T. Sowden. "Bird Sounds and Their Contributions to Perceived Attention Restoration and Stress Recovery." *Journal of Environmental Psychology* 36 (2013): 221–228.

Reggio, Godfrey. *Anima Mundi.* DVD. Miramar, 1992.

Reggio, Godfrey. *Anima Mundi. Letterbox. Audio recording.* Seattle: Miramar Productions, 1992.

Reid, Roddey. *Confronting Political Intimidation and Public Bullying: A Citizen's Handbook for the Trump Era and Beyond.* N.p., 2017.

Rheingold, Howard. *The Virtual Community: Homesteading on the Electronic Frontier.* Cambridge, MA: MIT Press, 2000.

Richardson, Ingrid. "Mobile Techsoma: Some Phenomenological Reflections on Itinerant Media Devices." *Fibercultures* 6 (2005): n.p.

Rimke, Heidi. "Introduction—Mental and Emotional Distress as a Social Justice Issue: Beyond Psychocentrism." *Studies in Social Justice* 10, no. 1 (2016): 4–17.

Ringmar, Erik. "Audience for a Giraffe: European Expansionism and the Quest for the Exotic." *Journal of World History* 17, no. 4 (2006): 375–397.

Riskin, Jessica. "The Defecating Duck, or, the Ambiguous Origins of Artificial Life." *Critical Inquiry* 29, no. 4 (2003): 599–633.

Robins, Kevin. *Into the Image: Culture and Politics in the Field of Vision*. East Sussex: Psychology Press, 1996.

Roell, Craig H. *The Piano in America, 1890–1940*. Chapel Hill: University of North Carolina Press, 1989.

Rogers, Katharine M. Agents of the Devil. In *The Cat and the Human Imagination: Feline Images from Bast to Garfield*. Ann Arbor: University of Michigan Press, 1988.

Rogers, Katharine M. *The Cat and the Human Imagination : Feline Images from Bast to Garfield*. Ann Arbor: University of Michigan Press, 1998.

Rohman, Carrie. *Stalking the Subject: Modernism and the Animal*. New York: Columbia University Press, 2008.

Rosenthal, Elisabeth. "Cat Lovers Lining Up for No-Sneeze Kitties." *New York Times*, October 6, 2006.

Rossiter, Ned. "Creative Industries, Comparative Media Theory and the Limits of Critique from Within." *Topia* 11 (2004): 21–48.

Rothenberg, David. *Why Birds Sing: A Journey Into the Mystery of Bird Song*. New York: Basic Books, 2006.

Rothfels, Nigel. *Representing Animals*. Bloomington: Indiana University Press, 2002.

Rothfels, Nigel. *Savages and Beasts: The Birth of the Modern Zoo*. Baltimore: Johns Hopkins University Press, 2008.

Rundell, John. "Modernity, Humans and Animals: Tensions in the Field of the Technical-Industrial Imaginary." *New Formations* 76 (2012): 8–20.

Rutsky, R. L. *High Techne: Art and Technology from the Machine Aesthetic to the Posthuman*. Minneapolis: University of Minnesota Press, 1999.

Said, Edward W. *Culture and Imperialism*. New York: Vintage Books, 1993.

Sandhu, Khushboo. "Cell Phone Tower Radiation May Be Killing Plants and Animals." *Ludhiana Newsline*, March 13, 2007, http://cities.expressindia.com/fullstory.php?newsid=226423 (accessed August 20, 2018).

Sardar, Ziauddin, and Sean Cubitt. *Aliens R Us: The Other in Science Fiction Cinema*. Sterling, VA: Pluto Press, 2002.

Saul, John Ralston. *A Fair Country: Telling Truths about Canada*. Toronto: Penguin Canada, 2009.

Saum, Lewis O. *The Fur Trader and the Indian*. Seattle: University of Washington Press, 1965.

Sayer, Derek. *The Violence of Abstraction: The Analytical Foundations of Historical Materialism*. London: Basil Blackwell, 1987.

Scarry, Elaine. *The Body in Pain: The Making and Unmaking of the World*. New York: Oxford University Press, 1985.

Schiller, Dan. *How to Think about Information*. Urbana: University of Illinois Press, 2007.

Schoell, William. *Creature Features: Nature Turned Nasty in the Movies*. Jefferson, NC: McFarland, 2008.

Schwartz, Hillel. *The Culture of the Copy: Striking Likenesses, Unreasonable Facsimiles*. New York: Zone Books, 1996.

Scranton, Roy. *Learning to Die in the Anthropocene: Reflections on the End of a Civilization*. San Francisco: City Lights Books, 2015.

Michigan, Sea Grant. "Avian Botulism." Michigan State University, http://www.miseagrant.umich.edu/explore/coastal-communities/avian-botulism/ (accessed February 20, 2018).

Seatter, Robert. "The Cello and the Nightingale." *BBC News*, March 25, 2016, http://www.bbc.com/news/magazine-35861899 (accessed August 21, 2018).

Sebeok, Thomas A. *Essays in Zoosemiotics: At the Intersection of Nature and Culture*. Leiden: Brill Academic, 1975.

Sefton-Green, Julian. Initiation Rites: A Small Boy in a Poke-World. In *Pikachu's Global Adventure: The Rise and Fall of Pokémon*, ed. Joseph Tobin, 141–164. Durham: Duke University Press, 2004.

Serpell, James. *In the Company of Animals: A Study of Human-Animal Relationships*. Cambridge: Cambridge University Press, 1996.

Serres, Michel. *Angels, a Modern Myth*. Trans. F. Cowper. Paris: Flammarion, 1995.

Serres, Michel. *The Parasite*. Trans. L. R. Schehr. Baltimore: Johns Hopkins University Press, 1982.

Serres, Michel. *Thumbelina: The Culture and Technology of Millennials*. Trans. D. W. Smith. London: Rowman and Littlefield International, 2014.

Serres, Michel. *Variations on the Body*. Trans. R. Burks. Minneapolis: Univocal Publishing, 2012.

Shell, Marc. "The Family Pet." *Representations (Berkeley, Calif.)* 15 (1986): 121–153.

Shepherd, John, Phil Virden, Graham Vulliamy, and Trevor Wishart. *Whose Music? A Sociology of Musical Languages*. London: Lattimer New Dimensions, 1977.

Shepherd, John, and Peter Wicke. *Music and Cultural Theory*. Malden, MA: Polity Press, 1997.

Shildrick, Margrit. *Leaky Bodies and Boundaries: Feminism, Postmodernism and (Bio) ethics*. London: Routledge, 1997.

Shukin, Nicole. *Animal Capital: Rendering Life in Biopolitical Times*. Minneapolis: University of Minnesota Press, 2009.

Simon, Clea. *The Feline Mystique: On the Mysterious Connection between Women and Cats*. New York: St. Martin's Press, 2003.

Singer, Dorothy, and Jerome L. Singer. *Imagination and Play in the Electronic Age*. Cambridge, MA: Harvard University Press, 2005.

Singer, Peter. *Animal Liberation: The Definitive Classic of the Animal Movement*. New York: Harper Perennial, 2009.

Slemon, Stephen. "Unsettling the Empire: Resistance Theory for the Second World." *World Literature Written in English* 30 (1990): 30–41.

Sloterdijk, Peter. "Rules for the Human Zoo: A Response to the Letter on Humanism." *Environment and Planning. D, Society & Space* 27, no. 1 (2009): 12–28.

Smith, Adam. *The Theory of Moral Sentiments*, ed. Ryan Patrick Hanley. New York: Penguin Classics, 2010.

Soper, Kate. *What Is Nature? Culture, Politics and the Non-Human*. Oxford: Blackwell, 1995.

Sorenson, Sue. "Battle or Gratitude? Attitudes Conveyed to Children by Pokémon, Bakugan, and Magic Tree House Books." *Peace Research* 41, 2 (2009): 5–27.

Sorkin, Michael. See You in Disneyland. In *Variations on a Theme Park: The New American City and the End of Public Space*, ed. Michael Sorkin, 205–232. New York: Hill and Wang, 1992.

Sparke, Penny. *As Long as It's Pink: The Sexual Politics of Taste*. Kitchener, ON: Pandora Press, 1995.

Pets, Spruce. The. "How to Be a Responsible Cat Owner." https://www.thesprucepets.com/cats-4162124 (accessed August 21, 2018).

Staedter, Tracy. "Octopus Inspires AI Robots on a Mission." https://www.seeker.com/octopus-inspires-ai-robots-on-a-mission-1771111049.html (accessed January 19, 2018).

Stallard, Brian. "Singing Primate Expose the Mystery of the Human Language." *Nature World News,* June 11, 2014, https://www.natureworldnews.com/articles/7529/20140611/singing-primate-expose-mystery-human-language.htm (accessed August 22, 2018).

Stallmen, Richard. "The GNU Manifesto." 1985, https://www.gnu.org/gnu/manifesto.en.html (accessed August 20, 2018).

Stamps, Judith. *Unthinking Modernity: Innis, McLuhan, and the Frankfurt School.* Montreal: McGill-Queen's University Press, 1995.

Stap, Don. *Birdsong.* New York: Scribner, 2010.

Sterne, Jonathan. *The Audible Past.* Durham: Duke University Press, 2003.

Sterne, Jonathan. "The Cat Telephone." The Velvet Light Trap: A Critical Journal of Film and Television 64 (Fall 2009): 83–84.

Sterne, Jonathan. Out with the Trash. In *Residual Media,* ed. Charles R. Acland, 16–31. Minneapolis: University of Minnesota Press, 2007.

Stibbe, Arran. "Language, Power and the Social Construction of Animals." *Society & Animals* 9, no. 2 (2001): 145–160.

Stoler, A. L., ed. *Haunted by Empire: Geographies of Intimacy in North American History.* Durham: Duke University Press, 2006.

Stuff on My Cat. http://stuffonmycat.com/ (accessed August 21, 2018).

Tennant, Roy, John Ober, and Anne G. Lipow. *Crossing the Internet Threshold: An Instructional Handbook.* Berkeley, CA: Library Solutions Press, 1994.

Tenner, Edward. *Why Technology Bites Back: Technology and the Revenge of Unintended Consequences.* New York: Vintage Books, 1997.

Tester, Keith. *Animals and Society: The Humanity of Animal Rights.* New York: Routledge, 1991.

Thacker, Eugene. *The Global Genome.* Cambridge, MA: MIT Press, 2005.

Theall, Donald F. "Speaking into the Air: A History of the Idea of Communication." *Canadian Journal of Communication* 26, no. 3 (2001): n.p.

Theberge, Paul. *Any Sound You Can Imagine: Making Music/Consuming Technology.* Hanover, NH: Wesleyan University Press, 1997.

Thomas, Keith. *Man and the Natural World.* Harmondsworth, UK: Penguin, 1992.

Thomas, Nicholas. Objects of Knowledge: Oceanic Artifacts in European Engravings. In *Empires of Vision: A Reader,* ed. Martin Jay and Sumathi Ramaswamy, 141–158. Durham: Duke University Press, 2014.

Thompson, J. *Eric S. Maya Hieroglyphic Writing: An Introduction*. Norman: University Press of Oklahoma, 1966.

Thorburn, Elise D. "Cyborg Witches: Class Composition and Social Reproduction in the GynePunk Collective." *Feminist Media Studies* 17, no. 2 (2017): 153–167.

Thrift, Nigel. *Knowing Capitalism*. London: Sage, 2005.

Thrift, Nigel. *Non-Representational Theory: Space, Politics, Affect*. New York: Routledge, 2007.

Tiessen, Matthew. Human Desiring and Extended Agency. In *Ecologies of Affect: Placing Nostalgia, Desire, and Hope*, ed. Tonya K. Davidson, Ondine Park and Rob Shields, 127–142. Waterloo: Wilfrid Laurier University Press, 2011.

Tobin, Joseph. Introduction. In *Pikachu's Global Adventure: The Rise and Fall of Pokémon*, ed. Joseph Tobin, 3–11. Durham: Duke University Press, 2004.

Tobin, J., ed. *Pikachu's Global Adventure: The Rise and Fall of Pokémon*. Durham: Duke University Press, 2004.

Tofts, Darren, Annemarie Jonson, and Allessio Cavellaro. *Prefiguring Cyberculture: An Intellectual History*. Cambridge, MA: MIT Press, 2003.

Trevor-Roper, Hugh. *The European Witch-Craze of the Sixteenth and Seventeenth Centuries*. London: Pelican Books, 1969.

Tucker, Abigail. "Opinion: How Cats Evolved to Win the Internet." *New York Times*, October 15, 2016.

Turkle, Sherry. *Alone Together: Why We Expect More from Technology and Less from Each Other*. New York: Basic Books, 2010.

Turner, Fred. *From Counterculture to Cyberculture: Stewart Brand, the Whole Earth Network, and the Rise of Digital Utopianism*. Chicago: University of Chicago Press, 2006.

Twine, Richard. *Animals as Biotechnology: Ethics, Sustainability and Critical Animal Studies*. London: Routledge, 2010.

Tyler, Tom. "Deviants, Donestre, and Debauchees: Here Be Monsters." *Culture, Theory & Critique* 49, no. 2 (2008): 113–131.

Tyler, T., and M. Rossini, eds. *Animal Encounters*. The Hague: Brill Academic, 2009.

Uddin, Lisa. "Canine Citizenship and the Intimate Public Sphere." *Invisible Culture: An Electronic Journal of Visual Culture*, no. 6 (2003), http://www.rochester.edu/in_visible_culture/Issue_6/uddin/uddin.html.

von Uexküll, Jakob. *A Foray into the Worlds of Animals and Humans, with A Theory of Meaning*. Minneapolis: University of Minnesota Press, 2010.

Väliaho, Pasi. *Biopolitical Screens: Image, Power, and the Neoliberal Brain*. Cambridge, MA: MIT Press, 2014.

Van Wyck, Peter. *Primitives in the Wilderness: Deep Ecology and the Missing Human Subject*. Albany: SUNY Press, 1997.

Virilio, Paul. *Politics of the Very Worst: An Interview by Philippe Petit*. Trans. Michael Cavaliere, ed. Sylvère Lotringer. New York: Semiotext(e), 1999.

Wainio, Carol. *Carol Wainio: Persistent Images*. Toronto: Art Gallery of York University, 1998.

Waldau, P., and K. Patton, eds. *A Communion of Subjects: Animals in Religion, Science, and Ethics*. New York: Columbia University Press, 2006.

Warnell, Philip. Writing in the Place of the Animal. In *Nancy and Visual Culture*, ed. Carrie Giunta and Adrienne Janus, 144–163. Edinburgh: Edinburgh University Press, 2016.

Weik von Mossner, Alexa, ed. *Moving Environments: Affect, Emotion, Ecology, and Film*. Waterloo, ON: Wilfrid Laurier University Press, 2014.

Wells, Paul. *The Animated Bestiary: Animals, Cartoons, and Culture*. New Brunswick, NJ: Rutgers University Press, 2009.

Wernick, Andrew. *Promotional Culture: Advertising, Ideology and Symbolic Expression*. Thousand Oaks, CA: Sage, 1991.

Wernick, Andrew. Vehicles for Myth: The Shifting Image of the Modern Car. In *Cultural Politics in Contemporary America*, ed. Ian H. Angus and Sut Jhally, 198–216. New York: Routledge, 1989.

Whitehead, Nadia. "Did Human Speech Evolve from Bird Song?" *Science*, June 12, 2014. http://www.sciencemag.org/news/2014/06/did-human-speech-evolve-bird-and-song, accessed April 5, 2018.

Whitehouse, Andrew. "Listening to Birds in the Anthropocene: The Anxious Semiotics of Sound in a Human-Dominated World." *Environmental Humanities* 6, no. 1 (2015): 53–71.

Whiteside, Kerry H. *Divided Natures: French Contributions to Political Ecology*. Cambridge, MA: MIT Press, 2002.

Wikipedia. "African Wildlife Foundation." https://en.wikipedia.org/wiki/African_Wildlife_Foundation (accessed January 2018).

Wikipedia. "History of YouTube." https://en.wikipedia.org/wiki/History_of_YouTube (accessed October 2016).

Wikiquote. "Talk: Margaret Atwood." https://en.wikiquote.org/wiki/Talk:Margaret_Atwood (accessed December 15, 2017).

Wilkinson, Eleanor. "On Love as an (Im)properly Political Concept." *Environment and Planning. D, Society & Space* 35, no. 1 (2017): 57–71.

Williams, Edgar. *Giraffe*. London: Reaktion Books, 2011.

Wills, David. Meditations for the Birds. In *Demenageries: Thinking (of) Animals after Derrida*, ed. Anne Emmanuelle Berger and Marta Segarra, 245–263. Amsterdam: Rodopi, 2011.

Wilson, Alexander. *The Culture of Nature: North American Landscape from Disney to the Exxon Valdez*. Toronto: Between the Lines Press, 1991.

Winner, Langdon. *Autonomous Technology: Technics-out-of-Control as a Theme in Political Thought*. Cambridge, MA: MIT Press, 1978.

Winslow, E. G. "Keynes and Freud: Psychoanalysis and Keynes' Account of the 'Animal Spirits' of Capitalism." *Social Research* 53, no. 4 (1986): 549–578.

Wittgenstein, Ludwig. *Philosophical Investigations*. Oxford: B. Blackwell, 1958.

Wittje, Gavin. "Deleuze Conference: On Media and Movement." Department of Anthropology, University of California, Berkeley, http://gavinwit.googlepages.com/Deleuzeconference (accessed December 4, 2017).

Wolch, Jennifer R., and Jody Emel. *Animal Geographies: Place, Politics, and Identity in the Nature-Culture Borderlands*. London: Verso, 1998.

Wolfe, Cary. *Animal Rites: American Culture, the Discourse of Species, and Posthumanist Theory*. Chicago: University of Chicago Press, 2003.

Wolfe, Cary. *Before the Law: Humans and Other Animals in a Biopolitical Frame*. Chicago: University of Chicago Press, 2012.

Wolfe, Cary. *Critical Environments: Postmodern Theory and the Pragmatics of the "Outside."*. Minneapolis: University of Minnesota Press, 1998.

Wolfe, Cary. *Zoontologies: The Question of the Animal*. Minneapolis: University of Minnesota Press, 2003.

Wolfe, C. T., ed. *Monsters and Philosophy*. London: College Publications, 2005.

Wolfenbarger, Josh N. "The Culture of Cell Phone Charms." by truefaith7. July 18, 2016, https://bellatory.com/fashion-accessories/cell-phone-charms (accessed July 31, 2018).

Wordsworth, William. "She Was a Phantom of Delight." https://www.poetryfoundation.org/poems/45550/she-was-a-phantom-of-delight (accessed August 18, 2018).

Wray, Britt. *Rise of the Necrofauna: The Science, Ethics, and Risks of De-Extinction*. Vancouver: Greystone Books and David Suzuki Institute, 2017.

Wuerthner, G., E. Crist, and T. Butler, eds. *Keeping the Wild: Against the Domestication of Earth*. Washington, DC: Island Press, 2014.

Yang, Jeff. "Internet Cats Will Never Die." *CNN*, April 2, 2015, https://edition.cnn.com/2015/04/02/opinions/yang-internet-cats/ (accessed August 21, 2018).

Zarrelli, Natalie. "When Squirrels Were One of America's Most Popular Pets." *Atlas Obscura*, April 28, 2017, https://www.atlasobscura.com/articles/pet-squirrel-craze (accessed August 20, 2018).

Zielinski, Sarah. "The Giraffes That Sailed to Medieval China." *Science News: Magazine of the Society for Science and the Public*, October 1, 2013, https://www.sciencenews.org/blog/wild-things/giraffes-sailed-medieval-china (accessed August 20, 2018).

Zylinska, Joanna. *Bioethics in the Age of New Media*. Cambridge, MA: MIT Press, 2009.

Index

Page numbers in italics refer to illustrations.